The Interaction of Economics and the Law

Edited by
Bernard H. Siegan
University of San Diego School
of Law

Lexington Books
D. C. Heath and Company
Lexington, Massachusetts
Toronto

Library of Congress Cataloging in Publication Data

Main entry under title:

The Interaction of economics and the law.

Includes bibliographical references.
1. Trade regulation—United States—Addresses, essays, lectures. 2. Economics—Addresses, essays, lectures. I. Siegan, Bernard H.
KF1600.A7515   343'.73'08   76-1223
ISBN 0-669-01340-4

Published simultaneously in Canada.

Printed in the United States of America.

International Standard Book Number: 0-669-01340-4

Library of Congress Catalog Card Number: 76-1223

Contents

v

Preface

The law and economics course for spring semester 1976 at the University of San Diego School of Law consisted of a series of lectures and seminars conducted by distinguished academicians from institutions in various parts of the country. The public was invited to attend the lectures, and they are reprinted in this book. The lectures cover subjects of current interest and are intended to augment the professional and general education of law students.

Much of the lecture series was devoted to evaluating the performance of government, a matter of obvious importance to all citizens and surely to lawyers, whose input in public affairs is usually greater than that of the average person. The series probed the operation, benefits, costs, and consequences of government regulation. Essential to such analysis is comprehending the operation of the economic system in the absence of regulation, and the lectures contributed considerable insights into that process.

The course in law and economics is a recent supplement to our law school's curriculum. In addition to providing general background information on the functioning of legal institutions, the subject can add in other ways to the training of lawyers. It is not likely to improve appreciably a lawyer's performance in drafting documents and handling the ordinary probate, tort, and contract actions that never go beyond the trial stage. But some students will probably become judges or government officials and many will advise clients as to the state of the law and present arguments before trial and appellate courts. For these groups in particular, subject matter of the kind represented in the lecture series should prove to be highly beneficial.

Let me suggest three reasons why law and economics is an important subject in law school. First, regardless of whether or not the opinions so indicate, judges frequently are guided by pragmatic considerations in making decisions. Economics can help show the benefits and detriments of various courses of action. Second, economics has a role to play consistent with acceptable practice in decisions on constitutional issues. Third, the study of economics provides for a more balanced law school curriculum. I shall explain each of these points separately in the following sections.

I

During many years of law practice, I found that predicting judicial decisions was a frustrating exercise. Lawyers spend hours speculating upon how the judges will rule. The difficulty is that no one person can be certain as to the thought processes of another. Contrary to what some might believe, it is not a matter solely of analyzing and evaluating the legal precedents; there are often important extraneous factors. Strict construction of laws and precedents appears to be more a hope or goal than a reality. Judges may seek to resolve the controversy before them fairly and reasonably with limited concern for the applicable rules. On occasion, their personal predilections and ideology may be decisive. In matters that have significance beyond the interest of the parties to the suit, frequently the most crucial element relates to the pragmatic consequences of a proposed opinion. What impact will a decision one way or the other have on the future conduct of affairs?

That judges are concerned with more than just the precedents is often revealed in the inquiries and comments they make during the course of the proceedings. It happens that after spending weeks or months studying for the legal arguments, lawyers arrive in court only to find that much of their preparation has been for naught. The judges seem as or more concerned with the impact of a ruling than with the legal distinctions. The final opinion, however, is not likely to reveal any of these "extra-legal" considerations.

Sometimes when existing precedents are overruled, or matters of wide significance decided, judges will buttress their legal conclusions with materials from the social sciences. Only then does the public become aware of a procedure that may be more the rule than the exception in judicial decision-making. If pragmatism is inherent in the process, it behooves the future advocate or jurist to prepare accordingly. One means to that end is an appreciation of economic analysis with its concern for costs and consequences. Its use might determine the outcome of litigation.

Some will contend our form of government is in peril when the court substitutes its judgment for the legislature's, and any influences leading to that result should be discouraged. The question presented has long troubled judges and commentators and does not lend itself to ready solution. Regardless of the answer—and it is not my purpose to give one in these pages—it is doubtful that change will occur. The practices I have described are so common and accepted and have prevailed for so long that only flagrant abuses provoke any serious complaints in the legislatures. Self-restraint can limit these judicial proclivities, but experience suggests that this quality is not a dominant characteristic of judges, nor should it be when protected rights are at stake. Moreover, courts have to engage in legislating when they change the rules or prior interpretations of them to make the law current and relevant.

Most major cases brought before high courts probably can be decided either way. Once we accept that proposition, it is evident that judges operate with great leeway and, if they wish, can achieve their legislative propensities through a select construction of the precedents. For Justice Holmes these practices were to be expected and not to be deplored:

[I]n substance the growth of the law is legislative. And this in a deeper sense than that what the courts declare to have always been the law is in fact new. It is legislative in its grounds. The very considerations which judges most rarely mention, and always with an apology, are the secret root from which the law draws all the juices of life. I mean, of course, considerations of what is expedient for the community concerned.[1]

Given these conditions, it would seem incumbent upon the lawyers arguing cases to submit in addition to the expected legal arguments, other material available to support their cause. This would include economic analysis of the facts, as appropriate.

Much current litigation is brought by environmentalists, consumerists, and proponents of certain social causes. These groups are reluctant to confine their arguments to the cases and precedents, and often insist that the protection of special concerns should dominate the judicial response. For lawyers opposing or representing these interests, reliance on the precedents is not enough. They should be able to submit other information bearing on the appropriateness and desirability of existing or proposed rulings. In such instances, the input of economic analysis by both sides may lead to a more balanced and satisfactory outcome.

II

For a long period in our history, opinions of the U.S. Supreme Court relating to economic and social legislation were replete with economic reasoning. During this time, the doctrine of substantive (or economic) due process was in vogue, and the courts sought to preserve economic liberties from encroachment by the legislature. The concern of most of the justices was directed at the right of the businessman, employer, and worker to be free of regulatory restraint. Consumers, competition, and monopoly were discussed in these cases and often with considerable insight.[2] Substantive due process was rather abruptly terminated in 1937, and only on rare occasions since then has its basic philosophy surfaced in opinions of the U.S. Supreme Court.[3]

The high Court has subsequently adhered to the rule that economic and social enactments carry a strong presumption of constitutionality, and that as Justice Lewis Powell recently advised, "the constitution does not require that legislation on economic matters be compatible with sound economics nor even with normal fairness."[4] In light of this policy, the role of economics in evaluating legislation is limited in certain areas of constitutional law. A greater opportunity for the employment of economic analysis, however, is offered by some state courts which do not give the same deference to the legislature. The supreme court of Pennsylvania has asserted that it still accepts the tenets of substantive due process and maintains that the resulting difference between the federal and its state's constitutional laws represent a sound development which takes into account the fact that state courts may be in a better position than the federal judiciary to review local economic legislation.[5] "State courts, since their precedents are not of national authority, may better adapt their decisions to local economic conditions and needs."[6] The Maryland high court appears to be in accord,[7] and the Alaska supreme court has recently proceeded on a similar course[8] by formulating an equal protection standard under which judicial deference to legislative classifications "is strikingly diminished."[9] As the grounds for challenge to legislation widens, the opportunity for the employment of economics increases.

Nor is the door completely closed to such considerations in all litigation brought before the U.S. high Court. About a month prior to Justice Powell's observation, a majority opinion engaged extensively in economic theorizing in bringing the advertising of prescription drugs within the protection of the First Amendment.[10] In striking down a Virginia statute effectively forbidding the advertising of prescription drug prices, Justice Blackmun's opinion delves into the role of advertising and its economic significance in our society.[11] As the Virginia case shows, the determination of constitutionality must be made within the context of the patterns and behavior of existing society. Professor Kurland refers to constitutional interpretation in this manner:

The document is not a series of rules—even abstract rules. It always has been read—and has to be read—in terms of the constantly changing political, social and economic conditions that give rise to the issues that come before the Court. Constitutional limitations like all law are a reflection of the needs of a society. The law does not create the society, the society creates the law.[12]

It is incumbent on the court to ascertain and weigh or balance interests, values, events, and circumstances presented by constitutional controversies. Try as they might, judges cannot avoid the process. Thus, as in the Virginia advertising case, they will continually be confronted with the eternal judicial dilemma of whether the court is being asked to substitute its judgment for that of the legislature or to enforce fundamental rights. Much of the time the answer must be subjective. Some of the most vigorous conflicts in the Supreme Court have raged about this very basic issue. Brandeis and Holmes, strong opponents of the values encompassed in substantive due process, continually accused their colleagues of substituting their judgment for that of the legislators but did not hesitate to do so when their own value system decided that individual rights were at stake.[13]

Except as they might conflict with existing interpretations, there are few principles as to what is appropriate or necessary for inclusion in constitutional analysis. Professor Karst believes the courts have a responsibility to be all-inclusive:

The fact is that there are no interests worthy of constitutional protection which are at the same time beyond description. Of course, as social forces create new problems, new interests will appear at first only indistinctly. But it should be the special task of the courts to make an effort to define those interests so that they can be served effectively. Indeed, the articulation of the interests may be an even more important function for the courts than the balancing process itself. Once the interests are identified, the public has ways of assuring that the proper weights are assigned.[14]

In exploring costs and benefits, economic analysis can be highly pertinent to the inquiry. It may also cause judges to express and expose economic predilections in their opinions and thereby subject these views to public scrutiny. Such input may offset popular platitudes of the day which appear at times to pose a regretable temptation for the judiciary.

III

There are many different positions in the world of economics, and the perspectives presented in a classroom will depend to an extent upon those of the instructor. Neutrality in such a controversial area is difficult if not impossible to achieve. This should be no greater cause for alarm in graduate than undergraduate school, and especially not in law school. Because the law is a distillation of competing interests and values, the content of most law courses likewise depends on the attitude of the instructor and the texts used. Whether the subject be torts, contracts, corporations, legal ethics, or constitutional law, among others, the teacher has great latitude as to the material his students will read and what they will discuss. The final authorities on constitutional.law are the justices of the U.S. Supreme Court and they regularly display sharp disagreement as to what constitutional provisions mean. The subject of economics, therefore, presents little more difficulty on this score than do the more conventional law school teachings.

Courses in law and economics are of recent origin in most of the law schools where they are offered. They tend to present a different orientation than do some other newcomers, such as courses on environmental law, consumers' affairs law, and poverty law. It is not unusual for these other courses to present arguments urging certain changes in society involving a greater role for government. Depending upon the instructor, many conventional legal studies may also present persuasive proposals for reform. Given the weight of such advocacy in today's curriculum, courses in economics should be a welcome addition. Economics provides material by which to measure proposals for new laws or regulations. In contrast to the attitude prevalent at times in law courses, many economists emphasize the virtues of private as opposed to governmental solutions for society's problems. Its presence should allow for a wider and greater balance in the curriculum, giving strength or weakness to ideas elsewhere presented.

During the series, a significant number of students disclosed to me they had never before been exposed to the perspectives presented in many of the lectures. Their college degrees notwithstanding, some had no prior acquaintance with the numerous published studies containing information critical of existing regulatory policies and practices, and were only dimly aware of the possible adverse side effects resulting from governmental controls over the economy. Yet, as citizens and lawyers, their lives will be greatly influenced if not dominated by regulation.

The lecture series served to narrow this educational gap. The students heard distinguished academicians question many popularly accepted notions and present other approaches to pressing issues of the day. The point, of course, is not that students should agree; only that they should know. Law schools are and should be a place of dissemination, consideration, and evaluation of the ideas related to the institutions which make up and bind our society. It is in this respect perhaps, that the lecture series contributed most to the creation of wiser lawyers and better citizens.

University of San Diego
School of Law

Bernard H. Siegan
Distinguished Professor of Law

Notes

1. O.W. Holmes, *The Common Law* (1881), p. 35.

2. See i.e., *New State Ice Co. v. Liebmann*, 285 U.S. 262 (1932); *Nebbia v. New York*, 291 U.S. 502, 539 (1933) (dissenting opinion of Justice McReynolds).

3. R.G. McCloskey, "Economic Due Process and the Supreme Court: An Exhumation and Reburial," *The Supreme Court Review* (P.B. Kurland, ed., 1962): 34.

4. Concurring opinion in *Usery v. Turner Elkhorn Mining Co.*, 96 S.Ct. 2882, 2906 (1976).

5. *Pennsylvania State Board of Pharmacy v. Pastor*, 272 A.2d 487, 490 (1971).

6. Ibid., p. 491.

7. *Maryland Board of Pharmacy v. Sav-A-Lot, Inc.*, 311 A.2d 242 (1973).

8. *Isakson v. Rickey*, 550 P.2d 359, 362 (1976).

9. Ibid.

10. *Virginia State Board of Pharmacy v. Virginia Citizens Consumer Council, Inc.*, 96 S.Ct. 1817 (1976).

11. Ibid., pp. 1826-30.

12. P.B. Kurland, "The Private I: Some Reflections on Privacy and the Constitution," *University of Chicago Magazine* (Autumn 1976), p. 7.

13. The abortion cases dramatically illustrate the quandary. Compare the majority opinion of Justice Blackmun and concurring opinion of Justice Douglas with the dissents of Justices White and Rehnquist. *Roe v. Wade*, 410 U.S. 113 (1973) and *Doe v. Bolton*, 410 U.S. 179 (1973). Consider also the majority opinion of Justice Douglas and dissenting opinion of Justice Black in *Griswold v. Connecticut*, 381 U.S. 479 (1964) and of Justices Powell and Marshall in *San Antonio Independent School District v. Rodriguez*, 411 U.S. 1 (1973).

14. K.L. Karst, "Legislative Facts on Constitutional Litigation," *The Supreme Court Review* (P.B. Kurland, ed., 1960): 75, 81.

The Interaction of Economics and the Law

1

Law and the Economy

W. Allen Wallis

Let me begin by quoting something written forty years ago by Walter Lippmann. It summarizes better than I can the theme of this chapter,

For more than two generations an increasingly coercive organization of society has coincided with an increasing disorder. It is time to inquire why, with so much more authority, there is so much less stability; . . . .

It is not a mere coincidence that the cult of a directed civilization should be accompanied by a general foreboding that modern civilization is doomed. Why should it be that, in a time when men are making the prodigious claim that they can plan and direct society, they are so profoundly impressed with the unmanageability of human affairs? . . . .

They find that the more they organize, the more general is the disorganization; the more they direct affairs, the more refractory they become. They find the directed society harder and harder to direct. For they have reached the point where the organization is too elaborate to be managed. The attempt to regulate deliberately the transactions of a people multiplies the number of separate, self-conscious appetites and resistances. To establish order among these highly energized fragments, which are like atoms set in violent motion by being heated, a still more elaborate organization is required—but this more elaborate organization can be operated only if there is more intelligence, more insight, more discipline, more disinterestedness, than exists in any ordinary company of men. This is the sickness of an over-governed society, and at this point the people must seek relief through greater freedom if they are not to suffer greater disasters. . . .

The essential difference between the faith that our generation has embraced and the faith that it has forsaken is to be found in what it thinks some men can do to manage the destiny of other men. The predominant teachings of this age are that there are no limits to man's capacity to govern others and that, therefore, no limitations ought to be imposed upon government. The older faith, born of long ages of suffering under man's dominion over man, was that the exercise of unlimited power by men with limited minds and self-regarding prejudices is soon oppressive, reactionary, and corrupt. The older faith taught that the very condition of progress was the limitation of power to the capacity and the virtue of rulers.

For the time being this tested wisdom is submerged under a world-wide movement which has at every vital point the support of vested interests and the afflatus of popular hopes. But if it is true that men can do no more than they are able to do, then government can do no more than governors are able to do. All the wishing in the world, all the promises based on the assumption that there are available omniscient and loving autocrats, will not call into being men who can plan a future which they are unable to imagine, who can manage a civilization which they are unable to understand.

1

The fact that the whole generation is acting on these hopes does not mean that the liberal philosophy is dead, as the collectivists and authoritarians assert. On the contrary, it may be that they have taught a heresy and doomed this generation to reaction. So men may have to pass through a terrible ordeal before they find again the central truths they have forgotten. But they will find them again, as they have so often found them again in other ages of reaction, if only the ideas that have misled them are challenged and resisted.[1]

Now, another quotation, this one delivered only last week by the governor of New York, a liberal Democrat elected a year ago after a New Deal, populist campaign ". . . Our goals are less government; less spending; fewer government employees; less interference in the lives of our citizens and businessmen and a new spirit of cooperation by all individuals in government." Perhaps the governor has found again those central truths whose loss Mr. Lippmann lamented.

Lippmann was not alone forty years ago in his prophecies. Here is another prophecy of forty years ago, this one from a speech delivered in January 1936 by Franklin Delano Roosevelt: ". . . we have built up new instruments of public power. . . . [S]uch power would provide shackles for the liberties of our people."

That prophecy of FDR's has materialized to a degree that scarcely anyone foresaw in 1936. I heard it over the radio when it was given, and it made an indelible impression on me. One reason the prophecy struck me so forcibly when I heard it was that it exactly fitted in with what I had learned as a graduate student in economics at the University of Chicago from 1933 to 1935, from such faculty members as Aaron Director, Henry Simons, Lloyd Mints, and—above all—Frank Knight, and from such fellow graduate students as Milton Friedman, Homer Jones, and George Stigler.

Before I discuss FDR's prophecy, I want to quote it again. What I have just read to you consists of phrases from two sentences. They give a central thought of the two sentences, but to avoid charges that I have twisted the meaning by taking phrases out of context, I will read the two sentences in full: "In 34 months we have built up new instruments of public power in the hands of the people's government. This power is wholesome and proper, but in the hands of political puppets of an economic autocracy, such power would provide shackles for the liberties of our people."

The prophecy was made when the 1936 election was on the horizon. It amounted to saying that the powers of the government had been built up in such a way that there was no choice but to reelect FDR, since others might misuse the power. That, if true, would have meant that the people had already had their liberty to elect someone else shackled. It meant, as Al Smith put it at the time, "If you are going to have an autocrat, take me."

In the forty years since FDR made his remarkably prescient prognostication, American life has changed drastically. We talk a lot about changes in technology, in farming, in urbanization, in standards of living, in health, in education, in communication, and so on. But surely none of these changes is as great as the changes that have come about in the relation between people and government.

When FDR made his prediction, there were innumerable areas of private life into which the federal government did not intrude, on the grounds it was prohibited by the Constitution; and many other areas were left to the states, again because of the Constitution.

In 1935, for example, when the administration was drafting the first social security legislation, there were the gravest doubts within the administration itself that the law could be written in such a way as to be acceptable constitutionally. Frances Perkins, secretary of labor, who was in charge of drafting the legislation, tells in her memoirs that she got a tip on how to write the bill so that the Supreme Court would uphold it. Where did she get the tip? Straight from the horse's mouth, from a justice of the Supreme Court, Justice Stone.

Today, in contrast, it is hard to think of any area of private affairs in which the federal government is reluctant to intervene. There are a few areas where the courts still constrain the government, but these are almost exclusively the domains that are important to the academic-journalistic complex—namely where their personal and rather commercial interests in free speech are threatened, or where election or law enforcement procedures seem disadvantageous to those who are vaguely described as "disadvantaged." And the courts themselves have thrown off virtually all self-restraint: it is rare for a court today to refuse to intervene in a situation because it is outside the jurisdiction of the courts.

Recently Alexander Solzhenitsyn was quoted as making a statement about the Russian government that is too nearly true of ours, that it dislikes any relations between individuals which it does not supervise. It is not, of course, "the government" as an entity that wants to supervise in this country. Rather, for almost any relations between individuals there is some group which has a special interest in supervising, and the influence of special interests in our system of government is so strong that generally they get their way. (By "special interests" I refer not only to commercial and economic interests but to such organizations as the Sierra Club, Common Cause, Ralph Nader and his multifarious franchised activities, organized religion, higher education, and so forth.)

We assure ourselves and our children that ours is a government of laws, not men. Well, sometime stop and check up on the "laws" that are regulating you, and see whether this is true. When you are making out your federal income tax return, for the most part, you have to work with an intricate body of rules and regulations handed down by various Internal Revenue employees, tax court officials, and federal judges.

The tax laws that Congress has enacted make some general statements, but to apply these to the infinite variety of individuals and circumstances requires elaborate interpretations. If you or your business has anything but the simplest kind of return, there is a chance that it may be reviewed. A review involves sitting down across the table from a man—not a law. And the review includes a lot of horse-trading: "I'll give you this if you'll give me that"; "if you hold out on this point I can make it more expensive for you than it's worth."

The taxpayer always fears that it may not be wise to press too hard because if he annoys the Internal Revenue man he can find himself in worse trouble, not only for himself but for others connected with him. Besides, he fears that if he wins this time, they will really be "laying" for him next time. Whether these fears are often realized is beside the point; the point is that the fears are of men and human emotions, not of laws.

The ordinary taxpayer is almost without effective recourse from the decisions an IRS agent makes, because of the costs in time, in legal fees, and in the psychological strain that arises because, fortunately, most people still respect (or fear?) the government enough so that it is by no means a matter of indifference to them to be at odds with it, even if they win eventually. Indeed, publicity may cause damage that never will be corrected by exoneration, however complete.

What I have said about the tax laws, namely that the regulations governing you with the force of law are mostly the edicts of officials, applies in almost every field. The Occupational Safety and Health Act is an excellent example—or should I say "horrible" example?—of government by men rather than by law. The Environmental Protection Act is another. As for automobile safety, let me remind you that Congress was never hebephrenic enough to legislate those squawk-and-balk interlock devices on cars, nor the $100 bumpers either.

Although Congress passes the basic laws on which the mountains of regulations rest, it would be naive to think that Congress gives every law thorough scrutiny. Look at the 1969 tax law and then tell me whether you believe that *your* congressman studied all of it. Do you think he even read all of it? Do you suppose any single congressman, even Wilbur Mills himself, studied every bit of it?

How many other equally voluminous bills were enacted at the same session of Congress, and do you suppose that all of them were carefully studied in full? Did your congressman scrutinize the appropriations for health, education, and welfare, or for the Defense Department? Or the Employee's Retirement Income Security Act, another two- or three-hundred-page monstrosity?

If you know how Congress works you realize that there has to be, and is, division of labor. Committees and subcommittees control most of the legislation. Within the committees and subcommittees the staff are sometimes more influential, at least on the bulk of the legislation, than the members themselves. And in the crucial all-night session at which a final bill is actually worded, the staff often is supplemented by outsiders with special knowledge of—and interests in—the bill.

All of these developments confirm the wisdom of the Founding Fathers in limiting narrowly the powers of the federal government. They did this only partly from antipathy to governmental control of private affairs. To be sure, such antipathy was strong at the time, because of direct experience in the preceding hundred years. But an equally powerful reason for restricting the power of the federal government was the realization that the form of government they wanted—a democratic government—cannot endure if it intervenes extensively into the affairs of the people. Democratic processes—representative processes, if you prefer—simply cannot handle complex, highly technical matters satisfactorily.

A democratic government cannot design efficient automobiles, it cannot design a sound energy policy, it cannot eliminate prejudice and discrimination, it cannot manage transportation, it cannot assure the soundness of investments or the accuracy of information about them, it cannot guarantee the effectiveness and safety of medicines—it cannot, in short, do most of the things that our government undertakes to do.

Congress, perhaps partly in recognition of its own incapacity to do all the things it undertakes to do, has come increasingly during the past forty years not to legislate itself but to delegate to thousands of employees the right to make what are effectively laws, and the right to enforce them.

Another important fact about representative government that the Founding Fathers recognized is that direct election by the people is likely not to produce the most competent representatives to carry on the people's business, and furthermore is likely to promote demagoguery.

Thus, in the Federalist Papers one of the features described with pride, as an argument for accepting the proposed constitution, was that the people could not get directly at the government. Only the House of Representatives was to be elected directly by the voters. Senators were to be elected by state legislatures; the president and the vice president were to be elected by a special electoral college; and judges were to be appointed by the president and the Senate.

Perhaps in an unconscious response to the weakness of government by representatives elected by the people, there is currently a strong movement toward government by the judiciary, which is now the only part of the federal government that still is not elected by the people. Whatever the reason, the fact is that a great deal of administrative business is now done by the courts.

It has been recognized for fifty years or more that the courts revise the Constitution through their interpretations and reinterpretations, and it has been recognized for perhaps twenty-five years that, in effect, the courts legislate in innumerable matters, including apportionment of Congress, legislatures, and school districts, and criminal law and the operation of prisons, but it has not been widely recognized that currently the courts are assuming many administrative functions that formerly were regarded as executive responsibilities.

The meaning attached to the phrase "rule of law" is, in fact, coming to be in practice the opposite of what we have traditionally understood by the phrase. Traditionally, the ideal of the rule of law has been that all men were equal before the law, regardless of rank, position, race, religion, income, occupation, or any other characteristic; the law was blind. The ideal of the rule of law has precluded retroactive legislation, and it has precluded laws intended to burden or benefit some people differently from others.

The term "rule of law" now is coming to mean that all activities and relations between people should be regulated by law. It is argued that in an interdependent society any action of an individual and any transaction between individuals necessarily affects other members of the society, so it is intolerable that there should be any activities or transactions that are not regulated by society. Since human beings cannot exist except in a society, and a society is by definition interdependent, it follows that "Whatever is not compulsory should be prohibited." This is coming to be the new meaning of "the rule of law"; instead of protecting freedom, the new rule of law annihilates freedom.

Last spring a colleague clipped items from newspapers for a month or two to illustrate the kinds of government intervention that are now commonplace. Since I am interested in economics, these examples relate to the economy; but just as many could be found relating to education, medicine, politics, or almost any other field.

One clipping reports that the Federal Communications Commission wants to limit to three hours the amount of network programming that a local station can show between the hours of 7 and 11 P.M., but to exempt certain types of programs.

The Department of Health, Education and Welfare is reported to be requiring the University of California at Berkeley to replace 178 white males with 97 women, 20 blacks, 42 Asians, 10 Chicanos, 0 American Indians, and 9 others. This is to be done within thirty years.

Another item mentions the effect of the minimum wage rate, then $2 per hour, in causing unemployment, especially among the young and blacks, and above all among young blacks.

The U.S. Customs Service imposes huge fines on businesses, and says that it needs to do this in order to negotiate more effectively with the businesses on what fines they will actually pay.

An article on the effects of prohibiting the use of DDT mentions a great increase in the prevalence of malaria in Ceylon and of a harmful moth in the forests of the Pacific Northwest.

The possibility that wage and price controls will be reinstituted has led some businesses to raise, or at least fail to lower, prices when they did not feel that such increases were advantageous in existing circumstances.

The regulation of retirement benefits and investment procedures will raise pension costs of the Consolidated Edison Company by 14 percent.

The controller of the currency warned banks not to take large deposits from people who might try to eliminate Jews from the boards of the banks.

The food stamp program, currently running at about $4 billion per year, is expected to be $5 billion in the next fiscal year. It is estimated that sixty million people will be eligible in fiscal 1977, although only fifteen million are now receiving the stamps.

The governor of New York complained that New Yorkers are not getting all the food stamps they could, so he set up a toll-free telephone line to call for advice on how to get them, and set a goal of an additional $100 million a year in food stamps.

Government allocations of capital have created a variety of vested interests. Federally guaranteed loans now amount to $200 billion, and in addition there are $50 billion of direct loans outstanding.

A number of local governments have banned the use of phosphates in detergents.

Licensing boards are expanding the number of occupations that must be licensed, and also the number of types of business that must be licensed the way liquor stores and taxis are now.

The federal government increased the support price for milk, leading to a 2 percent rise in retail prices. This was done after the president vetoed an even larger increase that had been passed by Congress.

In 1975 the government changed the effective date for automobile pollution standards from the 1977 models to the 1978 models. One reason was that the devices the government plans to require seem to boost the amount of another pollutant. This change was made after two years of warnings to the government, and after far greater costs have been incurred than would have been if 1978 had been the original target date. Indeed, no sensible person attempting a basic technological innovation sets a date and introduces the product on that date whether or not it works reliably and whatever it costs.

There is a shortage of natural gas in New England and surplus gas in Alaska, but the only ships capable of carrying it are registered under foreign flags, and foreign-flag ships are not allowed to carry goods between United States ports.

Several states have introduced controls over all land near seashores. These amount to the states' taking joint ownership of the property without compensation.

A number of cities have passed laws prohibiting growth, or at least limiting the number of new buildings that can be built.

The government is appropriating large and growing subsidies to maintain passenger service on the railroads. The resulting costs per passenger mile are such that most passengers, if offered the choice, probably would prefer to pocket the subsidy and find some other way to travel.

The Securities and Exchange Commission is attempting to form a single central market for securities, covering the entire country.

The Securities and Exchange Commission plans to require a great deal of additional detail in the quarterly reports of corporations, and to require some degree of auditing of these quarterly reports.

The Environmental Protection Agency is proposing rules to make jet airplanes quieter, at a cost estimated at $880 million.

So much for the clippings. Here is a more detailed example, from the field of health.

The Food and Drug Administration's regulations, together with certain acts of Congress, have changed the United States from a leader to a substantial laggard in developing new medicines. The therapeutic areas in which this U.S. drug lag is most pronounced are the cardiovascular, diuretic, respiratory, antibacterial, and gastrointestinal areas. In appearing before a Senate committee a year or so ago, Dr. William Wardell of the University of Rochester Medical School testified as follows:

The U.S. was at least the 30th country in the world to approve the broncho-dilato metaproterenol; the 32nd country to approve the anti-cancer drug adriamycin; the 41st country to approve the anti-mania drug lithium carbonate; the 51st country to approve the antituberculous drug rifampin; the 64th country to approve the antiallergic drug cromolyn; and the 106th country to approve the antibacterial drug co-trimoxazole.

Even when a drug is finally admitted to the U.S., the indications for its use are often ridiculously restricted and out-of-date. For example, the U.S. has more restrictions on the use of co-trimoxazole than any of the 107 countries in which the drug is currently marketed. Here, it is still only approved for the short-term treatment of chronic urinary tract infections. More important medically are situations in which this drug may be life-saving, in some of which no other effective therapy is available. Such situations were recognized as early as 1962, but are still essentially unknown (and certainly unapproved) uses in the U.S., some 12 years later.

Perhaps the most astonishing recent example of the unrealistic gap between regulatory philosophy and medical practice is that of propranolol. It is hard to believe that an advisory committee was still debating the approval of this drug for angina at a time when a physician's *failure* to use this drug (e.g., as a trial in most patients prior to coronary artery surgery) would be regarded as substantially suboptimal medical practice. The regulatory fate of this drug, for an indication (angina) in which it has long been a therapy of choice, bodes ill for its regulatory chances in an equally important indication, hypertension. In this latter respect, American regulatory philosophy is already a decade behind medical practice.

Another manifestation of the changing concept of the rule of law is the litigation explosion. So-called public interest law firms, which might as accurately be called "champerty corporations," are only a small part of this explosion.

In the past decade, the legal expenses of the typical corporation have risen about twice as much as its sales revenues. Legal costs often are around a quarter to three-quarters of a percent of sales.

There has been a striking growth in the number of law suits filed in federal district courts. For the five years 1968-73, the number of environmental suits rose at a compound rate of 45 percent per year, or by a factor of 6.4 for the five years. Securities regulation cases grew 24 percent per year, by a factor of 2.9. Antitrust cases, 11 percent per year, a factor of 1.7. Labor law cases, 7 percent, a factor of 1.4. Patents, copyrights, and trademarks, 2 percent, a factor of 1.1. Fair employment practice cases, of which there were over 1,000 in 1973, were not even recognized as a separate category in 1968, but all civil rights cases (most of which probably do not involve businesses) grew at an average annual rate of 36 percent, or a factor of 4.7 over the five years.

These law suits are just the tip of the iceberg. The real business of most lawyers, of course, is to prevent law suits. So corporations are swarming with lawyers, who read or even write the outgoing mail, package labels, advertisements, instruction manuals, public speeches, press releases, and employment manuals, and in fact monitor nearly every detail of corporate practice. And the costs of these lawyers probably are the lesser part of the total costs incurred from delay, wasted motion, and bureaucratization. They generate an attitude that production, service, and quality are less important than procedures, legalisms, and protecting your flanks.

Possibly as lawyers, you welcome this reversal of the concept of the rule of law, for it creates a huge market for lawyers. But I do you the honor of presuming that you do not welcome it, that it concerns you as much as it does me.

What concerns us is a powerful movement away from limited government and individual freedom; and toward pervasive government and collective control of all activities. It is a shift away from a rule of law; toward a rule of officials: A shift from laws passed by elected legislatures and enforced in courts under the constitutional and common law guarantees that we call "due process"; toward regulations, orders, and directives issued by appointed government employees and enforced by them. It is a shift away from judging conduct by criteria of propriety, prudence, and intent; toward judging conduct by consequences, even when the consequences were beyond the knowledge or control of the person judged. It is a shift away from trust in good faith, competence, and responsibility; toward reliance on detailed prescriptions by government and documentation by individuals of their actions, intentions, and motives.

In short, the problem is what Walter Lippmann called "the sickness of an overgoverned society."

Can we cure that sickness, or at least slow its advance?

Public opinion polls, the pronouncements of new governors from California to New York, editorials in traditionally liberal newspapers, and many other signs suggest that there is a deep and pervasive mood in the land that yearns for some relief from this sickness of over-government.

But what of the political institutions through which such relief would have to come? Are they capable of bringing it about, even if a considerable majority of the people want it?

I have grave doubts that our political institutions have that capability. The reason for my doubts is that our system of government is one in which minorities rule.

It is possible for any individual to gain enormously if he can harness the coercive powers of government for his particular advantage, perhaps through funds to support his industry or profession, perhaps through giving him cheap loans, perhaps through increasing some welfare program such as Social Security, perhaps through protecting him from competition, perhaps through tax advantages.

If even a small percentage of the voters in a congressional or legislative district share a common interest that can be served through the coercive powers of the government, and if they will vote for or against a candidate almost solely on the basis of his stand on the issue of overriding importance to them, most candidates will have to support this interest or be replaced by someone who will. Most congressmen could not win if, for example, a block much above 5 percent of their supporters were to shift to their opponents.

When a legislature made up of members elected under these conditions convenes, it is quite probable that no single law could get a majority vote. As the legislators get down to work, groups in favor of one measure or another will attempt to find other groups with whom they can form coalitions, each group agreeing to support the other group's pet measure in return for support of its own pet measure. As the legislative season progresses, gradually some measures will command majorities and be enacted. Professor William Riker, of the University of Rochester's Political Science Department, has pointed out that at the end of such a legislative session it is quite possible that almost every legislator and most of the public would prefer that all the legislation of that session be wiped off the books. This is because the cumulative effects of the many measures benefiting others probably will offset the effects of the few measures benefiting any one person. Yet our political processes are such that each session will inevitably pass a good many laws.

The only effective protection against this, if representative government is to be preserved, is a series of self-denying ordinances, by which it is agreed that certain areas simply are not subject to legislative action. For, as Walter Lippmann said, the attempt to legislate in these areas "multiplies the number of separate self-conscious appetites," thus leading to an unstable and ultimately self-defeating situation.

Such self-denying ordinances are, of course, exactly what the Founding Fathers attempted to achieve when they wrote the Constitution of the United States. They specified certain powers for the federal government, and prohibited it from doing anything else. But with the passage of time a series of measures, each seeming good and proper at the moment, have eroded the proscriptions until today it is difficult to name an area which the federal government does not regulate.

Perhaps I *seem* to be saying that our sickness of over-government cannot be cured. Perhaps I *am* saying that. But if I am, I am saying it as a challenge to your generation. When I was your age, I really believed that the impossible merely takes a little longer. I hope that Lippmann was wrong when he wrote that "men may have to pass through a terrible ordeal before they find again the central truths they have forgotten." But I have no doubt that he was right when he said that "they will find them again, as they have so often found them again in other ages of reaction."

Note

1. W. Lippmann, *The Good Society* (Boston, Mass.: Little, Brown and Company, 1943), pp. 38-41. Copyright 1936, 1937, and 1943 by Walter Lippmann. Reprinted by permission of Little, Brown and Company in association with The Atlantic Monthly Press.

The Economics of Protecting Americans from Foreign Competition

Warren F. Schwartz

I realize initially that I made a mistake in the title. I called it "The Economics of Protecting Americans from Foreign Competition" and one of my standard practices is to disclaim any expertise in the field of economics. In this case, my enthusiasm overcame my prudence. I am one of a growing number of law professors who have become intrigued with the field of economics because we feel, in a sense, that we have no choice but to become intrigued with it; but we usually are very careful not to include ourselves in the group of experts. So I will call this "The Law and Economics of Protecting Americans from Foreign Competition," and I will then have an opportunity to draw on my genuine expertise and not parade before you as an "expert."

All the economics you are going to get from me is fairly straightforward, not at all technical, and, on the whole, economics which is widely accepted. I suppose at the very outset I should also confess a general point of view, because for those of you who propose to come to these lectures week after week, you will, no doubt, discern a trend and that is, depending upon how you feel about it, what I call a "healthy skepticism" toward government intervention. People more impatient with the point of view call it being a "right-wing kook." You will have, in fact, paraded in front of you, of which I am the second, a variety of "distinguished right-wing kooks," also called "The Chicago School" although I did not attend it.

It is a sad story we have to tell, and it is a story that I for one do not find emotionally congenial. I was brought up with a strong belief in the government as a source of organized compassion for people who care a great deal about other people and wish to make the lot of the less fortunate better; that it was the way in which the good impulses of the society would somehow or other be organized and expressed. As I have become interested in economics, as I have examined government action of various kinds, I have become increasingly skeptical of the benefits that it affords and, I confess, increasingly libertarian in my own views, increasingly persuaded that most of the creative forces in society are those of individual action. There are indeed things for the government to do; but the widely accepted notion of what the government can do well is, in my judgment, materially exaggerated. I am, indeed, a skeptic; I am, indeed, in the eyes of otherwise sensible people, a "right-wing kook" and I am uncomfortable as a "right-wing kook." I found the other view much more congenial.

It is interesting when you read, for example, the *Washington Post*—what they are constantly crying about is the do-nothing Congress. The failure to pass that bill which will, once and for all, dramatically make the world better. One of the curious messages that you will be hearing from me is that much of the good that can be done in the years ahead will be in not passing bills that are proposed; not having that form of government intervention that has been suggested; and, to a very considerable extent, disassembling much of the government mechanisms which now exist. It is not a hopeful Kennedy-like note that "we are going to get in there and really make it a better world tomorrow." It is the unhappy note that, in balance, much of the efforts to effect radical change through governmental action have been failures.

I would like to put this discussion, which is specifically on the economics of protecting Americans from international trade, into the general perspective of somebody who approaches legal issues from the point of view of economic analysis.

The first question that arises is "Why are we all attracted to it?" It is, in terms of its technical content, a hateful kind of exercise. I have never been able to read graphs; I am almost hopeless at mathematics; and I find it really quite a dismal business. Why in the world am I engaging in it when I can be reading and distinguishing cases which is a pleasant occupation for lawyers? It is really a functional matter; it is an itch. The itch is essentially to move yourself back from this legal system and ask yourself "Is it any good?" And when you ask the question, you want it to mean something more than "Do I like it?", "Do I like the outcome?" You want a systematic method of appraisal. What many of us have become increasingly uncomfortable with is words like "fairness," "justice," "equity," being thrown around, and when you try to find out what is the point of view that underlies words of that kind, what is the theory, the legal literature, the legal scholarship that is taught in law schools is, in my judgment, remarkably barren. What economics offers, essentially, is a focus on two questions and by asking those two questions you can step back from this legal system and ask yourself in some significant way "Is this a good or a bad law?"

The first question is, if you introduce a particular legal provision, what would be the effect on the allocation of resources? Which means simply what will you have more of, and what will you have less of in the society? What will get produced? Will you, in the aggregate, produce more or less? By and large the simple message that the economist gives you is that whatever else you can say about the disagreements that exist in the society about what is good and what is bad, it is better to produce more than to produce less. It is better, if you will, to be efficient than to be inefficient; it is better to maximize the total social product. If nothing else, it gives you that. It can indeed be said of many legal provisions that they are not in that sense efficient; they decrease the total wealth of society.

The second question is what will be the effect on the distribution of wealth when you introduce a particular legal provision? If you do something, somebody is going to get richer and somebody is going to get poorer. The reason why the economic contribution to that is only partial is that economics, and to be candid no discipline of which I am aware, has much to say about how to answer that question. In other words, we have no basis for saying how the wealth of the society ought to be distributed. What economics does tell you is that one consequence of changing the law will be that you will have that effect; you will affect the distribution of wealth. Focus on it, it is a relevant consequence. What you choose to make of it is a matter of value.

The immediate piece of legislation which I will analyze is the Trade Act of 1974, which substantially reenacts or changes the governing rules with respect to international trade as conducted from the United States. The approach which I have just described causes you to first look at the legislation and identify the consequences. What is going to happen?, and, if possible, quantify the results. Who is going to get richer? What is going to be the effect on the allocation of resources? Then you have the very difficult question of assigning some degree of value to those consequences. The difficulty lies in assigning economic values to the consequences of the political process—i.e., to something which is never bought or sold. (I compare political processes with market transactions below.)

If you have a public education system that is provided at a subsidized price, like the University of Virginia Law School where I teach, nobody ever gets around to buying it so you don't know what it is worth and you don't know what I'm worth. If you have a public subway in New York City in which the fares represent only a fraction of the actual cost because there is a substantial public subsidy, one thing you do not have is any test in terms of people spending their money as to what it's really worth. If you build the Kennedy Center in Washington, or the other great marble halls, nobody ever pays for them and you never know what they're really worth. If you try to appraise legislation, you have the problem of assigning some degree of value. So, as I say, what you have to do is identify consequences, assign values to them, and then (a point often left out) you also have to determine what are the costs of the government legislation. There are essentially two kinds of costs. The first is the actual cost of the machinery, that is, in the case of international trade, the International Trade Commission, and the Special Representative for Trade Negotiations, and a whole bunch of people living in Geneva and negotiating, and other people in the White House who counsel the president. Presumably all of those people, if they were not doing that, could be doing something else of use. So the cost to society is the foregone benefit of their time when they are devoting it to this particular activity.

The other inevitable cost of any kind of government action is the undesired consequences that it creates; and there are always undesired side effects. I think a point that is often missed when evaluating some kind of a governmental or legislative solution is the great value of the private solution which the government solution overcomes or supersedes.

We have a great tradition that (I must say I am mystified as to the cultural origins of it) commercial transactions, exchange between people, is a kind of sordid, perhaps necessary, evil in which people motivated by profits present themselves at their worst. It is a kind of seedy business, this business of seeking profit, and it really isn't anything you ought to be very proud of or proclaim. I would suggest to you just the opposite: that voluntary exchange, that is what people will do without the government getting into it, has much to commend it. One has to commend it first of all precisely because it is voluntary. If I decide that I want to buy a German car, I want to buy a German car because I like it better. Nobody is making me buy it; nobody is making someone sell it to me. It is a free act and I presumably seek it out as I seek out employment or all the other voluntary arrangements. The beautiful part about it—it's the old invisible hand—is it really works. By my seeking out my gain, and you seeking out your gain, we are both better off, a point frequently lost. The point that is always made about trade is that somebody is taking advantage of somebody else. What happens in trade is that both parties gain individually. Both are better off essentially because they can specialize in what they do best and consume what they like most, because people are different. They can exploit individual differences to make both of them better off without anybody telling them to do it. That is at the heart of all trade, and is at the heart of international trade, and is that creative process which the government supersedes when it intervenes. The other thing that this individual action does to a remarkable extent is produce a very elaborate and sophisticated social organization, again without compulsion. The very motivating force for the organization is the desire for profit.

The third point about trade is that it also gives you highly quantitative data as to preferences on the consumption side and possibilities on the production side. It is not like going into a subway without paying a fare; you do not know how much the ride is really worth. If you have to pay for it you know what it is worth. So that the data that markets generate are highly quantified. I acknowledge in a moment that there are good reasons nevertheless to have government in this trade process, both in international and domestic trade. Essentially those reasons are what are called externalities or market imperfections. The basic idea is that in some buying and selling all of the costs and benefits are not taken into account. Theoretically in the field of international trade you have a so-called infant industry when you are just beginning to learn how to make something. Some company will learn all about how to do it, but it won't really be able to sell everything it learns; some of it will "spill over" to other companies which won't pay for it, so you need some form of government protection for the industry in its "infancy."

There are all of these elegant theories of why you need to supersede private exchange. It is, however, true that the variables implicated by these theories are very difficult to measure. Moreover, when you actually have the legislation, it is very rare that you have any kind of finding that indicates these externalities, approaching the magnitude necessary to justify the law, have, in fact, been found.

I would now like to turn to the Trade Act having, I hope, at least sketched the basic analysis. I think it is fair to say that, with respect to the provisions of the Trade Act of 1974, you cannot justify the law in terms of the kind of market imperfections or externalities that I have talked about. That is, the elegant economists' case for having these provisions simply does not exist. It would appear that these are "inefficient provisions." The interesting question is why our political process produces outcomes like this, and more interestingly, what might we do to change the form of political organization to decrease the likelihood of this kind of outcome.

Now a word about the background of how international trade is conducted in the United States in order to appreciate what the Trade Act of 1974 is. It has been traditional, since the '30s, but more particularly after the Second World War, to have a statute passed which does two things. First of all it authorizes the president to negotiate reductions in existing trade barriers. By trade barriers I mean essentially tariffs (a tariff is an amount of money that is charged on importation) or quantitative limitations which restrict the amount of goods which can be imported. The president (actually members of the executive branch under the authority of the president) entered into agreements reducing these in a series of negotiations, recently multilateral negotiations, that are conducted under the auspices of the General Agreement on Tariff and Trade. In the same bill in which the president is authorized to negotiate reductions in these trade barriers (tariffs and quantitative restrictions) various forms of protection are afforded to American industries that might be adversely affected by international competition. At the outset, much of this protection was protection from the precise consequences of the reduction in trade barriers pursuant to the agreements. It has now become more and more general.

I would like to refer briefly to the various forms of protection of American producer interests which are contained in the present trade bill. The first, and perhaps most important, are substantive limitations on the negotiations themselves. The president cannot agree to reduce tariff rates to a rate below 40 percent of the rate existing on January 1, 1975. If you ask me what economic theory tells me that 40 percent of the existing rates is in the national interest I would say I haven't the slightest idea. If you were going to do it as an economist you would have to say, "O.K., we look at tomato paste or we look at sponges (you ought to look at the tariff schedules sometime, they are really quite funny) and you'll find that you've got a 17 percent ad valorem tax." Now if you were going to be a really elegant economist, you would say, "Well the externalities encountered in making sponges or tomato paste, that is the 'spill over' benefits that they don't capture in selling tomato paste is sufficiently great to warrant a 17 percent tariff; if you have a 17 percent ad valorem tariff you can increase the price of tomato paste sold by domestic producers and they're going to sell a larger percentage of the market." It's all of that. Really what you must ask yourself is, "Is all of that extra money which we're charging the American consumers buying something good for the country that wouldn't otherwise be bought?" That is what "externality" means. I told you there are all these fancy theoretical arguments; but nobody has made them, and there is no reason to believe that they would lead to the conclusion that every tariff up to 40 percent of its present level is paying its way in social goodies. But that is what the statute says.

The other thing that the statute does is impose upon the executive branch what is called a sector negotiating objective, which in rough terms means that within each product class you have to get about as much as you give. That is, if you decrease tariffs in a particular sector so that imports increase, you should receive concessions in foreign tariffs resulting in increased exports in the same sector of a like amount. There is no sense to that either—no reason why in a negotiation of this kind it has to balance within a sector. Indeed, the critical point is that most of the things that we are "giving up" in these negotiations— that is reducing our trade barriers—we would be better off eliminating even if we got nothing in return. They are bad things for the country; but, in any case, there is no reason why this notion of getting as much as you give within a sector makes any sense.

The other aspect of this that represents considerable protection for American producer interests is the procedural role that they are assigned in the negotiations. This bill sets up various industry advisory committees which represent the interests of the industry in negotiations. It is obvious from reading this bill that in both substantive and procedural terms the interest that is getting underrepresented is the consumer interest, because the people who pay more when you have tariffs and when you have quantitative restrictions are the consumers. The consumer interest is not represented in the substantive limitations on the negotiations, nor is the consumer interest represented in these procedural requirements that are laid out which give a very substantial participatory role to representatives of the affected industry in the negotiating process.

The second aspect of what the bill does is provide a very materially increased amount of relief to American producers—indeed to American firms, to American workers, to American communities—who are "adversely affected" by international competition. The law in this regard has been changed to greatly facilitate the granting of relief, and, in particular in the case of an industry, as the law is now phrased, the industry is eligible for relief in the form of a quantitative restriction or increased tariff whenever it is determined, "that an article is being imported into the United States in such increased quantities as to be a substantial cause of serious injury, or the threat thereof." It is not obvious why, if an industry is being "injured" by foreign competition, it is entitled to have a quantitative restriction or a tariff imposed. The concept of injury in this sense does not correspond to any economic or any other theory that I know of. People lose out competitively all the time and are injured. Why it is that injury in the form of rivalry from international trade should qualify for this kind of relief is not plain. Incidentally, as a matter of history (by no means "incidentally"), as this law read originally it was required that the injury be the result of increased imports that resulted from trade concessions. The law has now been expanded so that any industry which suffers injury from increased imports is entitled to relief, and just recently the first such determination was made by the International Trade Commission. It used to be called the Tariff Commission, but it has been changed to the International Trade Commission to give it at least an air of impartiality in all of this.

Similarly, there has been a considerable liberalization of the grounds of eligibility for what is called "adjustment assistance" which can be gotten by firms or by workers adversely affected by international trade. And, in addition, at a very late stage in the bill, there is a brand new idea introduced—adjustment assistance for communities. If a community is now adversely affected by international trade, then substantial forms of government assistance, in the form of loans and grants and technical assistance to new and established businesses, in order to create employment opportunities in the area, is available.

The combination of the restrictions on the concessions that the president can make and the availability of relief in the case of increased imports reflects a kind of basic operating conclusion in the political process which is really contrary to fact. The basic idea that the present trade restrictions are beneficial to the country, should only be eliminated if we get something equal in return, and only if no domestic producer interests are "too much injured." If you read through the legislative history, this kind of Alice-in-Wonderland view is the orthodoxy to which everybody speaks, and the outcome is as I suggested. As I said in fact, most of these provisions that we are "bargaining away" we would be better to just get rid of on our own. This negotiating process has created a strange game. The game is that you cannot just get rid of it, because if you just get rid of it you lose it as a bargaining chip. For that reason, there has been virtually no unilateral change in any of these restrictions.

Another thing that the trade bill does is make a number of changes in various technical provisions governing international trade—that is, subsidies, dumping, unfair competition, and the like. I don't want to go through all of these because they are fairly technical. I would like, however, to isolate one phenomenon on which there has been a radical shift in what could be called a protectionist direction and that is with respect to the problem of foreign subsidies—the question of goods originating abroad being subsidized by the foreign governments. The Act comes down against subsidies far more severely than the preceding law. It treats the issue as if it is a more or less straightforward enactment of a sensible idea. In fact, however, the subsidy problem, or the problem of subsidization by foreign governments of goods sold in the United States, is enormously complex. Almost certainly in balance, where you come out is that we should not do anything about it. The reason why it is complex at best is, first of all, it is often very unclear what a subsidy means. The statute uses the word "subsidy," but, for example, it is difficult to know what "neutral" tax treatment is. If you treat foreign sales more favorably than domestic sales, is that a subsidy? If the government builds a road to a port, is that a subsidy? Indeed, if the government educates people who go to work for exporters, is that a subsidy? But, even if you put that aside, the fact of the matter is that if the foreign government is subsidizing the goods, American consumers are paying less for them. The benefits are real. And what do we care?

If the foreign government is correcting externalities just as we are through tariffs, the reason why the foreign government is subsidizing is because it thinks it is buying something good. It thinks it is terrific to have people as wheat farmers in Europe because it is a socially desirable thing—farmers are hearty democrats and if they move into the city they will become corrupt. If it wants to pay to have them on the farms, then it is going to pay part of the cost of the things they produce and the American consumers get it cheaper. So why not? Why shouldn't I get cheap dairy products and cheap wheat from abroad if the Europeans are foolish enough to subsidize them? Why don't I get part of that as a consumer? Or, at least, why don't I arguably get it? The only way in which the country as a whole could be worse off because of subsidies is if they were used in something called a predatory way. The notion is roughly that you subsidize until you drive all the Americans out of business and then you have a monopoly and you charge great, big monopoly prices. The answer is that it doesn't work because it is too expensive and if you do that, and then you go back to charging monopoly prices, what happens is that the American producers come back in and you never get your monopoly prices.

In any case, the argument on which the subsidy point is made is that subsidized competition is "unfair" to American producers. Well, it is unfair in the sense that the foreign government is kicking in part of the price. It is also unfair to the American consumer not to let him get the benefits of that. There is no way, incidentally, that you can use a subsidy to increase your sales in the United States without letting the American consumer capture part of that.

There is an entirely new procedure with respect to subsidies, whereby the president is called upon to take retaliatory action against foreign governments that practice subsidies. That is a very dangerous provision because the word "subsidy" is loosely used, raising all of the difficulties that I have described.

More significantly, we have on the books something called a countervailing duty statute which permits, on importation, the levying of a "duty" equal to the amount of the foreign subsidy, even if there is no "injury" to an American industry. This statute has long been recognized as having a tremendous potential impact. What the Department of the Treasury, which has authority to administer it, has done is simply get complaints of its violation and not do anything about it because they realize that it is a very dangerous provision. The Bill for the first time obliges the Treasury Department, when it gets a complaint that there has been a subsidy paid abroad, to act formally in disposing of it. It now has to issue an opinion as to whether it is a subsidy, and whether it is going to impose a countervailing duty. Given the expansiveness of the statute, and the Treasury

Department has made it plain before that it does not want to impose subsidies in all the cases that fall within this very general statute, the Treasury is now going to have to justify that in some systematic way. The result will be at least the nuisance of litigation and conceivably a very substantial increase in the incidence of imposing countervailing duties.

The point I would like to conclude with is that if you are talking about the economics of protecting Americans from foreign competition, the economics of deciding whether existing law is justified in terms of widely accepted economic theory is relatively uninteresting. You cannot make a case for these restrictions or, at least, it has not been made. So the really interesting question is the same one across the entire public sector: Why these political outcomes? In this case you may well have the simplest one to explain, although the theory I am about to advance does not explain a lot, and that is the simple reality that producer interests—that is the American producers who would benefit from these restrictions—are much better situated politically to give effect to their preferences than are consumers. The producer interests can identify the stakes; the stake for each producer is much higher; they can be organized in a way that can gain political expression. You do not need to go into the dramatic cases of the dairy producers contributing to political campaigns. It is obvious that producer interests who want to maintain restrictions have a stake that they can identify and advance politically. The consumer interest could not be more poorly constituted to gain effective political expression. If I was to ask you what products you are paying a higher price for because they are subject to a tariff, you would not have the vaguest idea. I do not know either. We would be dumb if we knew because what's it worth to us to know? Suppose we knew? What could we do? We could try to influence a congressman, and he could try to have an effect on the whole political process and that would be dependent upon many people with small interests doing the same. It is literally not worth it. We are rational as consumers not to be informed and not to be active in the political process because the payoff to us is not worth it; but it is worth it to the producers. The really interesting question is what you can do in a general way, if you can do anything, to restructure government decision-making so that concentrated, identifiable interests do not gain too much from the political process at the expense of widely dispersed, difficult-to-quantify interests.

There are really two classes that are the easiest to impose upon—the general class of consumer who, as a result of one of these things, pays a little bit more; and the general class of taxpayer, if you go the subsidy route, who as a result of one of these programs, along with everything else, ends up paying a little bit more. The beneficiaries of the action are in a much better position to identify the particular thing that is causing them to gain and to marshal political support. People who are paying as consumers and taxpayers are not as effectively represented; and, in a sense, international trade is just one example of what I think is a central, general government phenomenon of how you go about not letting the government speak too much for "special interests."

Individual Constraints and Incentives in Government Regulation of Business

Henry Manne

In recent years there have been increasing efforts by scholars interested in regulation to formulate rigorous theories of regulatory behavior with analytical and predictive powers [5]. The model I want to propose here derives fundamentally from the analytical apparatus generally accepted in economic analysis; the postulates adopted here are those found in the first few chapters of any basic textbook in microeconomic analysis.

These usually begin with the assumption that, at least in terms of aggregate human behavior, individuals act in their own self-interest. This does not mean, as some oversimplifiers have suggested, for example, that self-interest is to be equated with hoarding all the money one can possibly get. Charity, benevolence, the interests of others, and the value of forgone opportunities, among other subjective factors, may all enter the self-interest calculus of any individual.

My second introductory note is that the only "interests" we can recognize in developing a useful analytical model of bureaucratic behavior are those that "belong" to individual human beings, the ultimate units of analysis. That notion often surprises people familiar with aggregative constructs like "the corporation," "the university," "the Federal Trade Commission," or "the United States." As a matter of shorthand we do often refer, without loss of clarity, to such collectivities as though they were individual entities; it is simply not efficient to go through a full individualistic analysis every time we refer to an aggregate. In economics, for example, when we refer to "an industry," it is not generally necessary to review the whole body of analysis known as the Theory of the Firm.

Nonetheless, anything we say or imply about firms that does not take cognizance of the fact that actual decisions are made by and in the interests of the particular individuals making them will often lead to wrong conclusions. A substantial literature in the field of corporations, especially on the subject of "corporate social responsibility," has clearly demonstrated the fallacy of assuming that corporations, though properly viewed as aggregates for certain purposes, should be for all purposes. They are not themselves decision-making units, and their "behavior" can never be adequately understood in these terms.

The identical point must be made about government agencies. These come in varied sizes and structures, though for our present purposes it will be sufficient to keep in mind the traditional or conventional agencies we are most familiar with, particularly the major federal agencies such as the Interstate

23

Commerce Commission, the Federal Power Commission, and other rate-making agencies regulating a single industry or field.

Another borrowing from economics, so-called property rights theory, is newer and almost revolutionary in the power it has given economists to analyze areas previously closed to them. Unfortunately for people interested in interdisciplinary matters, and particularly those of us interested in law and economics, the economists who developed property rights theory gave it a name that has a quite different connotation for lawyers than for economists. I will, however, use the phrase in the newer, economists' sense of the terms.

What economists mean when they refer to property rights is the total set of institutional and legal constraints and incentives that effect an individual's behavior vis-à-vis property or relations with other individuals [1]. A simpler way of talking about this concept of property rights would be to refer to privileges and claims as they really operate in action, in other words, to the *real* as opposed to a theoretical or purely doctrinal legal system. I underline the word "real" to distinguish it from the matters of pure form lawyers are fond of confusing with the law as it operates in the objective world.

For instance, economists would analyze the power of burglars to gain something by breaking into houses and stealing, at a certain cost (mostly the disutility of punishment discounted by the probability of being caught and convicted), as a "property right" of burglars. Thus the phrase "property right" does not have the connotation of legitimacy a lawyer would give it. In economics this is an analytical concept and has nothing to do with legitimacy. It is a kind of existential concept of what, in fact, people can do to benefit themselves, given the costs of doing it.

Let me elaborate a bit more what is meant by property rights so that there is no misunderstanding. Property rights, for instance, can exist in the political sphere just as well as in the economic sphere, though they may assume quite different forms. An illustration of a "political" property right would be the right to vote. A person's right to vote may, in this context, be something of a considerable value to the person who has it, or it may be of very little value. Some people care so little for it that the cost of exercising it is greater than the benefit they assume they will get from its exercise. As a result such persons do not vote. Nonetheless, we would still call the right to vote a property rights of citizens.

The First Amendment also gives property rights to individuals. For instance, the right to lobby or advocate political causes in myriad ways is a part of an American citizen's property rights. The right to advertise commercially is, on the other hand, a highly attenuated property right given much less constitutional protection.

A lot of confusion has, I think, arisen in this connection. Criticisms that Ralph Nader has sought to interfere with the private property system illustrate this point. In the present context, this is a misreading of what a private property system, broadly viewed, really is. Ralph Nader's private property includes his rights to try to influence Congress, to gain voters to support his position, and to get out and make speeches. These are all property rights belonging to Ralph Nader by virtue of the United States Constitution.

The fact that I disagree with his facts and his logic or that his exercise of his rights decreases the value of the property rights of General Motors' shareholders does not make them any less property rights of Ralph Nader. After all, every time General Motors sells a car, that decreases to some extent the value of the property rights that Ford Motor Company shareholders would otherwise have. And it is really the same thing with Nader. Everyone's property right may have a positive economic utility or positive welfare value to that individual and a negative one to another person. In this same sense we may say that Nader's exercise of his political property rights has had negative externality effects on General Motors, but the law does not require Nader to internalize these costs.

In positive economics we often utilize cost/benefit analyses in which we add up the aggregate of all the individual pluses and minuses of given behavior. If the pluses are greater than the minuses, and the benefits are greater than the costs, we conclude that the action is, *ceteris paribus*, socially desirable. In politics, and in the field of regulation, this counting is quite difficult to do. The principal reason is that we simply have no identifiable units by which to count. We do not have a single medium of exchange, like money, that allows us to measure utility and disutility to different individuals. It may even prove impossible ultimately to develop a true science of politics because we cannot know whether an outcome is desirable or undesirable since we cannot measure the pluses and minuses. Still, some helpful analysis is possible, as we shall see, and occasionally even some measurement.

Other kinds of political property relevant to a full positive theory of regulation include the right to organize political pressure groups, various judicial procedural rights, Constitutional guarantees of a hearing and notice before administrative rulings are made, the right to appeal administrative decisions to courts, freedom of the press, freedom to publish materials pro or con on a given position, etc.

Still a different type of political property would include, for example, the special powers of a chairman of a particular appropriations committee in the United States Senate to deal with a particular area of regulation. This chairman obviously can exercise tremendous authority over the individuals in that agency who want to maximize their budget and must go to the right committee chairman to accomplish that. Therefore, we should anticipate that they would have something to exchange for his political (financial) assistance. It does not seem so unfamiliar to call this chairman's power a property right.

Still another type of rights in political power are bureaucratic powers. Here I would first include the right to job security. All things being equal everybody prefers more job security to less, but because of Civil Service rules, people who are relatively more interested in job security than in other forms of reward tend to be attracted to those kinds of jobs, and they will, therefore, "spend" more to protect them, a matter discussed further below. Still another property right of bureaucrats is the right to make rules, regulations, and interpretations. These are very important since they are the very meat (or should we say the "cleaver?") of regulation. They provide the most significant utilities or disutilities which bureaucrats use directly or in exchange to maximize their own interests.

A valuable property right of high level executives in government agencies is the right to assign jobs to different people. This power can be critical, since when an assignment has either economic utility or disutility to another person, some sort of mutually beneficial exchanges of the right is both possible and likely, another proposition taken directly from basic economic principles but certainly no less applicable in this context.

A more peculiar kind of property right, more significant in many government agencies than one might at first believe, is the right to behave either nicely or badly to people who have to apply for favors and rulings of one sort or another. Normally we do not think of that as a right; yet consider the post office. You wait in line for twenty minutes to buy 13¢ stamps; you get to the head of the line and are told that there are no more 13¢ stamps; you can get thirteen ones, but they won't fit on your envelopes; you growl (that is your right). Still the basis for an exchange transaction might well exist. Suppose there actually are a few 13¢ stamps around, but only the official behind the barred cage can decide who will receive them. His or her right to be nice or not to be nice to the individual in line is an economic utility that every such official has—and often seeks to maximize.

Another important bureaucratic property right is the right to take a private job, say in a law firm or in industry after leaving the government job. That right is sometimes constrained by various laws, however. For instance, the degree of constraint on taking post-government jobs in industry is higher among officials of the Department of Defense than it is among those who have worked for the Federal Trade Commission. The latter, who tend frequently to be lawyers, are generally free to take a job with a law firm with which they have just dealt, though there may be a restraint on the particular cases they can handle for a period of time afterwards.

One other "right" (in the purely positive economic sense of the term) is very important, that is the right (or the "power," if there are Hohfeldian purists around) to take a bribe. In other words, the potential is there for anyone who values the assumed gain more than the payoff discounted by the assumed risk of a particular punishment. We should expect some of that behavior to occur. Economists can predict that if a person walks down a street with no one else in sight and finds a $20 bill lying on the sidewalk, the tendency will be for the individual to pick it up and keep it. Just so with bribes. We do not know how often it occurs (the general absence of publicity about crimes implies nothing about the amount of such activity), but the greater the anticipated reward (a function of the value of the favor the official can bestow), the more often it must occur.

Up to now we have dealt with generalized political rights, Constitutional rights, the rights of elected officials, and the rights of appointed officials. But there are also nongovernment property rights we must deal with in analyzing the total picture of government regulation. So we look at the rights of the individuals who deal from the outside with the individuals in government. What sort of property rights do they have vis-à-vis an agency and the agency's production? First, some rights are provided by the basic enabling legislation. Usually some kind of substantive rules are mandated in those acts; provisions relating to notice and hearing, for example, and a variety of other rights may be determined by the underlying legislation.

Another kind of right that the outsider has—the other side of a coin already mentioned—is the right to hold open to individuals in government positions promises of jobs, wealth, travel, respect, and so forth; that is, the right in a sense to offer, legally or illegally, something of value. Again I am using "right" in the economic sense of something that can in fact be attempted and which is deemed valuable by the individual with that power. Economic theory suggests that individuals will utilize these property rights to maximize their own positions. Economic theory further tells us that normally we maximize by making exchanges with other individuals.

Individuals on the outside of an agency have a set of rights similar to but the converse of some of those mentioned for agency officials. They may be unkind, unfriendly, and uncooperative to agency officials. They also have the right to smile and to decide whether pushing will be more effective than pulling.

This concludes a fairly short summary of some of the property rights more actively exchanged and therefore usefully considered in developing an economic theory of individual behavior in bureaucratic situations. The parallel with economics is not coincidental; we are in fact merely encountering another type of exchange, which is what economic theory developed to explain. In conventional economic illustrations, individuals have money and individuals have goods; some people will sell goods for money, some people will give up the money for goods; some people will work for a certain wage, other people will pay that wage to get individuals to do a job.

The similarities are obvious, but it is very important to notice that there are some differences as well. First the variables we have to deal with are probably more complex, more varied, and simply more numerous in the political sphere than in the comparable economics sphere. Generally when we are discussing economics, we can talk about markets for grain or automobiles or gold in the same general terms. In politics we do not yet have a theory developed enough to make us feel confident with such generalizations. Reliable predictability as well as reliably testable hypotheses are still somewhat elusive. Each of the property rights mentioned above has peculiar characteristics that we know very little about; that is we do not really know how they are distributed, marketed, valued, exchanged, or used. We do not know how the political market for these various goods, or bads, really functions. In economics we talk about competition and monopoly, how price is determined, how production functions are determined, and we talk about the behavior of firms. Nothing quite so straightforward is as yet clearly available to us in the political arena.

William Niskanen's pioneering work in this area, entitled *Bureaucracy and Representative Government* [4], was restrictive in terms of the kinds of individuals that it dealt with and consequently of the property rights upon which it could focus. But it still illustrates, I believe, the potential for a full blown theory of political property rights. Niskanen identified legislators (all of them) as the most significant consumers of agency production. This was not necessary to his theses, but it did allow a more narrow focusing on an exchange relationship. He analogizes the government bureau or agency to a firm that produces an economic good and has customers. Its production is the flow of rules and regulations, and for Niskanen, as mentioned, the consumers likely to give most in exchange for the production of the agency are legislators. It is a legislative committee, as mentioned above, that controls the budget of an agency, and an agency head interested in effectuating his own political property rights will cater to that consumer.

Traditionally every agency had to deal with two committees, one with substantive jurisdiction over the legal powers of an agency, and the other with power over the agency's budget. That had the effect of dividing the control of the agency among two committee chairmen (with everyone on each committee getting a little throw-off as well). Ironically reformers bent on improving the "efficiency" of Congress amalgamated these two functions in many cases so that the same committees that had substantive responsibility also were given responsibility for an agency's appropriation—exactly the wrong direction to go if they wanted to make agencies behave more responsibly rather than less.

Not only did Niskanen view a very narrow set of interested parties, he also failed to note that legislators have an interest in nonregulation as a valued "product" of an agency too [7]. Indeed one reason legislators like bureaucratic regulation of private activities so much is because they have considerable power to stop or reverse a particular line of regulation if it becomes beneficial to them to do so. Because of their power over the agency executives and staff through budget controls, legislators are in a position to turn the regulatory voltage up or down or on or off, depending on what is in their own interest. So we are logically led to ask what could they be interested in.

The answers are many. As we have noted, they can get organized political support; they can get contributions to their campaigns; they may even get occasional black satchels full of money, or numbered Swiss bank accounts. All of those things must happen, though I have no information regarding frequencies or amounts. But it should be clear that the greater the regulatory pressures, the greater the power that legislators (and to a much lesser extent, members of the executive branch) have over private interests, and the more of their "product" they can sell, either by way of protection from harm or as a specific good that somebody wants.

From legislators, let us turn to the bureaucrats themselves, though we must take note at the outset that there are several separate groups of bureaucrats often having conflicting property rights and interests to protect. For present purposes, however, we shall consider only two sets. Starting at the top, there are the appointed officials. Their terms of office are generally rather short. They are generally close to the presidential political scene, and they have usually gotten their positions either as a reward for political favor or in exchange for an expectation of political favor in the future. They tend to be people "on the make," as it were, and often their interests will not coincide with the interests of the career staff bureaucrats. In fact, it is not too surprising to hear a chairman of an important federal agency, as occurred recently in the Civil Aeronautics Board, loudly proclaim the virtues of deregulation and indeed of abolishing his own agency, particularly if as a result of such behavior he feels that he moves himself closer to becoming secretary of transportation or of commerce or ambassador to England. We should expect him to say what the president wants to hear, since it will be in his interests to go along with whatever the president's political position is, even if that conflicts with what might be viewed by some as the agency's "interest."

Could we expect the same from the staff bureaucrats, the professional civil servants? Not commonly. Indeed, when a former chairman of the Federal Trade Commission was heard to say that there should be significant deregulation within his own agency, we may be sure that permanent staff members of the Commission were thinking of throwing sand into the Xerox machines or of running out of paper on which to print the chairman's press release. Their interest lay only in preserving the system of regulation. And if it were pointed out to them that this regulation may be needlessly costing the public vast sums of money, it would make little difference. Under our postulates they will generally behave as though the regulation is desirable, regardless of the facts. Only in this way can they protect their jobs and their own self-interest in the marketplace of political property rights. And rationalizations are cheap.

The main concern for the career staffer, as indicated earlier, is with security and secondly with not making waves or work for themselves. I suppose that these notions are fairly obvious and one can understand that it is not in their interest to behave in any other way. After all, they do not get rewarded for being bold and imaginative; they can only get into trouble. That is why any "old hand" in Washington will tell the potential career bureaucrat that it is always safer to say "no" than to say "yes," to deny a request rather than authorize it. There is less chance of getting into trouble and less chance of having to explain why something unusual was allowed. Say "no," and put the burden on the petitioner to go to court or wherever, or drop the matter, or let somebody else decide it. And one also can take quite a long time saying "no." We might predict other behavioral characteristics for lower echelon bureaucrats as well. In fact just about every cliche about bureaucrats can now be explained; "Don't make waves." "Stay out of trouble," "Avoid controversy," "Keep a low profile."

Part of their interest maximizing behavior will be to develop make-work projects and to delay all decisions as long as possible. They will favor a system of promotion by seniority rather than by merit because a merit approach creates competition and makes comparisons necessary, and that in turn requires some objective basis for judging the value of the work that people are doing. That is not desirable for people who want neither to do much nor to be noticed.

Finally, we would expect these functionaries to be extraordinarily legalistic, much more so indeed than any lawyer, law student, or law professor. In fact, they will often be so mechanically legalistic in their thinking that the true sense of what is intended becomes irrelevant.

The annals of horror stories about bureaucracy are full of such cases where no one looks behind the meaning of a rule. "Apply the letter of the law." Probably the best known case of recent vintage was the OSHA inspector inspecting a one-man (and the phrase is used literally) company, a single male individual who had a garage operation subcontracting to make a small component for someone else. He had no one else working for him. But OSHA rules require that every concern have separate bathrooms for men and for women, and the OSHA inspector therefore required that a second bathroom for women be installed—even though there was no one to use it. Now *that* is legalistic, but he was "just following the rules." That case, however, became a *cause celebre*, and I suppose OSHA backed down.

In the literature on bureaucracy, the group generally considered most important and the most complicated to deal with is comprised of the individuals and firms directly regulated [8]. It would be nice if, as Ralph Nader does, we could oversimplify the matter and view their interest as concerned absolutely with having a government policed cartel. But logic and intellectual honesty do not allow that. Among others interested in what administrators do are the customers of the regulated industry, neighbors of the firms regulated (as in pollution cases), and suppliers to the industry (as with labor). Underestimating or disregarding these other interests (and intra-industry conflict as well) has led many observers into a naive trap referred to commonly as "the agency capture theory." Nader and others like him have used this "theory" more for antibusiness propaganda rather than for any analytical purpose.

The name most frequently associated with this theory is not an economist nor a political figure at all but a fairly well known New Left historian, Gabriel Kolko. There is historical and logical merit to Kolko's argument, though certainly not as much as he suggests. Kolko, for instance, would give full responsibility for the adoption of the Interstate Commerce Act to the railroads themselves [2]. Kolko has exaggerated considerably, and there have been significant modifications to his findings by other careful researchers. Still there is no question but that his thesis holds up as a partial explanation of what has happened, and industries undoubtedly still seek regulation or nurture it in order to avoid competition.

There is a peculiar "economic good" that businesses try to produce privately but which they rarely if ever succeed in doing. This is the formation and preservation of monopolies or cartels. In producing this particular "good," centralized governments have a tremendous comparative advantage. The benefits of private cartels, private price-fixing arrangements, and even mergers designed to beget monopoly profits, generally do not survive long enough to warrant the activity. The cost of creating and maintaining such arrangements is greater than the benefit that comes from having them. If every firm in an industry merges and we have a monopoly that can charge a monopoly price, then, unless entry into the industry can be controlled, new entry will certainly occur and the monopoly will have to sustain the tremendous costs of inefficient size. Further, the private costs of preventing entry can be prodigious. However, if the government restricts the new entry into the industry, that cost may be much less. Still the government officials will presumably seek the maximizing "price" for this service, and if they be monopolists, the usual theory of monopoly pricing should yield some insights.

The government can more simply and cheaply restrict entry into an industry than private firms can by such devices as licensing and numerous other forms of regulation. For instance, the SEC regulates the amount of capital that brokerage firms must maintain; that is a neat way of keeping a large number of small brokerage firms from competing. The Federal Trade Commission puts restrictions on the very kind of advertising that may be most efficient in aiding entry into an industry. In these and many other ways firms already in an industry may benefit from regulation; but they will pay for this benefit.

Still, there are conflicting interests among the member firms in any regulated industry, just as we find in private cartels, and the market for government protection is not a simple or straightforward one.

In the theory of cartels the first great problem of the would-be monopolists is determining how to cut up the pie. Everyone realizes that by getting together they can make a larger aggregate pie for themselves than they presently have (though smaller for everyone else). But the job of determining how to cut up the larger pie and policing the agreement often requires greater costs and efforts than the cartel benefits warrant. The important point to note, however, is that that phenomenon does not cease to exist just because a government agency protects firms against competitive entry or cartelizes the industry in some other way.

Different firms still have different production costs and consequently have differing optimal prices. Or they may prefer different levels of production; and they may have different comparative advantages in quality, size, or other features. The fact is that in most industries each firm has different production preferences since each will generally have distinctive comparative cost advantages. Thus there can be no simple way in which "industries" can dominate agencies set up to regulate them. It must be true that for some firms within an industry (but rarely, if ever, all of them) it will be in their interest to have regulation. That does not mean by a long shot, however, that regulation will or can secure a perfect monopoly or cartel arrangement for each member of the industry. The conflict which destroys private cartels merely becomes part of political competition under regulation.

Similar conflicts may exist among individuals within a given corporation, thus further confusing the optimal production function of an agency. The interest that the top executive of a corporation, for instance, has in certain kinds of regulation may be quite different from that of the shareholders. This is particularly true in rate-regulated industries. Executives of power companies, and to some extent banks, insurance companies, and railroads, are generally thought to lead a more relaxed life than their counterparts in more highly competitive businesses. They seem to talk more about corporate social responsibilities, and they are also prone to longer vacations and shorter workdays than their counterparts in nonregulated industries.

Executives working short hours and taking long vacations may not be acting in the interest of the shareholders of the utilities. On the other hand, there is little if anything the shareholders can do about this, since the firm's position is protected by the governmental device of not allowing another firm to enter. Consequently, since no one has any interest in displacing inefficient executives in these industries, tender offers and "raids" are almost unknown, and there is little that the shareholders can do about the matter.

Small wonder then that as soon as someone starts to talk about deregulation, the top executive officers of the regulated companies speak almost with one voice decrying the "utter chaos and confusion" that would follow deregulation of their industry. For a recent illustration of this point, see newspapers two days after President Ford made his suggestion in 1975 to experiment with competition among airlines, both in fares and for routes. Within two days the chief executive officers of all but one major carrier in the country had written a public letter to the president in very strong terms complaining that he was about to ruin the greatest air transport system in the world.

Another kind of conflict in regulation arises because one firm's profit may be another firm's higher cost [6]. The Interstate Commerce Commission deals frequently and on a friendly basis with spokesmen for the trucking industry, including the Teamsters Union. Both those groups like ICC regulation, one because it keeps new competition from coming in and competing for their routes at lower rates, and the other because this ultimately generates higher wages. On the other hand, people who ship a lot of freight by truck are not totally without political power. They too have property rights, and most, but not all, would prefer lower rates for their shipments. The result of these competing vectors is unpredictable a priori, and even *ex ante*, after all the political events have occurred, we still cannot say with certainty who has had how much influence.

Still we can say some things that may be helpful. Those identifiable groups for whom the net cost over benefits are less than the net costs to others will generally tend to dominate [8]. Sometimes a winning group can be readily identified. For instance, regulation of three television networks is facilitated because only three firms have to reach an agreement among themselves and with the agency. Furthermore, their production functions are probably more alike than one would find, for instance, in the airline industry. On the other hand, the cost of politically organizing everyone who would like a chance to start a competing television station, or would like some change in the rules regarding advertising on television, would be extremely high. As a result we should expect producer interests to dominate over consumer interest in broadcast regulation.

But this cannot always be the case. Ralph Nader, labor organizations, Common Cause, and many other organizations illustrate how agencies became beholden to someone other than a regulated industry, even if that group does not happen to represent "the public," whatever that may mean. An agency may be a captive in some kind of contractual sense of somebody, even Ralph Nader, and certainly in many areas we have observed in recent years that somebody is not the industry.

I want to mention one other group's property interests in regulation before turning to some very tentative conclusions. That group is very powerful and plays a large role at every point in the whole scenario of an exchange of political property rights. That group comprises the established lawyers in private practice who specialize in a particular area of administrative law. Lawyers have just about as much interest in continuing a system of regulation as do members of Congress or permanent staff bureaucrats. Indeed, it is very difficult to find lawyers in private practice (as opposed in the main to lawyers who are in-house counsel for corporations) ever openly advocating repeal of a regulatory law they help "administer."

Some tentative conclusions now seem in order about where we are in the development of an economic theory of regulation, or of a theory of markets for political behavior. We have in economics, as mentioned earlier, a comprehensive and sophisticated apparatus for dealing with conventional types of economic behavior. But it is often of limited practical value because it has not been integrated with the kinds of institutional data I have been addressing here.

We know, for instance, that for a given supply of a good there is a market clearing price and that owners of the goods will try to find that price in order to maximize their returns. But all of that becomes much less valuable in formulating policy when the government is determining what the supply will be, or when individual producers are not free to compete simply by determining their own most efficient production rates, or when the most efficient pricing system for their production is illegal [3]. So, even though we have a body of economic doctrine—and a philosophy to go along with it—much remains to be done to make that economic theory more realistic and more useful.

We are a long way from developing the same degree of cohesiveness and academic acceptance of basic tools in the political field that we seem to have in economics. At the same time it is also fair to say that we are beginning to know a lot more about the regulatory system than we did previously. We are beginning to understand, for instance, that there is a lot more to the matter than an industry simply "buying" market protection through government regulation. We also know that the regulation such efforts leads to will not produce perfect monopolies. Competing and conflicting interests will generate political equilibria hardly likely to be optimal from the "pure" economic point of view. But we cannot readily predict or even describe those political equilibria.

I close with one prediction. As the true nature of regulation and the full applicability of the theory of property rights to regulation become better understood by scholars interested in such matters, I think we will hear more of them advocating deregulation. But I do not think that will make much difference, just as I do not think it made much difference that heretofore they strongly advocated regulation. They are not highly valued consumers of this governmental service, and generally they will be outbid by those willing to pay more to get what they want. There is no light of hope showing at the other end of the tunnel. We are, however, beginning to understand a little about the shape and size of the tunnel.

References

1. A.A. Alchian, "Some Economics of Property," RAND P-2316 (Santa Monica, California: The RAND Corporation, 1961).

2. Gabriel Kolko, *Railroads and Regulation 1877-1916* (Princeton: Princeton University Press, 1965).

3. Roland N. McKean, "Property Rights Within Government, And Devices to Increase Governmental Efficiency," *Southern Economic Journal* 39, 2 (Oct. 1972): 177-186.

4. William A. Niskanen, Jr., *Bureaucracy and Representative Government* (Chicago: Aldine-Atherton, Inc., 1971).

5. Sam Peltzman, "Toward a More General Theory of Regulation," *Journal of Political Economy*, forthcoming.

6. Richard A. Posner, "Taxation by Regulation," *The Bell Journal of Economics and Management Science* 2, 1 (Spring 1971): 22-50.

7. Richard A. Posner, "Theories of Economic Regulation," *The Bell Journal of Economics and Management Science* 5, 2 (Autumn 1974): 335-358.

8. George J. Stigler, "The Theory of Economic Regulation," *The Bell Journal of Economics and Management Science* 2, 1 (Spring 1971): 3-21.

Improving Economic Policy

Herbert Stein

Although this chapter is titled "Improving Economic Policy," I am really going to discuss *not* improving economic policy. That is, I am mainly going to discuss economic planning. Of course, it is much easier to talk about things that would not improve economic policy than it is to talk about improving economic policy because improving economic policy is much more difficult. What can be said about improving policy is very simple, but to carry it out is difficult.

I will discuss the current wave of interest in national economic planning and then, after I have said what it is and explained why I do not think much of it, I will suggest some of the kinds of things that might be done to improve economic policy. I certainly do not start from the assumption that economic policy is in no need of improvement. I had enough experience with it to know that we do not manage nearly as well as we would like or nearly as well as we sometimes pretend that we do.

Let me start with the question of economic planning. As you may know, there has been a surge of interest in the idea of national economic planning in the United States in the last year or so. There seems to be a cycle of waves of interest in national economic planning. We had a good deal of interest in the subject in the early 1930s and then again after World War II, and then again in the early 1960s; usually in situations where there is a feeling something is wrong with the performance of the economy, and obviously this is a feeling that has been widespread in the last year or so.

Almost the whole problem of discussing economic planning is in defining what it is. People have quite varied ideas of what it might mean and many of the people who discuss it, especially those who are most for it, have no idea whatever of what it might mean except that planning is a good word and they are for it. It has a certain sound of modernity and rationalism. As long as the subject is undefined, it is very difficult to discuss, and also very difficult to object to. I am going to give some possible definitions and select what seems to be the most relevant one.

There was an article in the magazine section of the *New York Times* (January 25, 1976) by Professor Robert Heilbroner about economic planning, in which he maintained that despite my complaints about it, which he cited, and complaints by some other people, planning was inevitable. Then he went on to indicate some of the kinds of planning that he had in mind. One thing he says early in the piece is that, for example, we might have a plan to limit inflation, and this would involve this and this and this and this.

If what we are talking about is the possibility that we would have a plan to limit inflation, we have had not only a plan but many plans to limit inflation. Planning to limit inflation has been a staple of economic policy for decades, if not centuries. (This of course indicates another very relevant thing about planning which many of the proponents of planning forget, and that is that there is a big difference between planning to do something and doing something.) We have had a lot of plans to deal with inflation but we have not really succeeded in dealing with inflation. My point about the Heilbroner example is that a good deal of what people are urging upon us as being important and new and desirable aspects of planning consists of things that we do and that government does.

I was reminded when I read his article of the fact that when I was in the White House the mess used to serve a Mexican lunch every Thursday; that went back to the time of Lyndon Johnson who was a fan of Mexican food. So you can say we were doing planning in the White House: we planned to have Mexican food for lunch every Thursday. If that is all people mean it is like saying that we wake up and discover that we have been planning all along, just like the famous Frenchman who woke up in surprise to discover he had been speaking prose all his life.

I think we have to be somewhat more specific about what we mean by planning before we can discuss it. I have a list here of eight possible meanings of planning. Basic in any discussion of planning are statements of what the government should do. The first is that the government should do something that it is already doing, as is evidenced by Mr. Heilbroner's example of having a plan to limit inflation. A second and very common meaning (which of course is very hard to object to) is that government should do better. Whatever the government is doing or is going to do it ought to do better. It ought to act with more information, more rationality, more foresight, more objectivity, and more certainty and stability.

A third meaning (which may be an aspect of the second one) is that the government should coordinate its policies better. There is a view that the government is an enormous enterprise and there are several million people who are all doing different things, and with different objectives in mind, and that they all ought to be "regularized." Somebody ought to decide what all the priorities are and make sure that everybody is playing on the same team (not only playing on the same team but presumably that everybody should be playing the same position on the same team). So, coordination is one of the key words when people talk about the need for economic planning.

Sometimes what they mean is that the government should provide some particular benefit. This is clear in an article that Senator Javits wrote. (I am going to be referring from time to time to a bill which is called the "Humphrey-Javits Bill," the "Balanced Economic Growth and Planning Act"). Senator Javits wrote an article in the *Wall Street Journal* explaining why we need planning and what it all seemed to come down to was that he was in favor of health insurance: "Look at Sweden—they have a planned society (which is incorrect, but anyway)—and they have a health insurance plan too." So that is a possible meaning of planning. Another meaning is that the government should control some particular thing, like air pollution. Then we get into what I think are more useful and relevant meanings of planning.

First (this is really sixth on my list), the government should provide some comprehensive general guidance and influence over the behavior of the economy. At this particular point we get away from, "they should do this particular thing or that particular thing," or, that, "it should do what it already does, better," and say, "government should exercise general comprehensive influence over the economy."

The seventh meaning is that it should not only provide this comprehensive and general guide and influence but it should enforce compliance where there seems to be, or there is a danger of there being, a significant departure from the guidance that the government provides.

Finally, there is the notion that the government should exercise comprehensive mandatory controls over the system. The last three of these meanings of planning are distinguished from each other by the degree of control that is exercised. They range from, on the one hand, merely setting out a plan for the operation of the economy, and perhaps exercising certain moral suasion over the private sector, to the last, which would involve comprehensive and mandatory controls.

I cannot discuss all of these possible meanings under the head of planning, partly because there is not time, but partly because it would not be relevant. There is no point in discussing propositions that are simply based on error, such as the proposition that we should have a plan for checking inflation. And there is no point in discussing a kind of Stalinist system. All of the proponents of planning would reject that notion; they would say that we are not for mandatory controls because such controls have a bad name in this country. I suppose most of them would say, and probably sincerely, that they would be against national economic planning if they thought that the upshot of the national economic planning would be a move into mandatory comprehensive controls of a totalitarian type like the Russian system.

It is interesting to note that some of the people who would oppose total mandatory controls, nevertheless favor the idea of guidance. Of course many of the people who favor planning without the mandatory controls believe that one advantage of the guidance system or the more or less voluntary system is that the centrally arrived at plan, will, inevitably, be wrong at a number of points. They believe that if the conformity to the plan is voluntary, the private sector will conform to the plan in those cases where the plan is correct and not conform to it in the cases where it is incorrect. That seems to me a groundless belief, as many of the beliefs in this field are.

It reminds me of the kind of argument we used to have about incomes policy before we went to price and wage controls in 1971. There were many people who said we ought to have a kind of voluntary incomes policy; the government would set out some guidelines, and people would be expected, and business and labor unions would be expected, to comply with them voluntarily. When you said, "Well, but these guidelines would not be relevant and realistic in all cases; you can't set out a simple set of rules which would be efficient for determining prices and wages in all circumstances," they would then say, "Well, since the system is voluntary, people will not adhere to them, will not observe the guidelines in the cases where the guidelines would give the wrong signal." But there is no reason to expect that if people are free to obey, they will obey or comply only in the cases where it is, from some national standpoint, rational to do so.

I do not intend, either, to discuss proposals for specific benefit programs or controls, because each of those has to stand on its own merits. I am not going to take the position here that there are no circumstances in which the government should provide benefits or no circumstances in which the government should exercise controls over the economy.

However, I think it is also necessary to say that while every case of a proposed benefit, or a proposed control, needs to be examined on its own merits, it is usually not sufficient to do this. One needs to have a certain presumption about the desirability of expanding or not expanding the area in which the government provides benefits or extends controls. You can get into a situation where a number of decisions in particular cases, each of which might be wise when considered separately, would accumulate to a relationship between the government and the private sector that you would not like. So that what may be said about planning in general does have some relevance for specific proposals.

I think we come down here to two kinds of policies which might be discussed under the heading of planning. The first is, to improve the performance of established government functions in pursuit of those goals of the society which are recognized as being the proper functions of the government to serve. This includes the problem of coordinating the behavior of the various parts of the government, and I will return to that. But second, and the thing I will discuss mainly under the head of planning, is the formulation of a comprehensive plan for the performance of the private sector, not in every detail, but by major divisions.

For example, people who are proposing a plan now have used as an example that the government would draw up a plan which would indicate how many automobiles ought to be produced; but they would not say how many should be two-door or four-door, or how many produced by Ford, or how many by General Motors, and how many black, and how many gray, and so on. They would leave those details to the private sector, but they would provide some guidance on the total number of automobiles to be produced, and they would give guidance about the total amount of frozen food, but not how many peas, and how many beans, and so on.

There would be this comprehensive plan, the degree of detail not usually being specified, but obviously more detail than the government now makes decisions about, and the government would try to bring about conformity to that plan, by some combination of information, moral suasion, incentives, and compulsion. That, I think, is what is involved in the current proposals about planning. And I think that is what is the implication of the Humphrey-Javits bill, which is now the vehicle of the movement for economic planning in the United States.

Senator Humphrey has said that it is not his intention, nor is it his expectation from the bill, that it would extend the role of government or increase government control over the economy. It would just make the government do everything better that it is supposed to be doing anyway. Senator Javits' view, I have already explained, involves his preference for the expansion of some welfare programs. But I do not think these explanations can be taken as a real indication of what the implication of the bill would be. For one thing, many of the people who are more involved in the drafting of the bill than I think either Senator Humphrey or Senator Javits have given more ambitious descriptions of what their expectations are. If one reads the language of the bill, one can come to some notion of what the outcome would be if this bill became law, and an attempt was made to live with it.

The first question that needs to be asked is, why do people want greater economic planning? What is their view of the economic problem which leads them to believe that we need a new economic planning system, that we need in a rather fundamental way to change the relations between the government and the private sector of the economy?

I think this view is best described as the current radical chic view of the economic system. It is a view that is radically different from the established view, or the range of views which have strong scientific backing. It rejects both neoclassical economics and old fashioned liberal economics. It also describes as inadequate the neo-Keynesian view, or the view that we used to call the "new economics" when President Kennedy came in. (This is now the middle-aged economics, that people like Walter Heller and Arthur Okun represent.) It rejects all that.

It is a view that is easily affected by anyone and it immediately serves as a sign of a kind of modernity, of being "with it," and of not being old fashioned. It is the kind of view that is held not only by fashionable economists, by Galbraith and Heilbroner, but also by Hollywood stars who want to do good with their beauty and fame, and media pundits, and even some guilt-ridden businessmen.

A main element in this radical chic view is that the market no longer works, if it ever did work. The world is, and especially the United States is, increasingly dominated by large corporations; some will also say by large unions, but generally, the focus is on the large corporation. So we cannot count on a market system to serve the interest of consumers efficiently, and this of course, in their view, leaves the way open for more reliance on the government.

The multinational corporation is a favorite buzz-word in this view of what is wrong with the world, although no one, I think, has ever explained very persuasively what it is that is wrong with the multinational corporation. I think what is implied is that the multinational corporation has escaped both the discipline of the market, and the discipline of the national state.

A third proposition is that the world is dominated by what economists for many years have called "externalities." That is, it is dominated by conditions in which the decisions made by private actors in the market have effects which the private actor has no motive to take into account. The outstanding case is the environment. The person or the business whose smoke stack pollutes the environment does not suffer any damage from that pollution, and therefore has no financial interest in reducing it. Outside controls need to be imposed.

This is a situation of course, which everybody has recognized to exist for a long time, at least since four hundred years ago when the English government passed laws against throwing refuse out of second-story windows. That was a form of antipollution legislation. That situation is considered now to be the very essence of our lives.

A fourth element of the believed situation is that the world's economy has become enormously more complex, and this is believed to create the need for more planning, more government control. A fifth (I find that I'm making another list of things) and another dominant element in this thinking about the new condition of the world is that we are running into shortages. The view is that we are running out of things, and on that account the world is going to become poorer, or it is going to become rich much less rapidly than it formerly did.

This is a very important aspect in the whole view of the situation. I remember almost two years ago, when I was in the government, the president received a letter from Senators Mansfield and Scott, who were the majority and minority leaders of the Senate. It was a portentous letter saying that there is something wrong with the way the American economic system is organized, and we really should have a large meeting of all sectors of the government, and all parts of the private community, to figure out what is wrong and how to organize the economy so that it would work better. We agreed that it was not working very well but were rather skeptical about their view of what was wrong with it; but we said we would be glad to come and talk with them about it. When we got there (in the Capitol) we discovered that their whole concern was that we were running out of things and, particularly, that we were becoming dependent on the rest of the world. There was no mechanism, as far as they knew, in the private economy, which foresaw shortages and dealt with them.

Another example of how dominant this thinking is in the current wave of interest in planning is the statement by Leonard Woodcock of the UAW, who is a leader in the planning movement. He said he did not really become interested in planning until after the oil shortage hit us.

A sixth element in this new view of what is going on in the world is the view that the less developed countries have become not only much more economically independent, but also much more economically aggressive, so that they pose a new problem for the industrial countries, including the United States. Finally, as an aspect of some of these other developments, it is believed that we have an inflation and unemployment problem which is much more fundamental and structural than ordinary economists have thought it was.

That is, they are saying that because of these shortages and because of the aggressive action of those countries that supply us with raw materials, productivity will be rising less rapidly and costs will be rising more rapidly. This causes inflation, and it also causes unemployment because productivity will not be rising as fast as the wage expectations of workers, and this creates a persistent unemployment problem.

I think that these alleged descriptions of the state of the economy are, in general, not true, and if they were true, not relevant to the problem of planning. There is no evidence, for example, that the American economy or the world economy is becoming less competitive or more monopolized, except insofar as we are having government suppression of competition. The fact that the world has become so much more open than it used to be, that barriers to international trade are smaller than they used to be, is a force making for considerably more competition than we used to have. As far as the multinational corporation is concerned, it can be regarded and I think properly, as a way of making the world market work better. It is a way in which goods and technology and management move around the world across national borders much more freely than they otherwise would do. That is a force for competition.

As far as the externalities (like the environment) are concerned, I think one cannot deny that such externalities are among the reasons why we have government, but they are not a reason for having the government dominate our lives. The shortage story, which is so important, I think is entirely wrong. We are not running out of resources. The resources available to us are not less abundant than they were a hundred years ago, or two hundred years ago. It is true that we have been using up some things since the beginning of time, but as long as investment is going on, and research and development are going on, we are adding to the supply of productive resources available to the world's population, and adding to them more rapidly than we are using them up.

If the notion of a market economy was appropriate two hundred years ago in the time of Adam Smith, we have certainly not become any less affluent than in his time, and we are certainly not likely to be. The worry about the independence of the less developed countries is entirely extrapolated from the behavior of OPEC. I think we have survived and surmounted that, and it is unlikely to be emulated; at least it is unlikely that the countries that raise bananas and cocoa are going to be able to bring us to our knees by exploiting a monopoly of those things.

It is true that the world economy has become more complex, but to say that is an argument for planning really begs the basic issue, which is whether a complex system is better managed by the market than by the government. If you think the world is becoming more complex, that is an argument for more dependence on the market, and not an argument for more dependence on planning.

If we pass beyond this question and assume that the world has changed in some various respects, what do the advocates of planning expect or propose that it should do for us? What is really incredible in all the dicussion about planning in the last year or so is that there has been so little specification of what the planning is to be for; what are the objectives to which the planning is to be addressed?

One would think that the very essence of planning is that you have a goal, and plan to use various means and instruments in order to achieve that goal, and one would have thought that people who are devoted to planning, who think that we need more of it, would be prepared to state the goals before they set up instruments and processes for trying to achieve those goals. But that has not been the case at all. The Humphrey-Javits bill does not list goals, it lists a number of areas about which goals are to be developed. It says that the plan should be developed paying particular attention (these are only the subjects to which particular attention is to be paid; presumably there are subjects to which less particular attention is to be paid) to the attainment of the goals of "full employment, price stability, balanced economic growth and equitable distribution of income, the efficient utilization of both private and public resources, balanced regional and urban development, stable international relations, meeting essential national needs in transportation, energy, agriculture, raw materials, housing, education, public services, and research and development."

That is quite a formidable list. But as I have said, these are just areas, they are not objectives. They are not defined, they are not quantified. The bill would not tell us what is full employment (a subject over which there has been a tremendous argument for thirty years or so). Its authors think that balanced economic growth is a primary objective, a primary goal, because that is the title of the act, "Balanced Economic Growth and Planning Act." But nowhere is there any note, any idea, of what balanced economic growth means. Does it mean that growth should be as fast east of the Mississippi as west of the Mississippi, or equally fast in each of the fifty states, or that all industries should grow at the same rate, or at the rate indicated by some statistical table?

That kind of question can be asked about all of these objectives. So one cannot tell from anything that has been said, so far, what the goals are to which the plan would be addressed.

But you can say two things about the plan; if the legislation was adopted, if we embarked upon this process, we would have goals about a lot of things for which we do not now have government goals. Everybody agrees in some sense that we are in favor of balanced economic growth and we are in favor of an equitable distribution of income, but we do not have government goals about all these things. The legislation is an invitation and a mandate to have goals about all of these things, and therefore an invitation to have government policies, programs, benefit provisions, and controls, to achieve a much longer list of goals than the government is now concerned with. That certainly means an expansion in the area of government responsibility.

A second point that is also clear is that the objectives with respect to these various goals will escalate, because the objectives will be stated in a kind of political process, and if A says, "My objective with respect to these goals of equitable distribution of income is that the lower twenty percent of the population should have not less than ten percent of the income," his competitor in the election will have to say, "My objective is that the lowest twenty percent of the population should have not less than fifteen percent of the income, or not less than twenty percent, or maybe twenty-five," and that we will all be equal or at least more equal than others. That is just the nature of the political process—that once you commit yourself to having a stated objective with respect to some of these good things there is no limit to the ambitiousness of the objective that you come to. This is very relevant to the problem of inflation in the United States and any other country, because the more ambitiously these objectives are set, the more difficult it is to prevent inflation.

Suppose we pass over this point and say, "Once the objectives are determined, presumably a plan will be developed to achieve the objectives." At this point we get to a really difficult central problem, a problem of how to organize an economic system which is basically a problem of how to organize the use of knowledge. How do we assimilate and integrate the knowledge, about all the productive potentialities of the countries, and all the wishes of the people of the country, so that the productive potentialities are most efficiently used to achieve the most urgent wishes?

Professor Hayek wrote a definitive article thirty years ago on the uses of knowledge in society. He repeated much of it in a recent article on planning in the *Bulletin of the Morgan Guaranty Trust Company*. He complains about the fact that, while it seemed thirty years ago that we had a great intellectual discussion, and settled a lot of these issues, people are now raising them again, as if this debate had never occurred and as if there had never been any solution to it. But the fact is that the knowledge required to make decisions about the economy is all out there in the private sector. It is private people that have the knowledge about the productive processes, in which they are directly involved, and even more important, it is the private people who have the knowledge about what their own preferences are. These preferences are, in most views, the objectives of economic behavior. Still, of course, unless each of us operates in a

Robinson Crusoe manner, we need some knowledge that we do not have internally. We need to have knowledge about the productive potentialities of others, and about the preferences of others, and there are two possible ways of bringing all this knowledge together.

One is through the market, in which the individual confronts the rest of the world in terms of certain prices. He does not need to know, when he makes a decision whether to take coffee or tea, what is the rainfall in India and whether there has been a frost in Brazil and what is the exchange rate of the Brazilian cruzeiro, and so on. All he needs to know is that when he goes to the grocery store the price of coffee is X and the price of tea is Y. All the background information is summarized for him through the market in those prices.

The alternative way of integrating all this knowledge is to try to funnel it into the government, through a computer, and solve a million equations simultaneously. I think it is quite clear that the market system is the more efficient way of doing this. And I would have thought by now that everyone agreed that unless the objectives of the system are radically different from the objectives of the people who make up the system, those objectives will be better satisfied by the people operating in the market than by the planning process.

One central question in all this is, who does the planning? There is a kind of notion that the planning is a neutral process, that it is done by scientists, by economists, wearing white smocks and operating computers, and that they will produce a right answer out of their tables of logarithms. But that is not the case at all, of course. All these plans, even selections of alternative plans (if that is what is to be done) affect people, and affect people differently. People will have different opinions and derive different results from them, and so it is important who makes the decision.

The decisions will either be made by experts, in which case the process is very undemocratic, because these experts will not be elected and not be representative. Or they will be made by politicians, in which case one can count on a lot of the scientific aspects of the system falling through the grating. If we have to choose between decisions made by experts and decisions made by politicians, I think we should chose the politicians. They tend to be less arrogant, they are more competitive, (that is they have more differences of view), and they are easier to get rid of than experts are. Of course we do not have to choose between having the economy run by experts or run by politicians. At least for a large part of the economy, there is a third way, and that is the market.

My experience with price controls suggests to me that once the government gets into highly detailed and comprehensive management of the economy, as we did in the case of price controls, you get a combination in which a great mass of decisions are made by experts or bureaucrats, or experts who are not politically responsible, but there is enough political intervention or injection of political considerations into the process to make sure that the whole system does not operate with the kind of rationality that the experts might have conceived. So in a way you get the worst of both worlds.

And finally, let me say a word on the question of voluntarism versus compulsion. What proponents of planning in the United States commonly say is that they do not propose a mandatory system. They recognize that mandatory systems are not popular in the United States. The system would operate in some more gentle way. One notion is that the mere fact that the government has developed a plan which says how many automobiles and how many tons of frozen food ought to be produced will so commend itself to all the actors in the private market, that everybody will become impressed with the rightness of this plan. They will so feel the accuracy of the government's forecast and estimates of the proper relation between tons of frozen food and numbers of automobiles that they will spontaneously behave in conformity with the plan.

This is an idea borrowed from the French theory of indicative planning, which I think has been largely abandoned there, not having made much difference in the behavior of the French economy. It is extremely unlikely to be effective in the United States, because we do not start with this great respect for the estimates and forecasts made by government that might exist elsewhere. So, you get beyond that, and to the notion that conformity to the plan would be brought about by moral suasion, or leadership. One of the common phrases in this discussion is that the president should exercise moral leadership, which means that he should call the automobile companies in and tell them that he would like them to plan to produce twelve million cars next year, or whatever the number in the plan is, and that does have a certain influence.

It has a certain influence on certain kinds of companies. It has an influence on companies that are large and conspicuous and especially on companies that do a lot of business with the federal government. But, when you say that, you have said that it really is not voluntary, that it really is not moral suasion. It is an indirect form of compulsion which applies rather unevenly around the economy.

Beyond that, you can get into incentives. We provide tax incentives for this and that. For example, people who invest in the areas where there is a lot of unemployment would get special tax incentives under one of the president's new proposals. That is a form of compulsion also. To give or take away a valuable benefit like that is a form of compulsion, just as much as if there were controls. There is not much point in deluding ourselves with the view that what is proposed is purely voluntary conformity to a code of good conduct.

So, I would summarize my views on the planning business in four words. I think it is, if adopted and carried through with serious intent, likely to be inflationary, inefficient, coercive, and undemocratic, which is, I assure you, a balanced judgment.

I do not think we are going to have the revolution tomorrow, and I do not think we are going to have a comprehensive planning system. I do not think we are going to adopt the Humphrey-Javits bill. In fact, Senator Humphrey has said that he is about to revise the bill. I do not know in what direction, but I think in response to some of the complaints that it involves too much government control.

Partly, we are not going to get the Humphrey-Javits bill because it steps on too many toes. It takes too much power away from people in the government who have it, and transfers it to a number of people who are not on the scene now, that is, the Economic Planning Board, and all the people who now have the power are not going to stand still for that. That by itself is, in my opinion, sufficient reason to believe that we are not going to get the Humphrey-Javits bill. But also I see no evidence of its having rung any bells in the country, outside of Washington, New York, and some academic centers, because it does not deal with the problems that people are very interested in.

What is a cause for concern is not so much that this bill will be adopted, but that it reflects an attitude of mind which is widespread in the country, and that is that the market does not work very well. It means that when we have a particular problem we can turn to the government to solve it, as we have turned to government controls of one kind or another to deal with the energy problem. By a proliferation of this kind of selective controls, we will get into a position where the control is so pervasive that it can only be rationalized by some kind of overall plan.

Let me turn now to the other, and smaller end of the problem, that is, how to improve economic policy. I think there is no doubt that the economic policy is in need of improvement. There is no doubt that the economy has not worked in the last several years as well as we would like it to work, or as well as we have thought it would work, and that this defect is in part, maybe in large part, a matter of the inadequacy of government policy. That is the problem to which we should be addressing ourselves. I think that the planners are guilty of a very naive notion about what is wrong with policy and how it can be improved. They think that there are some people out there who know the answers, especially they themselves, and that it would only be necessary for them to point the answers out to have them adopted more or less by acclamation.

But the facts are that we do not know the answers, and that if we did know the answers they would not necessarily be adopted. So we have two things to do. First, we have to find better answers to the economic problems, which the planning process does not promise to do because all the planning process will do is to take into the plan the faulty information and inadequate analysis we now have. What we are deficient in is information and analysis, not plan. And second, we need to try to create the situation in the country where better answers will be accepted or demanded.

I can give quickly an example of this problem in both aspects. President Ford said in his State of the Union message that the American people have learned that if they want to keep the cost of living down they have to keep the cost of government down. There are two things to be said about that. First, that it is not necessarily true, and if the American people have learned it, they may have learned the wrong answer because you have to ask yourself, "Well, does that mean that to keep the cost of living down you have to keep the cost of government down whether or not you pay for the expenditures by taxes, or does it have something to do with the relation of taxes to the expenditures?" And if it has something to do with the relation of taxes to expenditures, does it have something to do with the way a deficit is financed, whether by borrowing from the public or by monetary expansion, and does it have something to do with the circumstances of the economy at the time in which the government increases the expenditures?

It has become, intellectually, a long and difficult question. If the American people now think they know the answer, they probably are wrong. Second, suppose they did know the answer, and regardless of whether the answer is correct or not, suppose they now know that the way to keep the cost of living down is to keep the cost of government down, does that mean that they will keep the cost of government down? Not necessarily, because everybody will say, as they always do, "Well, yes, we've got to keep the cost of government down, but not my program, not my benefit." The only way in which we can get together on a budget in which everybody gets his own programs protected is in a big budget. That is because we can reconcile all our demands in a large budget even though everybody would recognize that what we really want is a low budget.

We need to improve knowledge, and we need to improve public tolerance of sound policy, and I really do not have much to say about either of those things. As far as economic knowledge is concerned, we are terribly miserly in the resources we devote to the collection and improvement of economic statistics, and one can point to a number of cases in which policy has been misled by the inadequacy of the statistics. I will not go into that, because that is a somewhat specialized subject.

We are making very little progress, in fact hardly visible progress, in improving what economists know. Most of what we have learned in the past ten years is that we do not know as much as we thought we knew ten years ago. One could justify the devotion of a great deal more effort, more concentrated effort, more policy-oriented effort, on economic research that might pay off.

When I have said this in the past, some of my friends have complained that, while I take a very miserly view of government expenditures in general and of government functions in general, I do seem to have some soft spot in my heart for increasing government expenditures in economic statistics and government devotion of economic resources to economic research. They claim that shows a certain lack of objectivity on my part. But I would deny that.

And finally, probably the most important thing is the need to improve public attitudes towards public policy. We need to bring about a condition in which people take a more long-run and general view of economic policy and its consequences, in which they give more weight to distant consequences than they do now, in which they recognize that if they get benefits out of a system which are of particular value to them, others will also want benefits out of the system and that there are limits to the benefits that the system can provide without getting us into deep trouble. So, I think that aside from the fact that economists do not know as much as they ought to know, another major source of our difficulty is that the public is rather shortsighted and has a rather narrow view.

I once said, on a national television program, that I felt that the American people were ultimately responsible for inflation, because they did not tolerate, let alone demand, the kinds of politics that would stop the inflation. I have said many infuriating things during the time when I was chairman of the Council of Economic Advisers, but that seems to have been the most infuriating thing I ever said. I got terrific amounts of very violent mail, which amazed me because it should not be surprising to think that in a democratic society, the responsibility for what government does ultimately lies with the people. But it is the case.

Faith in the durability and success of democracy has always been faith in the possibility that people will learn. And I believe we are learning. We do learn from experience, and the only question is whether we learn fast enough and whether we know some ways to speed it up. Many of us here are engaged in an effort to speed it up, and I think this is ultimately a large part of the answer to our economic problem.

The Political Economy of Resentment

Wesley J. Liebeler

In 1971, Kurt Vonnegut wrote a short story which dramatizes the extremes to which egalitarianism has been carried in current social policy.[1] In it, in the interest of "fairness," the more talented and intelligent members of society were given handicaps to make them "average." For example, the U.S. "Handicapper General" required that a person with above normal intelligence wear a "mental handicap radio" which emitted noises that interfered with his thinking.

Similar treatment was meted out in that society to those similarly situated. There was a slight problem, of course, in that those who did not qualify for mental handicap radios were a little envious of those that did, resenting not being able to hear all of the interesting, different distracting noises that the Federal Handicappers send out over the air. Even in 2081, and in the hands of one as imaginative as Vonnegut, it is apparently impossible to stamp out all of the reasons for envy and resentment. There are some problems of "fairness" that apparently just will not admit of solution.

I do not hold myself out as an expert on Kurt Vonnegut. I think it is safe to conclude, however, that this story has something to say about the question of who in the community gets what and why they get it, or do not get it, as the case may be. Vonnegut may in fact have hit upon the only truly effective way to bring about any significant long-term redistribution of income. For there is good reason, I believe, to think that a redistribution of property holdings, even to the point of complete equality, would not have any great long-term effects. A significantly unequal distribution would very likely reappear in fairly short order. And my credulity would not be stretched by the proposition that there would be a high degree of correlation between the before and after identity of both the haves and the have-nots.

It is hard to avoid the conclusion that no government program can effectively redistribute income unless it is bottomed on schemes that are uncomfortably reminiscent of Mr. Vonnegut's Handicapper General.

Do I say "uncomfortably reminiscent" too quickly? Perhaps there are some who would prefer a world with similar, perhaps somewhat disguised, institutions in it, at least as compared to one in which they would feel compelled to compete and to have the results of their efforts compared with those of their fellows. Such comparisons must in some, perhaps in many, cases be to our own disadvantage. There must be those who so prefer, or else we would not see these equalizers as often as we do. For they are there, make no mistake about it.

For me, however, and for many others I suspect, there are problems with

49

Handicappers General no matter how well intentioned and competent their staffs may be; no matter how punctiliously they may comply with the Administrative Procedures Act, and no matter that the particular form the institution takes may be more subtle and somewhat harder to discern than the one articulated by Mr. Vonnegut.

These problems are first and foremost moral problems. They are also economic, political, and psychological in nature. And, of course, they manifest themselves inexorably in the context of legal institutions. Let me confine myself to a few general comments, primarily designed to raise questions on some of the moral, economic, and legal issues involved in the problem of income distribution.

As to the moral aspects of this issue we might ask, first, what can be said? Second, we might ask why is it worth talking about the question in this way?

First, it is often claimed that goods and services, or at least certain kinds of goods and services, are properly (which I take to mean morally) distributed on the basis of need. Take medical services for example. It has been argued that it is a "necessary truth," that the proper ground of distribution of medical care is ill health.[2] It is not clear what makes this a "necessary truth," but it has been suggested that "if among the different descriptions applying to an activity, there is one that contains an internal goal of the activity, then (it is a necessary truth that) the only proper grounds for the performance of the activity on its allocation if it is scarce, are connected with the effective achievement of the Internal Goal."[3]

If this activity is performed upon others, it is argued that the only proper criterion for distributing that activity is their need for it, if any. We may suppose that by the same token that this argument establishes the need of sick persons as the test of distribution of medical services that it also establishes a similar criterion for the distribution of barbering services, that is to say, barbering need, and perhaps automobile repair services and the like. Are barbers and mechanics different from doctors in this respect? And if so, why?

Are we to take this argument that need is the only "proper" test for the distribution of medical services to mean that doctors are to be required to allocate their activities in terms of this internal goal (the necessary truth) of medical care? Are we to conclude that doctors are less entitled to pursue *their own* goals, within the circumstances of their chosen field of specialization, than everyone else?

If these conclusions can not be accepted, and I do believe that they can be, then it must be the case that the "argument" that need is the only proper test for distributing medical services must be based on something other than the inherent nature of the practice of medicine. What?

The answer to that question is to me even less clear than the argument based on the inherent nature of the practice of medicine. Presumably it is simply that medical services are important; that sick people need them very much. But this is simply a statement that society should provide for the important needs of all of its members. This is a familiar claim. But the purpose of this discussion is not simply to restate that claim, or to deny it. The purpose is to ask whether or not there is any argument that can state a plausible moral justification for that claim.

I do not know that there is. The problem with the usual formulation that the American people are entitled to the best medical service that money can buy is that these arguments do not tell us how much money and, more importantly, whose money we are talking about. They do not pinpoint the source of the resources that are to provide these services. They look only to the question of allocation, apparently assuming that the wherewithal to perform will appear like manna from heaven.

But doctors, to whom medical services are in part attached, may have their own ideas as to the basis on which they choose to provide their services, as may barbers, mechanics, and many others. Some of these persons may prefer to provide their services to those who will pay them, or to those to whom they enjoy talking to the most, or on some other, perhaps to us irrational, basis which may be entirely personal to them.

Moving the claim back a step to the proposition that society—each of us acting together through some government agency—should provide for these services does not solve the problem. It merely broadens the group from which property is to be taken and obscures to some extent the coercive nature of the transaction involved.

But may not the members of this larger group also have rightful claims to their time (property) that are at least equal to those of the doctor, barber, or garage mechanic as against the claims of the sick, the hirsute, or those with ailing automobiles? One would think this to be the case, at least some of the time. The answer appears to depend in large part on how the members of the community came into possession of their wealth in the first place. If they have obtained it in return for services or goods provided to others in free and uncoerced exchanges, it is hard to see by what moral right others may make superior claims.

I would suppose that nonvoluntary exchanges are not favored by most sensible people.[a] If property obtained in that way could readily be identified, and if it could not for some reason be returned to the rightful owner, perhaps it could be put to good use in providing medical or other services to the community at large.

But most property holdings in our society come into existence because of voluntary exchanges. These voluntary exchanges would not occur if both parties

---

[a]It is not entirely clear that this is so. Most people would tend not to favor slavery or other nonvoluntary transactions by which wealth may be shifted from "poor" persons to "rich" persons. But many of those same people might not oppose, or might even support, the use of coercion, i.e., nonvoluntary transactions, to shift property from the "rich" to the "poor." While our tradition suggests, or seems to suggest, that the latter activity is more "desirable" than the former, there is no difference between them in terms of the use of force against individual persons.

did not benefit from them. If a person or a company of persons is able to discover some way of providing large benefits to others, he or they have the opportunity to become wealthy. They get this way by creating and transferring to others goods and services that those others value more than (or at least as much as) that which they receive in the exchange.

If a person has some particular ability that gives him a comparative advantage over others in performing tasks valued highly by others, he has an even better opportunity to become wealthy. A former UCLA football coach is reportedly being paid $200,000 a year to provide coaching services to a football team in Philadelphia.[b] I would like to receive $200,000 a year. But I have not been able to get anyone to pay me that on a voluntary basis, or I may add on an involuntary basis either.

Should we be envious of this football coach? Or resentful? Do we have any moral right to take some of that money that he is to be paid and use it to pay doctors to provide medical services to ourselves or to others? Do we have a right to take it to pay our rent? To pay for our vacations?

Voluntary or involuntary exchange transactions are not the only means in which people obtain holdings of wealth in our society. Some people find lost treasure, win at gambling, or strike oil. Others inherit large sums or receive gifts, foundation grants, or the like. Still others obtain wealthy spouses or spouses who are able to get high returns in voluntary exchange transactions in their own right, and who are willing to use some of those returns to keep our hero in the style to which he will become quickly accustomed.

As long as the holdings which our hero may acquire in these ways came into the hands of his benefactor in some legitimate way (such as voluntary exchange transactions with others), and so long as they are legitimately transferred to our hero, is there any room for complaint on moral grounds? Do we have any *right* to take these kinds of holdings away from others to provide for the medical care of ourselves or others? Or to make ourselves or others better off in any way?

If we have such a *right*, what is its nature? On what is it based? Or are we observing claims based on nothing more than force or the threat of force?

The question of how property comes to be legitimately held can be made enormously complicated. And it can raise issues that will stir great emotions and antagonisms. It appears that not all property has come to be held in what we could reasonably regard as just ways. Property acquired in involuntary exchanges seems to have been obtained in an unjust manner.

It appears to some that the most significant consequences in this regard flow from the existence of certain widespread involuntary exchanges that have occurred in the past.[4] Slavery, and the taking of land from native Americans, are

---

[b]After coaching the UCLA Bruins to an upset victory over number 1 ranked Ohio State in the 1976 Rose Bowl, Dick Vermeil was reportedly offered $1,000,000 on a five-year contract to coach professional football. He accepted that offer.

examples that are often used. The implications that follow from these events and similar events, if there are similar events, are not entirely clear. Robert Nozick puts the following questions raised by the existence of past involuntary exchanges:

If past injustice has shaped present holdings in various ways, some identifiable and some not, what now, if anything, ought to be done to rectify these injustices?

What obligations do the performers of injustices have toward those whose position is worse than it would have been had the injustice not been done? Or, than it would have been if compensation had been paid promptly?

How if at all do things change if the beneficiaries and those made worse off are not the direct parties in the act of injustice, but, for example, their descendants?[5]

These are difficult questions and there are lots more of them. The possibility has been raised that some holdings of wealth in contemporary American society may not be justly held. To put it very mildly, it would be difficult to figure out which ones, once it is assumed that such an inquiry would be relevant. It may also be, however, that even the requitement of what some would regard as a moral principle is subject to some sort of statue of limitations. It is also possible that some of those who were on the wrong end of past involuntary exchanges (or more likely their descendants) are better off (along, perhaps, with everyone else), at least in a material sense than they would have been if the involuntary exchange had never occurred.

I do not pretend to know the answers to such questions. But it does not take a great deal of reflection to see that infirmities such as those suggested above, if infirmities they really are, in no way justify, from a moral or any other point of view, the widespread and general schemes of wealth redistribution that are coming to characterize present day American society. On that point, I do not see that there can be any serious argument.

I suggest, however, that if the view that I have tried to sketch briefly, and which Professor Nozick calls the Entitlement Theory of Justice in Holdings,[6] is correct, that it would be well worthwhile to examine closely any infirmities in present holdings of wealth arising out of the past (or present for that matter) involuntary exchanges. The nature of any such infirmities could provide some clues as to the kind of wealth redistribution, if any, that may be morally justified.

Summarizing, to this point I have argued that no one-time redistribution of property holdings would have significant long-term effects and that any program that attempts to achieve an end-state result (such as equality or equality within certain limits of deviation) would most likely be required to engage in constant monitoring and intervention, not unlike that of the Handicapper General, in order to be successful. I have asked you to consider the nature of any moral principle that justifies the use of force to take property holdings away from one person and give them to others, including ourselves, for the primary purpose of making that other person or ourselves better off. I have suggested that there is no such moral principle, at least so long as the property holdings that we propose to take by force have been legitimately acquired by their holder.

While a complete statement of the principles of legitimacy in acquisition could be complicated, I have argued that property holdings acquired by any person or group of persons in voluntary exchanges with others do, perhaps with some highly unlikely exceptions, qualify as having been legitimately acquired. It seems, given the conditions that have been obtained in the United States for the relevant time last past, that the amounts that persons will receive in voluntary transactions with others will be roughly equal to the value of their marginal product.

I think that it follows, if the propositions that I have sketched are reasonably correct, that not only is there no moral principle upon which the redistribution of wealth can be justified in terms of need (or the fact that one person has less or more than another), but that there is or should be a basic presumption that, if observed, would prevent the use of coercion, by the state or otherwise, from taking any holdings of legitimately held wealth, no matter how large, simply to improve the welfare of other persons.

That is the end of the first part of a sketchy treatment of philosophy. In the second part, which will be much shorter, I ask the question of why it is worth talking about questions of income distribution (or redistribution) in moral terms. Such discussions will not have any effect on the "public servant" who seeks to advance his own purposes by promising to smite down the rich and the large in order to benefit the poor and the downtrodden. Or on union leaders, other price fixers, or other operatives who maneuver to prevent in various ways members of the community from engaging in voluntary exchanges that would be best for themselves.

While all of that may be true, I suppose it has never been thought necessary to justify a discussion of moral philosophy in an academic setting. Such discussions are the meat of the removed, cool-headed, rational, and objective members of the academy that we all are.

If I had not spent the greater part of the last ten years in the academy, it might come as some surprise to me that so few of my fellows there seem to have considered the basic questions to which I have referred. But they have not. We need not, I suggest, look far for the reasons.

The underpinnings of Professor Nozick's Entitlement Theory of Justice in Holdings is a structure that looks suspiciously like a free market. There is not much room for big government in this scheme of things. The free market has not found many apologists in the academic community for some time. The emphasis has been all the other way, toward government intervention, toward the increasing use of coercion, and away from the principles of voluntary exchange.

This has started to change, it seems to me, with the increasing interest in economics in many law schools. This is all to the good, but it does not, as far as I can see, herald any swing to market principles across the board, either in universities or elsewhere.

The health of the university does not, of course, depend on its being populated primarily by apologists for the free market. Indeed, under the principles of voluntary exchange we would not expect universities in general to be populated by apologists for any particular point of view. But it would be nice, it seems to me, if there was a greater understanding of, greater study of, market-oriented institutions, how they work, what causes them not to work at times, etc. And it would be nice if these studies were taking place on a broader scale than among graduate students in the economics department, and a relatively small percentage of law students.

One way to move in this direction is to broaden the claims for the market. Most economists and lawyers conversant in the field base their arguments for the market on efficiency considerations. I believe that they are correct in their view that as a general matter the free market is the most efficient way to allocate resources in a consumer-oriented society. But a lot of people think that efficiency is pretty thin gruel. Particularly may this be true of ourselves, and our colleagues, who are concerned after all, as academics ought to be, with the finer things.

I believe that the claims for the market should be broadened, whether that induces those who have been too fine in the past to take those claims seriously to do so now or not. For it is right to broaden them. If you do not believe that, then ask yourself what your attitudes toward markets (with which we may interchange the term "the principles of voluntary exchange") would be if it were demonstrated conclusively that some other institution that did not incorporate the principles of voluntary exchange were somehow more "efficient" than the market. While it is a difficult question to formulate precisely because of problems in thinking clearly about the meaning of "efficiency," to the extent that I can make the question intelligible I conclude that I would still prefer markets.

Perhaps we should treat the efficiency claims, true though they certainly are, as lagniappe and put it up front that institutions based on the principles of voluntary exchange are better than other institutions because they are the only ones that are consistent with freedom. I think that most of us believe that. Perhaps now that a professor of philosophy from Harvard has said so, we will be less reluctant to express these thoughts among our colleagues in the academy.

Much of Professor Nozick's book is an agenda for further work. I close my remarks on moral philosophy by suggesting that we engage that work with dispatch.

I want to go on now to give some examples of the work of Handicappers General, primarily in the area of antitrust and trade regulation. Before I do that, however, I want to offer a definition whereby we may be better able to identify the work of the Handicapper General when it appears among us. I also want to share a bit of history that may help to explain why so many people who are devoted to the finer things in life are so hostile to free market institutions.

First the history. It involves the comparison between Richard Arkwright and Samuel Crompton, which is drawn by the French man of letters, Paul Mantoux.[7] Arkwright claimed to be the inventor of the first successful mechanical spinning device. Whether he was or not, and Mantoux clearly believes that he was not, i.e., that he stole it from somebody else, Arkwright certainly put it to good use. He became, at the dawn of the Industrial Revolution, "the prototype of the great manufacturer, made rich by his own toil and his own inventions" as well as "the true founder of the modern factory system."[8]

Crompton, on the other hand, really was an inventor. Unfortunately, he appears to have had the business sense of a church mouse. He developed significant improvements on the machine then in use by Arkwright but could neither patent it nor keep it secret. So, he gave it to the public. A group of manufacturers promised a voluntary subscription as compensation and while the subscription was actually made, it appears that "some of the subscribers, once they had got hold of the model, did not feel bound to keep their word."[9] Crompton later invented a carding machine, but according to Mantoux, "it was hardly finished before he smashed it to pieces, exclaiming, 'they shall not have this too.' "[10] Needless to say, he died poor.

With this background let me turn to Mantoux's comparison of the two men:

Crompton was a man of remarkable intelligence and some culture, probably much above most of those who profited by his invention. But he was unable to reap any benefit from it. His very independent character, combined with a modesty which almost amounted to shyness, were not qualities which made for success; and he lacked some other qualities, such as the gift of organization and of leadership. The contrast between his life and that of Arkwright shows the difference there is between original research and discovery, and their clever adaptation to practical ends. In the South Kensington museum the portraits of the two men hang side by side. Arkwright with his fat vulgar face, his goggling heavy lidded eyes, whose expressionless placidity is belied by the vigorous line of the brow and the slight smile on the sensual and cunning lips, is the matter of fact businessman who knows how to grasp and master a situation without too many qualms of conscience. Crompton, with his refined and emaciated profile, his fine forehead from which his brown hair is tossed back, the austere line of his mouth and his large eyes, both enthusiastic and sad, combines the features of Bonaparte in his younger years with the expression of a Methodist preacher. Together they represent invention and industry, the genius which creates revolutions and the power which possesses itself of their results.[11]

What can be said for an institution, such as the market, which could reward the likes of Arkwright and leave a chap like Crompton in the poor house? Are not those who appreciate the finer sentiments entitled to be resentful of those vulgar, cunning, grasping men without conscience which constitute the power which possesses itself of the results of the original research and discovery of the modest, refined, and intelligent men of culture and independent character, some of whom at least are reminiscent of a combination of the younger Bonaparte and of the Wesley brothers? And are these finer types not entitled to harbor the same feelings toward the system that produces such unjust results? Whether we (or they) are *entitled* to such feelings and attitudes, it is clear that they are not in particularly short supply these days, nor have they been for some time considerably past.

I have never seen a single paragraph that unintentionally lays bare so clearly the causes of the general contempt which so many contemporary intellectuals have for market processes, for the principles of voluntary exchange as the one quoted above. As a general proposition, voluntary exchange places value on productive factors, including the work of individuals, in direct proportion as the members of the community at large find the output of such productive factors worthwhile to them. As compared to the captains of industry, indeed as compared to many sergeants of industry, the work product of most intellectuals is not valued highly under the principles of voluntary exchange. It is simply a fact that the ruminations of most English professors and philosophers and even of some law teachers are not much sought after by the community at large. It is a psychological necessity, based on the need to maintain his vision of self-worth, that the self-respecting (more precisely the non-self-respecting) intellectual reject a system that produces such results.

It is not surprising that so many college teachers pass the same judgment on the market that the market has already passed on them.

Let me move on now to attempt a definition of what constitutes the work of the Handicapper General and then to provide some examples drawn mostly from the current scene.

First the attempted definition: The product of the Handicapper General is to be found in any nonnatural event which raises the cost of engaging in voluntary exchanges when the parties to that exchange are entitled to the holdings which are the subject of the exchange and where the principal voluntary exchange does not directly involve others in significant involuntary exchanges.

Rather than trying to deal with this in general terms, let me lay out some examples that I think meet the definition, which can be refined later if necessary.

One of the most striking examples of the Handicapper General is to be found in the history of the French theater. At one time, shortly before the French Revolution, the state had a monopoly in this field. But, there began to grow up private theaters. It turned out that the citizens of Paris preferred to patronize many of the private theaters rather than go to the state theater. I suppose this was because for some reason they preferred to watch the performances put on by the private theaters rather than the ones that were put on by the state.

The state had a solution for that problem; it required all private theaters to hang a thin gauze curtain between the audience and the actors on the stage. Given that kind of handicap it is possible, perhaps, that state enterprise could compete with free market organizations. The desired result could be achieved simply by varying the thickness of the gauze as a function of the excellence of the performance.[12]

My first example from contemporary society is Civil Aeronautics Board (CAB) restrictions on charter flights. For many years the affinity group charter has been the most popular form of charter air flight. If you are planning a summer in Europe you join an organization that has such charters available, remain a member for at least six months, certify that you did not join the group to obtain the charter, go to Europe on the charter flight and then come home and drop out of the organization. Even though there are inconveniences to consumers in using this form of transportation, it is by far the most flexible form of charter available.

Recognizing this and noting that these charters "diverted" considerable traffic from scheduled flights, the CAB last year proposed to drop the affinity charter concept entirely.[13] The first reason given was that this form of charter was discriminatory because persons who were not members of affinity groups could not use this form of transportation. There is a certain irony to this, of course, because the only reason that such persons could not use this form of charter is prohibitory CAB regulations.

The second reason for abolishing the affinity group charter given by the board was that it was impossible to enforce the requirement that groups not be formed primarily for purposes of obtaining air transportation and that travelers have been a member of this group for at least six months before going on the trip.[14] My own casual experience convinces me that enforcement may have been *somewhat* of a problem. That hardly justifies the board's proposed "solution," which was to get rid of the most unrestricted form of charter transportation and thereby make it unavailable to everyone.

This all happened while I was director of the Office of Policy Planning and Evaluation at the Federal Trade Commission. We convinced the commission to file a memorandum with the board arguing that the "problem" could best be solved by making charters available to everyone on an unrestricted basis.[15] We thought that would solve both the discrimination problem and the enforcement problem. Under the FTC proposal there would have been no restriction at all and, therefore, no need for enforcement and no possible way in which discrimination could occur. Travel agents, or anyone else for that matter, could charter airplanes and sell tickets to anyone they pleased for whatever price they pleased. For some reason the CAB did not go this route.

The FTC proposal demonstrates, of course, that even though the affinity group charter seems to be relatively unrestricted there is a very simple way to make much less restricted charter flights available. Thus, the purpose of these CAB regulations is to make it less convenient to use charter flights, i.e., to increase the costs of engaging in voluntary exchange in respect of air transportation.

Other kinds of restrictions on different kinds of charters fill page after page of CAB regulations. The openly avowed purpose of these regulations is to prevent "diversion" of traffic from the scheduled carriers, stark recognition of the extent to which consumers would prefer unrestricted charter flights to other available forms of air transportation. The gauze screen here is in the myriad of restrictions that has been placed on charters, decreasing their value to consumers and protecting the revenues of the scheduled carriers.

If we call the restrictions on charter operations a gauze screen, the protection that the CAB gives existing scheduled trunk carriers from new entry must be characterized as an iron curtain.[16] I give you three examples:

World Airways, basically a charter operation from Oakland, has filed with the CAB an application for authority to transport passengers from coast to coast for approximately $90. This is the second World application. The first time World filed for similar authority the board simply refused to hear the matter for a period of years and then dismissed the application as stale: it had been there too long. You would not think that Handicappers General could do that sort of thing given the Administrative Procedure Act and all that. But the CAB actually had the gall to do it, and it got away with it!

The second application is still pending. It may be doubted that the board, even in this period of flirtation with "deregulation," will act favorably on that application because of the untoward effect it would have on American, United and TWA. (Since the time of this writing, the second World Airways application has been denied.)

My second example involves a most interesting fellow in England by the name of Freddy Laker. He is apparently one of the last free enterprisers in that part of the world and, in his attempts to fulfill that capacity, he has caused a proper amount of discomfort to the Handicappers General on both sides of the Atlantic.

Freddy has two DC-8's which he wanted to fly between New York and London, providing an "air bus" type of service for $125 each way. The CAB, with due regard for the welfare of its handicappees and none at all for the consumer, recommended that Freddy not be granted permission to do any such thing. Since the president has final say on international air transport matters, that recommendation was duly forwarded to the White House.

There was mild hope in some quarters that a president who is relatively enlightened in regulatory matters might actually allow Freddy to take to the air. But it has not happened and I doubt that it will. We all know what would happen to TWA and Pan Am if Mr. Laker were permitted to take people from New York to London, and vice versa, for a paltry $125

There is a final bit of irony to all of this. The British government, apparently anxious about what President Ford might do, has withdrawn *its* authority from Mr. Laker. The reason: His operation would have an adverse effect on the revenues of BOAC.[17] So it goes, as Mr. Vonnegut would say.

The third example, one which I particularly enjoy, is one with which most of you are probably familiar. There was once a venture called "Air Europe," which proposed to fly from Tijuana to Luxembourg. I understand that a lot of people in Tijuana want to go to Luxembourg, and vice versa. Obviously this operation was designed to entice people from all over California to travel cheaply to Luxembourg, from whence, we might suspect, they would soon depart for other points in Europe. Since they would not be operating out of the United States, they would not be subject to CAB regulation. The Luxembourg destination was designed to avoid landing restrictions "suggested" by the International Air Transport Association (the international air carriers cartel organization), and adopted by almost all European countries.

The reaction of our domestic Handicapper General in respect of air transport matters was predictable. A CAB spokesman characterized Air Europe as a "pirate" operation. Air Europe planned to refuel at Bangor, Maine, on one leg of the journey. The CAB tried to get the Federal Aviation Agency to deny use of FAA facilities to land at Bangor. FAA would not do it. Then CAB found an old regulation that they claimed gave them authority to control any operation that flew over the United States. The point at issue then became whether Air Europe could fly around the United States and still sell tickets (at a profit) for less than any of the cartel airlines.[18]

One point of this is that the CAB, in some cases at least, never needs to get you into court or even before the board. The harassment, threats, and uncertainty exemplified by the board's behavior in the Air Europe caper can increase the costs of starting any operation to the point where it will have significantly less chance to succeed. The board's staff is well schooled in such techniques.

There is a bit of humor in this example, however. It turns out that the two planes that Air Europe proposed to use were Freddy Laker's DC-8's! It shows you what a little entrepreneurial ability and a couple of airplanes can do. You can cause trouble all over the world. But so far Freddy and his friends have not been able to overcome the international operations of the Handicapper General. They never got off the ground.

My second contemporary example involves the Federal Communications Commission. Its restrictions on cable television are exactly analogous to the CAB's restrictions on charters. The three major networks are like the existing trunk air carriers; cable operators are like the charters or other potential entrants. The FCC has extended its jurisdiction to cover cable operators and is limiting their expansion and regulating them in such a way as to protect the major networks from more vigorous competition.

This sort of regulation over a communications system has interesting implications. During the course of the last year a gentleman from CBS who had responsibility for developing new programs for the CBS show "Sixty Minutes," met with some of the FTC staff who were working on a deregulation project for the commission. He wanted to get some ideas for a program dealing with the adverse effects of government regulation.

One of my colleagues suggested that they do a show on the effects of FCC regulation. There was an embarrassed silence, a shifting from side to side; I could not contain myself, I just laughed. I said, "Yes, I think that CBS should do that. Why don't you tell the American people how the FCC protects CBS, ABC, and NBC from the competition of the cable operators?" Needless to say, he seemed to be more interested in the CAB and the Interstate Commerce Commission.

There is in fact no real justification for the continued existence of the FCC. Its historic mission was to deal with the problem of conflicting claims to property rights in airwave frequencies.[19] Once those property rights have been defined, however, as they in effect have been, their enforcement is essentially no different from enforcement of other types of property rights.[20] The courts are thought to be adequate to this event in other areas; there is no reason why they could not handle this problem as well. And it is hard to see why the courts would have any interest in handicapping one particular group of broadcasters in order to protect another, unlike the Handicapper General at the FCC.[21]

Next is the Food and Drug Administration (FDA) restrictions on the sale of prescription drugs, with which we are all familiar.[22] Let me give you a case by way of an example of the Handicapper General at work.

There was a story in the Los Angeles *Times* early in 1976 about three cases in the United States District Court in Oklahoma.[23] Judge Luther Bohanon, of that court, had received three applications from cancer patients in Oklahoma and Kansas for orders permitting the importation of Laetrile from Mexico. The story said that the applicants had been taking this drug for cancer and that the FDA had tried to prevent them from bringing it into the country for that purpose. The drug has not been approved for such use by the FDA.

When I read the story I thought the cases probably involved people dying of cancer who had elicited Judge Bohanon's sympathy to the point where he had decided to enable them to have this drug to give them at least some psychic relief from their condition. I asked the judge for copies of any available orders or briefs in these cases.

It turned out that one of them involved a man who had complained, over two years ago, of a growth in his lower intestine. His family doctor had sent him to a cancer clinic which diagnosed cancer of the lower intestine. The patient was ordered to the hospital for surgery; no assurance would be given as to how much would be left of him after the operation.

He never showed up. He went to Mexico instead and went on a Laetrile regimen. *Two years later* we find FDA trying to stop him from bringing the drug into the United States for his own use. The papers in the case showed that he had had the growth cauterized and continued to take Laetrile. He was apparently cured![24]

FDA has now appealed Judge Bohanon's order enjoining them from preventing this patient from importing the drug into this country.[25] *Why*?

At first glance the FDA example seems different from the usual handicapping case. It is not clear who is really made better off by preventing this patient from importing Laetrile. I suppose that surgeons and cancer clinics might be resentful if it turned out that this drug was a cancer cure-all. But that does not seem to be a likely possibility and I am prepared to believe that most surgeons and the like would not really resent it if cancer could be cured in some way not involving their services, although that may be a debatable proposition.

Yet the case fits my definition clearly. FDA's actions increased the costs of voluntary exchanges between this cancer patient and the purveyors of Laetrile in Mexico, who presumably came into the possession of their drug in some legitimate fashion. The patient most likely had similar claims to the resources that he proposed to exchange for the drug. Nor does the transaction obviously involve others in involuntary exchanges, i.e., impose external costs.

Who benefits here in the same sense that the dull benefited from the distractions imposed on the bright in Vonnegut's tale of the Handicapper General? The precise analogue, of course, would be other people dying of cancer that could not be cured by Laetrile. There are other candidates as well. It seems to me that one group "benefiting" from the worsened condition of the patient and of the putative drug seller is made up of the regulators and those who, in many cases passionately, believe in this form of regulation.

I suggested earlier that the modern intellectual's rejection of the principles of voluntary exchange is based in large part on his dislike of the desserts which such a system would provide him. This, of course, implies that he has a vision of a better society, better that is than the one which would result from the free choice of members of the community expressed in voluntary exchanges. He knows, in short, more about what is better for people than those people know about that issue themselves. This being the case, there is no reason why doctors and their patients should be able to make decisions about whether to use a particular drug or not. That is a matter which can only be entrusted to those who know *better*.

My next example of the Handicapper General at work involves various state laws and regulations restricting the freedom of individuals from advertising the prices at which they are willing to make goods and services available to the public. There are many such restrictions. I focus on prescription drugs and eyeglasses.

It is obvious that restrictions on advertising the retail prices of such goods and services (or any goods and services for that matter) will increase the costs of engaging in voluntary exchanges.[26] How do consumers get information on the prices of prescription drugs or eyeglasses when those prices cannot be advertised? Let us assume that the consumer knows that there are substantial differences in price for the same product, which is not obvious in the absence of advertising. Armed with this knowledge the consumer can try to get comparative prices by telephoning various sellers. In some cases such information will not be provided over the telephone. If it is not, our searcher may have to go physically from store to store to get information on prices. That is rather a bit more costly than picking up a copy of the Los Angeles *Times*, as I did the other day, and finding an advertisement by a firm called Opti Cal offering to provide glasses to fit most single-vision prescriptions for $19.99.

These restrictions are designed to keep people from learning about the availability of low-price options for the service or product in question. Persons who believe that the price of the same drug, by *brand name*, is much the same everywhere, will probably shop at the most convenient place, which is just as likely to be a high cost local retail pharmacy as it is a more efficient, most likely chain or franchise operation. I have nothing against small pharmacies, many of which provide excellent service and advice, etc. I do not see why, however, government should prevent those who are willing to sell for less from telling consumers that lower prices are available. There is no reason in principle why this freedom to provide information should not be available to everyone, including doctors, lawyers, and dentists.

There is some movement on this front. The Federal Trade Commission has proposed two trade regulation rules that would strike down state laws restricting the freedom of the seller to advertise the prices of prescription drugs and prescription eyeglasses.[27] Several private actions have also been brought; the United States Supreme Court has recently held unconstitutional a Virginia statute prohibiting price advertising of prescription drugs.[28]

Other examples of the Handicapper General at work include:

1. Antisubstitution laws which in most states make it illegal for a pharmacist to fill any prescription calling for a particular brand of drug with an equivalent generic preparation. The basic purpose of these laws is to reduce competition between brand name drugs and generic equivalents; they raise the cost of engaging in voluntary exchanges with generic drug manufacturers.[29]

2. Local building codes and union work rules that prevent the most efficient technology, or at least the technology of choice, from being used in many situations. These codes and rules are designed to force builders to use more labor by requiring use of more labor intensive building materials and techniques and by reducing the type of work that can be performed by any particular worker.[30]

3. State laws that set milk prices at the wholesale and retail levels. In some cases the state does not actually set these prices but requires that sellers file with the state the prices at which milk will be sold. The filed price cannot be changed without prior notice, which, of course, gives other sellers a chance to match the change before it goes into effect. These states also have very elaborate laws

prescribing "appropriate" conduct for milk wholesalers: credit cannot be extended except on certain specified terms, free advertising for resellers is not permitted, etc. These legal provisions make it more difficult to engage in nonprice competition; price competition is hindered by the filing requirement. It is exactly what cartel theory would predict any cartel would do to try to enforce fixed prices.

Ralph's markets ran a full page in the Los Angeles *Times* last year asking the California Department of Agriculture to suspend the operation of this system, predicting that the price of milk would drop if these controls were eased. Retail controls were suspended for a period of time in the Sacramento area. Prices did go down. But the system remains in effect in the rest of the state; in fact it has recently been reinstituted in Sacramento.

The obvious purpose of this law, no matter what false protestations of public good may be offered in its justification, is to keep the price of milk up to prevent us from engaging in voluntary exchanges with Ralph's and similar stores to obtain milk at lower prices. This would be bad because some of the smaller stores might not be able to sell milk at such lower prices and make a profit.[31]

My last example of the Handicapper General principle is the attitude of antitrust enforcement agencies, particularly the Federal Trade Commission, toward success. Again I will make my point by way of a particular case. At some time in the recent past Procter & Gamble, which owns Folger's coffee, decided to try to extend its sales of that coffee into the eastern part of the United States. Folger's is popular in the west; Maxwell House, which is owned by General Foods, is the most popular brand in most sections of the east.

Procter & Gamble moved into Cleveland, Ohio, where Folger's had never been sold before. It cut prices, put on an extensive promotion, advertised heavily, etc., in an attempt to penetrate this market. General Foods responded by doing pretty much the same thing. That is how the great coffee war began. It spread to Pittsburgh, Philadelphia, Syracuse, and other points in that general area.

It was not long before the smaller coffee companies complained to the Federal Trade Commission. For it was clear that if this kind of price cutting kept on for very long, some of them would be in trouble. There is really no type of case that the FTC staff likes better than one involving a small firm discomforted by price cutting. The fact that there were two large firms fighting it out here created some problems, however, because of the obvious possibility that competition was actually going on in the Cleveland coffee market. And the exact type of law suit and the most appropriate remedy for this situation were not entirely clear at first.

But the staff was equal to the event. They decided to proceed not against Procter & Gamble, who had started all this in the first place, but against *General Foods*, on the theory that GF's response to the Procter & Gamble entry, i.e., price cutting and greater sales efforts, was an attempt to *foreclose* competition.

General Foods was able to engage in this "exclusionary" behavior, it was argued, because of the "power" of its Maxwell House trademark. One economist actually wrote that General Foods was "bludgeoning" its competitors (Procter & Gamble) with its Maxwell House trademark.

It was never clearly specified whence came this "trademark power." I would have supposed it had something to do with the fact that more people preferred Maxwell House than other brands of coffee, for whatever reason. The chief FTC economist was hard pressed to come up with any other explanation. He did think that advertising might be the *cause* of consumers' belief that they liked Maxwell House best, even though they presumably also had the opportunity to taste the stuff at some point along the way. The fallback position was that consumers *should not* drink so much Maxwell House because coffee was, after all, coffee.

With this as background you should not be surprised at anything, such as the remedy that the FTC staff proposed to solve this "problem." They proposed to require General Foods to license the Maxwell House trademark, royalty free, to any coffee maker (except Procter & Gamble) that wanted to use it, for a period of ten years with quality control to be the responsibility of the *licensee*. I know that this is hard to believe, but it is really true!

Perhaps the most fascinating thing is that the commission could not muster a majority to decide to do anything about this preposterous proposal. Two commissioners did vote to give it the death that it so richly deserved. One excused himself; another wanted to bring a Robinson-Patman proceeding against both Procter & Gamble and General Foods; still another wanted to attack a merger that General Foods had made back in the 1920s! But at least that split kept the complaint from being voted out. As far as I know the great coffee war still goes on. (In the spring of 1976, the personnel of the commission having changed and Commissioner Hanford-Dole having changed her mind on the dangers of low coffee prices, the commission voted out a complaint in this matter.)

So I leave you with the message that the Handicapper General is alive and well. He is with us all the time, sometimes in obvious ways and other times more deviously. I would ask you to reflect on the definition I suggested to identify his work. You may use it, if you wish, to find for yourself other events that qualify as the work of the Handicapper General.

Notes

1. K. Vonnegut, Jr., *Welcome to the Monkey House* (Dell, 1970).

2. Bernard Williams, "The Idea of Equality," in *Philosophy, Politics, and Society*, 2nd ser., Peter Laslett and W.G. Runciman (eds.) (Oxford: Blackwell, 1962), pp. 121-22; reprinted in Joel Feinberg (ed.), *Moral Concepts* (New York: Oxford University Press, 1969).

3. Robert Nozick, *Anarchy, State and Utopia* (New York: Basic Books, 1974), p. 233.

4. See Boris Bittker, *The Case for Black Reparations* (New York: Random House, 1973); Nozick, *Anarchy, State and Utopia*, p. 152.

5. Nozick, *Anarchy, State and Utopia.*

6. Ibid., p. 150.

7. Paul Mantoux, *The Industrial Revolution in the Eighteenth Century* (New York: Harper & Row, 1962).

8. Ibid., p. 220.

9. Ibid., p. 236.

10. Ibid.

11. Ibid., p. 237.

12. Marvin Carlson, *The Theatre of the French Revolution* (Ithaca: Cornell Univ. Press, 1966), pp. 12, 16.

13. See CAB, Advance Notice of Proposed Rule Making (Nov. 9, 1972); 37 Fed. Reg. 24193. The Notice of Proposed Rule Making was issued on October 30, 1974. See Statement of Wesley J. Liebeler Before the Administrative Practices Subcommittee of the Senate Judiciary Committee on November 7, 1974, pp. 5-6.

14. See CAB Notice of Proposed Rule Making, *supra.*

15. The FTC memorandum was made part of the record before the CAB in the Rule Making Proceeding notice of which was issued on October 30, 1974.

16. The CAB has uniformly resisted attempts by "outsiders" to enter the trunk airline industry. See Douglas and Miller, *Economic Regulation of Domestic Air Transport* (Washington: Brookings, 1974).

17. The Laker story is told in various issues of *Aviation Week* throughout the period 1974-75. It is discussed in my statement to the Administrative Practices Subcommittee of the Senate Judiciary Committee referred to in note 13 above.

18. Ibid.

19. See Coase, *The Federal Communications Commission.*, *Journal of Law & Economics* 2, (1959): 1.

20. DeVany, Eckert, Meyers, O'Hara, and Scott, "A Property System for Market Allocation of Electro-Magnetic Spectrum: A Legal-Economic-Engineering Study," *Stanford L. Rev.* 21 (1969): 1499.

21. The general approach to this problem outlined above is also discussed in Minasian, "Property Rights in Radiation: An Alternative Approach to Radio Frequency Allocation," *Journal of Law & Economics* 18 (1975): 221, and in Levin, "The Radio Spectrum Resource," *Journal of Law & Economics* 11 (1969): 433.

22. A market-oriented approach to prescription drug marketing is suggested

in Liebeler, "Critique of Crout, New Drug Regulation and its Impact on Innovation," in Mitchell and Link (eds.), *Proceedings of the Third Seminar on Pharmaceutical Public Policy Issues* (Washington, D.C.: American University, 1976), p. 261.

23. Los Angeles *Times*, January 9, 1976, p. 32.

24. Judge Bohanon found: "The Court is compelled to find from the testimony and the exhibits that plaintiff Glen L. Rutherford was in late 1971 suffering from invasive adenocarcinoma and that by the use of Laetrile, B17 or amygdalin (all being the same drug) his condition was cured, as there is no evidence to the contrary." Findings of Fact and Conclusions of Law in *Stowe v. United States* (CIV-75-0218-B, W.D. Okla., August 14, 1975).

25. This appeal is No. 75-1725 in the United States Court of Appeals for the Tenth Circuit.

Laetrile may now be used legally in Alaska, so long as the material used does not cross a state line beforehand. In refusing to block legislation permitting use of the drug, Alaska Governor Jay Hammond said, "The main question in my mind is how far do you go in protecting people from themselves?" Federal officials had urged Hammond to veto the measure. Federal efforts to continue to protect people from themselves and their doctors resulted in the indictment in San Diego on May 26, 1976 of sixteen persons on charges of conspiracy and smuggling Laetrile into the country from Tijuana. Los Angeles *Times*, June 23, 1976, p. 4.

26. See Stigler, "The Economics of Information," *J. Pol. Econ.* 46 (1961): 213. This increased cost will result in higher prices. See Benham, "The Effect of Advertising on the Price of Eyeglasses," *Journal of Law & Economics* 15 (1972): 342. Professor Benham found that prescription eyeglass prices were from 25 percent to 100 percent higher in states that prohibited advertising of eyeglass prices, as compared to states where such advertising was allowed.

27. Proposed 16 C.F.R. § 447, 40 Fed. Reg. 24031 (1975); see *note* "The State Action Exemption and Antitrust Enforcement under the Federal Trade Commission Act," *Harv. L. Rev.* 89 (1976): 715.

28. *Virginia State Board of Pharmacy v. Virginia Citizens Consumer Council, Inc., Law Week* 44 (May 25, 1976): 4686.

29. See Green, "Welfare Losses from Monopoly in the Drug Industry: The Oklahoma Antisubstitution Law," *Antitrust Law & Econ. Rev.* 5 (1972): 5.

30. The Federal State Commission Office of Policy Planning and Evaluation recommended that the commission institute a program to assess the costs of this type of "featherbedding" and to determine whether or not its incidence could be reduced by any action available to the commission. See 758 Antitrust & Trade Reg. Rep. A-6, H-1 (BNA, April 6, 1976).

31. See Knutson, "The Economic Consequences of the Minnesota Dairy Industry Unfair Practices Act," *Journal of Law & Economics* 12 (1969): 377.

The Economics and Politics of Airline Deregulation

Michael E. Levine

The fare from San Diego to San Francisco (a distance of 447 miles) is $32, which is 7¢ per mile.[1] That same trip, if you purchase your ticket out of state, will cost you $54, or 12¢ per mile. If you want to fly from San Antonio to Dallas, and you purchase your ticket from a CAB-certificated carrier, you will pay $37, or 15¢ per mile. If, however, you fly an intrastate carrier (Southwest Airlines), you will pay $25 (9¢ per mile), during the business day and $15 (5¢ per mile) on evenings and weekends. The Los Angeles to San Francisco fare is $25.50 intrastate (7½¢ per mile). The CAB published fare for the same route (which would be paid by a passenger who wanted to travel between Los Angeles and San Francisco and bought his ticket in another state) is $44, (13¢ per mile). The lowest fare in that market is $17,[a] (5½¢ per mile). What the high fares have in common is that they are subject to approval by the Civil Aeronautics Board, which is the federal agency responsible for the economic regulation of airlines.

What the low fares have in common is that they are offered entirely within states that have their own regulatory authority and have regulated less restrictively than at the federal level. In the case of Texas, authority is exercised quite lightly. In the case of California, regulatory authority was virtually nonexistent until 1965 (it now is quite extensive). This may seem surprising, the common wisdom is before regulation, markets were dominated by robber barons who charged high prices, ran monopolies or cartels, and victimized the public through high prices. This wisdom holds that we changed all that by instituting regulatory agencies whose function was to protect us from these rapacious gentlemen. The odd thing, of course, is that this view presumes that regulation was established to keep prices down, yet the evidence above suggests that regulation is associated with higher, not lower, air fares. Actually, recent scholarly analysis of the history of regulation suggests that regulation, at least in many industries (airlines being one of them), was established to keep prices up.

In these terms, the history of airline regulation is quite instructive. The bill which established the Civil Aeronautics Board was originally drafted by the Air Transport Association of America, which is the trade association of scheduled airlines in the United States. That bill, which was patterned on the act which instituted trucking regulation (the Motor Carrier Act of 1935), was designed to make sure that what was then considered to be an *excess* of competition in the airlines industry was eliminated. It did that by providing that no one could enter

---

[a]That is on Continental Airlines, which flies from Burbank to San Jose as part of its longer haul routes to the Pacific Northwest.

the airline business without the permission of the CAB, that no airline could raise or lower fares without the permission of the CAB, and that carriers must publish all fare changes in advance.[2]

This legislation has had major impact on the airline industry and major impact on the public. The impact on the public has, in my opinion, been mostly negative. The most conservative estimate I am aware of (which is almost certainly too low) puts the additional cost to the public of airline regulation at about half a billion dollars a year.[3] Less conservative estimates[4] range from $1½ billion to $3 billion a year, in extra cost to the public.

One way in which this regulation has been very effective has been by keeping new firms out of the airline business (which was one of the principal objectives of the airline supporters of the bill). In May 1938, when the act was passed, there were sixteen carriers certificated under the so-called grandfather clause of the act. This was a provision which said that if you already were in the airline business you could have a certificate. The number of trunkline carriers that have been licensed since 1938, a period in which the industry has grown several hundred times, is *zero*. There have been a number of mergers in the interim and the number of grandfather carriers has been reduced from sixteen to ten. This is, by anyone's standard, effective entry regulation. What it has meant, of course, is that for forty years, a firm with ideas and airplanes which thought it could make a profit serving the public was not permitted to do so. The CAB has from time to time certificated other classes of carriers, but it has carefully delimited their rights in an effort to make sure that they did not compete with the carriers which were originally certificated under the grandfather provisions of that act. We have had local service carriers (e.g., Hughes Airwest), and there are eight of those remaining. All cargo carriers have been certificated. Occasional charter airlines have been certificated. But anyone who wanted to offer mass market or long-haul transportation has found himself, for some reason, unable to persuade the board that he ought to be permitted to do so. This, I suppose, would be an acceptable (although perhaps lamentable in principle) state of affairs, if the existing carriers were providing the service the public wanted at the lowest possible fares. The evidence is, however, otherwise, as the fares and excess cost estimates given above suggest.

The absence of new competition has not been due to a lack of interest in entering the airline business. Indeed, a Senate report found that seventy-nine firms had applied between 1950 and 1974 to offer domestic trunkline service for the first time.[5]

To take the most recent and interesting example, a supplemental carrier named World Airways, which operates modern jet equipment, and has charter rights in the United States and throughout the world, applied in 1967 to the CAB to provide coast to coast service for $79, using Boeing 707's. The then existing fare was $145. World proposed to lower that fare to $75 once it received Boeing 747's, which it then had on order.

The board accepted the application (that is, took in the piece of paper) and ignored it. It held it for approximately six years without setting it down for hearing. The procedure by which one nominally gets entry into the business is that one has one's application heard before an administrative law judge and ultimately the board, and if "the public interest, convenience, and necessity" require it, the application is approved. It is interesting that the "public interest, convenience, and necessity" have never required the entry of a new trunk carrier, and World's application was no exception. Indeed, the "public interest, convenience, and necessity" evidently did not even require that World get a chance to present its case. And the board decided that, after the application had been on file for six years and no hearing had been granted it was "stale" and therefore the CAB dismissed it.

World refiled the application again at $89, changing it slightly. The new application requested permission to provide service from Ontario Airport and Oakland Airport to Newark, instead of from Los Angeles and San Francisco to Kennedy. World obviously was attempting to tailor the application so that it seemed less threatening to existing carriers. This did not fool the board, World's application was recently dismissed by using an extremely restrictive interpretation of the board's licensing powers to conclude that such service could not be approved.

A rather interesting feature of the board's original dismissal of World's application is that one of the reasons it articulated for not having heard the application for six years was that it was a very busy agency. Since there were very many more applications before the agency than it could possibly hear, the agency had to establish priorities. Under those priorities, it was much more important to decide who was going to provide through service between Memphis and Miami than it was to decide whether or not low-fare service should be permitted in the Los Angeles-New York market, because Los Angeles-New York service already existed. Therefore, World's application duplicated existing service. Anyone who appeared at an airline counter after 1967 with $79 in his hand and asked for a Los Angeles-New York ticket might have questioned whether existing service was duplicated, but under the board's interpretation there was nonstop service and there was certainly no need to waste the public's time by hearing another application. The board has been even more aggressive in eliminating competition in other cases.

Where the board for one reason or another has allowed some sort of new entry, fares have been, and remain, quite a bit lower than they are in general. For example, O. Roy Chalk, a gentleman with a fair amount of political influence, was operating a nonscheduled cargo airline between San Juan, Puerto Rico, and New York in the 1950s. The carrier was named Trans-Caribbean. Mr. Chalk managed somehow ultimately to persuade the board to grant him a certificate to carry passengers between New York and San Juan. This is "overseas" transportation under the act, rather than "interstate" transportation, and Trans-Caribbean is the only new long-haul carrier certificated since 1938 on noninternational rates. With Trans-Caribbean in that market, the fares dropped by more than half and have remained at 5¢ a mile or less, depending on what time of the week and what day you travel, (fares in markets of comparable distance elsewhere in the United States are about 8¢ a mile, and so the difference is about 40 percent). Trans-Caribbean later merged with American Airlines. The fares in that market, however, remain low and American Airlines operates profitably in that market.

Other effects of CAB regulation are that there are many fewer carriers than there otherwise would be, costs are quite high, and planes fly quite empty producing less intensive use of capital equipment. We have already noted that there are only ten trunklines. One local service carrier (Allegheny) has sufficiently expanded its short haul service between northeastern markets so that in some respects it is a trunk airline. But studies have indicated that an airline reaches minimum efficient size when it operates a fleet of between five and ten airplanes. All of these carriers of the ten (or ten and a half, if you count Allegheny) are very much larger than that. While it is difficult to predict exactly how many carriers we would have in a deregulated environment, it would probably be very much larger than at present.

The high costs of operating in a regulated environment are indicated both by the high fares I have identified and the fact that most airlines do not make large profits at those high fares. The reason they do not is that there is no regulatory control over the amount of capacity an airline can offer between the points for which it is certificated. Since fares are pegged, passengers will naturally take the airline which has a schedule operating at a time most convenient to them. Since the fares are set at a relatively high level, the airline can break even at low load factor. Therefore, carriers proliferate flights in an effort to capture passengers.

The direct operating cost (using the CAB's definition, which *includes* capital costs) to move a seat from New York to Los Angeles is in the neighborhood of $30. The fare is $180. Obviously, a genuine fare-paying passenger is a precious creature indeed. And if a 5 o'clock flight will entice him away from the flight he was going to take at 6 o'clock, a carrier operates the 5 o'clock flight even if relatively few passengers will use it. Only a few passengers at $180 (about seventy-five in a Boeing 747) will pay the operating costs of a modern aircraft between Los Angeles and New York. The result is that carriers operate very many planes, relatively empty. And they do that at very high per unit passenger fares, and about break even. Most make no more profit than they would in a competitive environment. The extra money goes to provide all these additional flights, as a result, costs are high.

This results in considerable capital waste. For the year ended August 1975, the CAB reported the load factor for domestic trunk airlines as 53 percent. That means that, on average, only 53 percent of seats on flights in that year were filled. That figure in itself suggests that there is a lot of empty space flying around, but it greatly understates the amount of waste that is taking place, because the board calculates load factor statistics using the number of seats actually in the airplane. If fares which are set quite high, and a carrier can break even flying relatively few passengers per flight, one way to compete for passengers is to offer relatively spacious seating. And if one carrier offers relatively comfortable seating, others must to stay competitive. Passengers might prefer more cramped seating at a lower price, but regulation does not offer them that option. A passenger must pay the high price and if he is forced to pay the high price, he chooses among carriers on the basis of space and service amenities, as well as the schedule frequency mentioned earlier.

The result is that the DC 10, which was designed to carry between 350 and 400 people, is operated by U.S. carriers with about two hundred and forty seats in it. The 747, which could carry as many as five hundred people, is operated with approximately 350 seats in it. When the board reports that, on average, 53 percent of the seats offered were filled last year, it understates the percentage of the potential capacity of the aircraft that was used. I have crudely estimated that percentage at about 39 for the year in question. This means that about 60 percent of the carrying capacity of flights operated was wasted. The numbers on which I base this calculation are not the maximum number of people that the FAA will allow you to put into these aircraft; that figure is uncomfortable. I am assuming a standard of operation which by my arbitrary standards is moderately comfortable.[b] So regulation causes considerable capital waste, even if you assume that under deregulation as few as 70 percent of the seats would be full. (There has been argument as to what the load factor under deregulation would be, but 70 percent is quite conservative.)

Under those circumstances airlines could accommodate 78 percent more business than they did last year without buying another aircraft. This fact becomes important when we discuss the politics of deregulation. But let us consider first whether regulation which results in such high fares and so much capital and fuel waste can be justified on other grounds.

The CAB and the industry make several sorts of arguments: without regulation, there would be cut-throat competition, all firms would lose money, and then the public would have no air service. This is difficult to believe, since there is an enormous basic demand for air travel. Why can't somebody manage to make a profit servicing it? A fallback to the second line position is then asserted: not everyone will go out of business, there will be one survivor who will have a monopoly and will use it to exploit the public. This argument ignores the principal technical fact about the airline business that created carrier demand for regulation in the first place, namely that entry into the airline business is very easy.

An airplane is a very mobile piece of capital equipment, mobility is its

---

[b]For example, I have assumed 34-inch seat pitch and nine abreast in a DC 10.

reason for being. If there is an opportunity to fly between two cities and make a profit, it is relatively easy to shift equipment into that market, contract for services, and enter. This should make continued profitable operation as a monopolist impossible, since the profits will attract competition. This rather crucial fact does not seem to deter those who argue for regulation. Their resilience is suggested by a third argument, namely that without regulation, service will be confined to the major routes. Everyone will want to fly between Los Angeles and New York and no one will want to fly from Los Angeles to Sacramento. But if all service is concentrated in the Los Angeles-New York market, it obviously will not turn out to be especially profitable, while profitable opportunities would continue to exist to carry passengers to and from Sacramento. Presumably, some carriers will pursue this opportunity. On the logic that underlies this contention, there would be no food stores in Sacramento, only in Los Angeles, because there are more people in Los Angeles than there are in Sacramento and all food stores would wish to locate in Los Angeles.

When all else fails, regulation proponents argue that deregulation would impair safety, and so we need economic regulation to protect lives and property. This argument ignores the fact that safety is regulated by a separate government agency, the FAA, which has nothing to do with CAB regulation. No serious scholar has yet proposed its abolition. Where we have had carriers without CAB certification, the safety record has, in general, been very good. California is an example. During its unregulated period, the safety record in California air travel was excellent.

If those arguments are unconvincing, what is the real source of opposition to airline deregulation? To identify and understand it, we must project the likely financial impact of deregulation on those who are connected with the airline industry. To do this, we must make a few assumptions. First, entry by new firms is easy. As indicated above, airplanes are very mobile. They are designed that way. Management personnel are available, operating personnel are available, and there is a large pool of military-trained pilots and mechanics. In particular, there are many more pilots who would like to and are qualified to fly jet equipment than there are pilot jobs in the present industry. And if a carrier wishes to avoid startup costs or long-term commitments, there are firms here and abroad that will lease aircraft, personnel, and know-how. Many existing certificated carriers contract for facilities to maintain their airplanes, make reservations, provide station servicing, and in some cases, even to fly their services. Braniff Airways, for example, bought Panagra. Braniff did not operate the type of aircraft Panagra owned, so Braniff has them maintained in Miami by a company that specializes in maintaining airplanes.

Airlines that operate to stations which they serve only once or twice a day often contract with other carriers to have station services provided. If Eastern has only two flights a day, and American has ten, it does not pay Eastern to employ a ground crew and ramp equipment. They employ only a person behind the counter, although in some cases they don't even do that. But the personnel on the ramp who are unloading the airplane and fueling will almost certainly not be employees of a carrier that makes only one stop per day. This sort of service is available to anyone who wants to get into the airline industry.

The second assumption is that the minimum efficient size of an air carrier is quite small. Carriers much smaller than those now certificated can operate at no cost disadvantage compared to larger carriers. In fact, the very largest carriers in the United States seem to have higher operating costs than the medium-size carriers. Whether that is due to excessive management or because the employees lose *esprit* or to some other factors is not well understood. But statistics suggest that the lowest cost carriers in the United States are in the low or medium-size range of the carriers presently certificated. Southwest Airlines in Texas, which operates six Boeing 737's, seems to operate at lower cost than the much larger CAB-certificated carriers.

If we make these assumptions, then the kind of world that can be projected as a consequence of airline deregulation strongly suggests the genesis of opposition to deregulation. First, of course, the CAB would have very little to do in a deregulated industry, so it is not difficult to see why the CAB has opposed deregulation.[c] As among the rest of us, self-immolation is not a common tendency among bureaucrats and there is little likelihood that someone whose justification for existence is managing an airline market will suddenly decide that management of an airline market is not an important thing to do.

Second, since the principal passenger-attracting strategy of a newly entering firm will be price competition, we can expect that new entry under deregulation will lower fares. This is especially true on long-haul routes where the relationship of fares to costs is particularly anomalous. Obviously, if prices are lowered, the cost relationships discussed above suggest that load factors will go up. The industry would begin to use its capital equipment more intensively. And in addition, new carriers would probably invent new price service options, in the same way that PSA pioneered no-frills low-cost service. Laker Airways' proposed trans-Atlantic Sytrain service is an example of the sort of long-haul service innovation that might be generated. As proposed, a passenger would show up at the terminal within eight hours of flight time to be accommodated on a first-come, first-served basis. This presumably was a service which would be most attractive to people with sleeping bags who do not mind airline terminals. But if time was not valuable to the passenger and fare level was crucial, the service might be very attractive, because Laker Airways was proposing to make it worth consideration by charging only $100 (when first proposed) between New York and London.

---

[c]The board has recently announced that it favors "carefully monitored" deregulation of certain services to take place very gradually. While often this represents an unusual bureaucratic willingness to contemplate morality, the specifics have not yet been revealed and the testimony in which the position was asserted seemed to assert a long enough period to ensure job tenure until retirement for almost everyone employed at the agency.

In the face of competition like this, many existing carriers obviously would be reduced in size. Many of them are too large to be efficient, and many of them have managements which are specialized toward getting along with the CAB, functioning in trade associations, and in influencing the Congress. Those are very useful skills in a regulated environment. But nobody much cares whether the president of a supermarket chain is a statesman. Investors and customers mostly want to know if he can run an operation that can sell food cheaply. Presumably similar skills would be desirable for people running deregulated airlines. Under deregulation then, present management might find themselves replaced, present carriers would probably shrink (or be replaced by some other carriers not nearly as large). Some carriers would go bankrupt because they could not adapt at all, or they would reorganize, causing losses to shareholders and lenders. A few national carriers of some size might continue to operate, much as do Hertz and Avis, but there would also be quite a few carriers that specialized in serving certain markets, much in the same way that small rental car firms offer you low cost services at relatively few locations without a national reservations network.

The big losers, obviously, would be some existing carrier managements and some providers of unsecured lenders capital. In the airline industry debt-equity ratios are quite heavily weighted toward debt, because the CAB has been able to protect capital very successfully. If an airline is in trouble, the board helps it raise rates and denies competitor applications for lower rates. In addition the board has tried to give troubled carriers new routes, particularly profitable monopoly routes, if available. In other words, the board does what it can to protect carrier health. It does this because it identifies the health of the air transport industry with the health of particular carriers, rather than with the health of consumers using the airlines. Also, because of the difficulty of obtaining a certificate and of the relatively small number of airlines permitted to operate on any particular route, owning a route certificate is quite valuable. For example, the right to fly between New York and Los Angeles is a very valuable asset. It should not be any more valuable, as indicated above, than the right to fly from Los Angeles to Sacramento or Bakersfield. (Under price competition, the value of the right to enter any market should be the same, because returns to investment should equalize as investment flows into markets that are profitable and seeks out new opportunities.) But certain certificates are worth a great deal, and lenders in effect lend against them. The carrier does not actually put up the certificate as collateral, but the lender is willing to lend to an airline like TWA, because TWA is an established carrier with "good" routes and the lender expects that the board will do whatever it can to keep TWA in business. Capital provided on these assumptions could obviously be rather insecure as the industry moved to a deregulated environment. The unsecured lender is particularly vulnerable. Equipment trust certificates (mortgages) would not be nearly as insecure. An aircraft can be transferred elsewhere and used whatever the financial capability of the original operator. Indeed, in the kind of growing market that I would project under deregulation, existing capacity would continue to be valuable.

Initially, capital sources might be reluctant to finance new or even existing carriers, but this would be counterbalanced by equipment available on a leased basis as secured lenders sought to put their existing aircraft to productive use. At first venture capital, and later more conservative equity and debt capital, would finance new operations as the level of uncertainty regarding the future structure and prospects of the industry declined. Ultimately, the rapid growth of air travel demand would attract new capital to firms demonstrating the ability to survive and prosper.

Airport operators would become more like independent entrepreneurs and less like instruments through which the carriers provide ground services to the public. A larger number of smaller carriers not legally committed to serve any point and not guaranteed the protection of the CAB would become ordinary customers of, rather than long-term contractors with, airport authorities, who in turn would make their own financing arrangements without depending on carriers for guarantees. Capital would be supplied to airport operators based on long-term demand for their proposed facilities. Fewer, if any, carriers would be provided with terminals uniquely suited to their requirements in return for long-term commitments, since long-term commitments on the part of the carriers would be less reliable than at present. On the other hand, civic monuments would be harder to impose on the carriers and the public if alternative service at lower fares reflecting lower airport charges was available at competing satellite airports. Smaller cities would make do with less elaborate airports than at present as fare levels directly reflected airport costs and could be compared with fares from cities with more realistic facilities. In addition, specialist carriers serving smaller cities would be less likely to use aircraft demanding costly and environmentally objectionable runway expansions.

Unionized airline employees, particularly pilots, might be sharply affected by deregulation. Smaller carriers are more expensive to organize, and multiple firms and free route entry make the strike weapon much less effective. A strike against a carrier whose service represented a relatively small percentage of the national total and could be replaced by competing carriers without route restrictions would not be sufficiently disruptive to generate political intervention. The level of wages which could be paid by a firm unable to recover its costs through an industrywide fare increase would tend to be competitive. Lack of route monopolies or oligopolies would eliminate monopoly rents available for capture by labor unions. And the existence of a large pool of eager and qualified unemployed pilots would make an attempt to organize the entire pilot population virtually impossible. The same would hold true for other classes of airline employees, although their present wages are undoubtedly much closer to competitive levels and the impact on their earnings would therefore be much less pronounced.

A significant decline in fares would undoubtedly lead to more intensive capital use as consumers opted for less convenient and comfortable price-quality options. Experience in markets where new entry has occurred, such as California and Texas intrastate markets or New York-San Juan, suggests strongly that most consumers prefer to pay less for less comfortable (higher-density seating, higher load factors, less inflight service) or less conveniently timed transportation than to purchase CAB-style service at CAB fares. (Of course, to the extent that sufficient numbers of travelers preferred other, more comfortable, service/price combinations to allow them to be offered at a profit, such options would be provided, in the same way that first-class service is provided now.) Since the calculations referred to earlier also suggest a 78 percent increase in trunkline revenue passenger miles could be absorbed without requiring new equipment (assuming a load factor of 70 percent), a move to price competition at higher load factors would temporarily terminate new equipment orders to airframe manufacturers. This state of affairs would continue for whatever period was necessary to produce actual or anticipated traffic growth requiring new equipment. If the price elasticity of demand for air transportation is as high, as I and some others believe it is, traffic would expand dramatically over time as fares came down. During this period airframe manufacturers would face severe cash flow problems, alleviated only by orders from international and foreign carriers. Manufacturer insolvencies might result, but these would almost certainly end in reorganizations rather than liquidations. Once existing capacity was absorbed, the manufacturers would face bright prospects. For one thing, much existing equipment, particularly older long-haul narrow-bodied jets, could not be operated economically in a high-density low-fare market environment. These aircraft would fall in capital value (producing losses to investors and lenders) as the market revalued them in an effort to keep their total operating costs competitive, but many would not be economic even at zero capital costs and would have to be replaced. Any further fuel cost increases (perhaps brought about by termination of domestic petroleum price controls) would accelerate this process. For another, the existing product lines of the domestic airframe manufacturers are well-suited in their present forms to high-density low-fare service, so no new capital investment in the airframe industry would be required to adapt them. Finally, traffic growth would be greatly stimulated by low fares, resulting ultimately in significant demand for new equipment.

The big gainers from deregulation would obviously be consumers and new entrepreneurs. Consumers would get air service at a fraction of present fares. We could barely imagine what the travel world would look like if the Los Angeles-New York fare was $50 or $75, if steelworkers could fly on their vacations, and so on. There would be an enormous expansion in the travel market.

The sources of political opposition to deregulation, then, should be obvious. The CAB is opposed to deregulation, financial institutions are opposed to deregulation, existing managements of certificated carriers are opposed to deregulation. The aircraft manufacturers have not come on record, but there is reason to believe that they are uncomfortable with it at least for the short run, and the labor unions are strongly opposed.

Should we take the prospect of deregulation seriously? The title of this chapter is, "The Economics and Politics of Airline Deregulation." Let us briefly consider further the politics and aspects of the problem. If new entrepreneurs and consumers are for deregulation, and the CAB, financial institutions, airport operators, existing managements, and the unions are against it, what is the likely end result? By whatever theory of political influence sinister or not one uses, well-organized groups with an intense interest in a problem typically have much more influence on the legislative process than those such as consumers with relatively diffuse interests and certainly more than new entrepreneurs who do not even have an identifiable interest in the business. There is, not surprisingly, very well-organized opposition to deregulation. There is not nearly as well-organized support. The national administration has introduced legislation which emphasizes price deregulation without allowing much entry. Since I think that the principal driving force behind lower fares is the prospect of new competition, I think the bill is inadequate, but it is probably stronger in any event than anything Congress will enact.

The relevant committees in Congress are dominated by people hostile to deregulation. The Senate Commerce Committee is chaired by Senator Magnuson, who is from Washington. The largest industry in Washington is Boeing. Regulation, you will recall, causes Boeing to sell more airplanes per passenger than they would otherwise. Increased future production from dramatic growth seems too speculative and too far in the future to induce manufacturer support for deregulation. Senator Magnuson's position on deregulation is thus fairly easy to divine. Similar analysis elsewhere in the committee structure of both houses of Congress suggests that there is little committee support for deregulation. There is actually considerable support in the Congress at large, but mostly from members who do not have an enormous influence on the committee process affecting this legislation. Since it is hard to imagine airline deregulation as the kind of issue which would produce a floor rebellion against the committee structure, to bring a bill out of committee, large numbers of mildly interested supporters will not produce a deregulation bill.

Some liberalization is taking place at the CAB in an effort to defuse what public pressure has been generated by media stories and congressional hearings by committees that do not have jurisdiction over the issue, there may be some liberalization of regulation by the board. It has, for example, recently proposed charter rules that finally will end the necessity to join a bird watching society in order to get cheap transportation. But the net result of all this, to my great regret, will be only somewhat liberalized policies and rules, perhaps some minor decline in fares as the board imposes somewhat higher load factor standards to make the carriers fill up the airplanes a little more, and perhaps some legislation exhorting the board to pay more attention to consumers. But the "Brave New World" of low fares enticing globetrotters drawn from every walk of life, is a long way in the future, if it exists at all.

80

Notes

1. All fares from *Official Airline Guide*, February 1976.

2. Civil Aeronautics Act of 1938, pp. 401, 403, 1002. 49 US Code 1371, 1373, 1482.

3. G.W. Douglas and J.E. Miller III, *Economic Regulation of Domestic Air Transport.*

4. See e.g. Testimony of W.A. Jordan in *Hearings on the Oversight of C.A.B. Practices and Procedures* (U.S. Senate, 1975).

5. See *Civil Aeronautics Board Practice and Procedure* (U.S. Senate, 1975).

Jury Composition: An Economic Approach

Alvin K. Klevorick

It is difficult to think of a society of heterogeneous individuals in which disputes would not arise. Hence, one set of public services governments usually provide consists of the facilities and processes for the resolution of such disputes. In the United States, the resources expended for these public services include, for example: the use of courthouse and administrative agency buildings; and the time of judges, prosecutors, public defenders, courthouse personnel, and members of administrative agencies.

Of course, not all disputes reach the stage where government facilities and services are called upon for assistance. Indeed, the nature and structure of the particular set of services provided by the government help to determine which conflicts will be resolved inside and which outside the framework of government institutions. For example, the structure of liability rules, the court-established precedents for similar cases, and the current extent of court delay—all characteristics of the government's dispute-resolution service would be among the factors a potential plaintiff in an accident case would weigh in deciding whether to go to court. Moreover, not all disputants will employ the same set of government institutions. Different processes and facilities will be used in settling different conflicts.

In resolving some legal disputes, society turns to a selected body of laymen—a jury—for the decision. This particular "government service"—the jury—is the focus of this chapter. In considering the use of the jury as a conflict-resolving instrument, several interrelated questions arise: How large should the jury be? What should the composition of this jury be; alternatively, how should members of the jury be selected? What voting rule should the jury use to reach its decision in resolving the dispute at hand?

As a result of several relatively recent U.S. Supreme Court decisions, these questions have taken on renewed interest in the United States. These decisions have upheld, under particular circumstances, the constitutionality of juries comprised of fewer than twelve persons and of decisions reached by nonunanimous twelve-person juries. My aim is to describe a theoretical structure which might help in addressing these questions of jury size, composition, and voting rule. My hope is that this statistical decision-theoretic model will be helpful in

This chapter is based on a paper originally prepared for an International Economic Association Conference on The Economics of Public Services, held in April 1974 at Turin, Italy, and published in M.S. Feldstein and R.P. Inman (eds.), *The Economics of Public Services* (London: Macmillan and Company, 1976).

82

organizing and clarifying thought about the relevant current questions concerning the jury.

The model will not be able to specify exactly how juries should be structured, but it will be useful in pinpointing the empirical information (or empirical guesses) needed to reach such decisions. It will suggest what data are relevant for making such choices and how different values for the critical quantities affect the choices made. Given the state of empirical research on the questions of jury size, composition, and voting rule, it seems reasonable to pursue the theoretical route a bit further. While the present model abstracts drastically from the richness of the jury as a social and legal institution, it is more attentive to two aspects which previous probabilistic models of the jury have suppressed: differences among jurors and the nonindependence of juror decision-making.

After describing the basic theoretical structure, we will use the model to examine how representative a jury should be. The question of jury representativeness was highlighted by the Supreme Court's opinion in *Williams v. Florida*. There the Court saw little problem with reducing jury size from twelve to six so long as the jury continued to be a cross-section representative of the community. In the Court's view, if the six members were representative of the community, the reduction in size would not substantially reduce the protection afforded the defendant.

Now, there is, to be sure, a spectrum of reasons one could offer for having representative juries. I shall describe a model of the most instrumental function of the jury: fact-finding. Then, drawing upon the economist's model of portfolio selection and using that model as a metaphor in viewing the question of jury composition, I shall examine the degree to which and the conditions under which jury representativeness serves this most instrumental function. While the functions of the jury have previously been debated at length, I shall also try, at the end, to suggest another reason for representativeness of the jury, one which I have not seen articulated elsewhere. This reason, which lies at the least instrumental end of the spectrum, focuses on jury representativeness as a political symbol, as a value in its own right.

The analysis focuses on the criminal jury, and it abstracts from the reverberations that institutional changes in the jury may have on the number of jury trials itself. For example, while we will assume that an erroneous conviction affects the total incidence of crime, we will not consider how this increase in criminal activity affects the number of criminal trials. I also do not explore how changing the efficiency of the jury would affect the extent and nature of plea bargaining. Especially since such a small fraction of criminal cases are resolved by means of jury trial, these questions which we put aside are very important.

The object of the analysis is a single case in which the individual has been charged with a particular crime. I shall assume that the jury which is chosen to hear the case has only three alternatives. It can find the defendant guilty of the crime, it can declare him innocent, or it can reach no decision (it can hang). In particular, the possibility that the jury might find the defendant guilty of a lesser charge is excluded from consideration. Our analysis takes the defendant and the charge against him as given and discusses the situation in which the jury faced with these three alternatives must be chosen before the in-court proceedings have begun. A simpler and narrower analysis would ask how to select the "optimal" jury after the in-court proceedings had already been completed. In contrast, the most general analysis would ask what kind of jury panel we would want *given only* the number of cases and the composition of charges to be evaluated. This last decision involves optimally choosing the panel from which juries for particular cases will be drawn.

The conclusions one reaches about optimal jury composition will depend on the level of analysis one chooses. It may, for example, turn out that a fully representative jury is optimal when one defendant is to be tried on a particular charge but not when another defendant is to be tried for a different crime. The degree of representativeness that is optimal for the juror panel as a whole may differ from that which is optimal for the jury for any particular case.

We must begin with a discussion of the variety of costs associated with running a jury system, including both readily monetizable costs (which I shall refer to as "economic costs") and less easily quantified costs (which, for convenience, I shall refer to as "noneconomic costs"). The monetizable economic costs represent the value of all the resources society devotes to the jury system, including the value of judges' time, lawyers' time, and the time of courthouse personnel; the value of courthouse space used for the trial and jury deliberations; the subsistence expenses and travel expenses of jurors; and the value of jurors' time. Since these costs are described in some detail elsewhere, I shall restrict myself to some observations about them.

First, it should be clear that in measuring the economic costs of the jury, one is concerned only with the incremental costs of using a jury. It would be incorrect, for example, to count the value of the entire time judges spend in cases tried to juries as a cost of the jury system. Given our assumptions, eliminating any jury trial currently taking place would mean replacing it by a bench trial. Hence, it is only the *extra* time the judge must spend for a jury trial rather than a bench one that should be assessed as a cost of the jury system.

Second, in considering the additional economic costs society incurs because it uses juries, it is useful to distinguish between the fixed costs and the variable costs of having a jury trial. The fixed costs are incurred as soon as it is decided to try a case to a jury rather than to a judge. In particular, these costs do not vary with the size or composition of the jury. For example, having juries decide cases requires an administrative structure to poll the community, determine who is eligible for jury duty, and maintain up-to-date lists of such people. Some of the costs incurred in establishing and operating this structure are independent of the number of people on each jury and the characteristics of those people, and hence they constitute a fixed cost of the jury system.

The variable costs of the system are those resource costs associated with running a jury which depend on the kind of jury one uses. The model developed here focuses on two particularly important sources of variation. First, the cost of running a jury varies with the number of jurors. For example, the daily incremental subsistence expenses of the jury can be expected to vary directly with jury size. Another resource cost which varies with the number of jurors used is the opportunity cost of jurors' time. It consists of the goods and services society foregoes because of their jury service—that is, the output that would have been produced by the jurors had they not been serving on the jury. This resource cost is the sum of the social marginal products of the jurors for the period for which they serve. The opportunity cost of jurors' time also provides an example of the second way in which the cost of a jury trial can vary. It will change as the composition of the jury changes. If, for example, the time required for a jury trial depends only on the number of jurors, then holding the number of people on the jury fixed, but replacing one individual with another whose social marginal product is higher or lower will change the jury's demand on society's resources.

The model described here focuses on the economic cost attributable to the use of jurors' time and particularly on the way that cost changes as the composition of the jury changes. I shall essentially treat all other costs of the jury system—judges' time, lawyers' time, use of courthouse space, and so on—as fixed and invariant with the size and composition of the jury. This simplifying assumption will help to highlight some ideas about jury size and composition.

Let us turn now to what we have called the noneconomic costs of the jury system, focusing again on an individual trial where the defendant has been charged with a particular crime. It will be assumed that there is a true state of nature: the defendant either did commit the crime with which he is charged or he did not. If we had perfect knowledge, we would know what that true state is. But we do not have such knowledge and the process we use to provide the decision-making unit—the jury—with data cannot be expected to yield such perfect information. The principal noneconomic social costs are the social costs of making mistakes in deciding whether the defendant is guilty in fact or innocent in fact. We are measuring the noneconomic social costs of the jury relative to the social costs a perfectly accurate fact-finder would engender. When the jury reaches the same verdict the perfect fact-finder would reach, no noneconomic social costs are incurred; when the two verdicts diverge, the jury has generated noneconomic social costs.

The jury can declare the defendant legally guilty, which I shall refer to as a conviction; or it can declare him legally innocent, which I shall call an acquittal; or it can reach no verdict. Social noneconomic costs are associated with convicting an individual who is, in fact, innocent and with acquitting a defendant who is, in fact, guilty. In statistical terms, if one regards the null hypothesis as the statement "The defendant is innocent," then these two possible mistakes are, respectively, the Type I error and the Type II error of classical statistical hypothesis testing.

The corresponding social costs are the costs of committing Type I and Type II errors. In the former case, when an innocent individual is convicted, the costs include the goods and services society foregoes if the punishment involves imprisonment (taking into account both what the individual would have produced and the resource cost of his imprisonment), the loss the innocent individual suffers as the result of being labeled a criminal, the effects on the total incidence of crime that ensue because the system convicts innocent individuals, and the effects on the social state of mind of having such a system. The social costs associated with a Type II error—the acquittal of a guilty defendant—include the cost of having an individual who has committed a crime free to commit another one and the effects on the total level of crime and on the social state of mind of having a system which acquits defendants who are, in fact, guilty. Of course, in computing the social cost of a Type II error, one must take account of the benefits society obtains from the error: the marginal social product of the truly guilty individual when he is free and the resource costs saved because he is not imprisoned.

There remains for consideration the set of cases in which the jury neither acquits nor convicts the defendant. Such a decision, or rather such a nondecision, could be considered a "mistake." The defendant is either innocent or guilty, and the jury does not declare which state actually obtains. To be sure, the resource cost of running a jury trial in which the jury hangs is real and will be counted among the economic costs discussed earlier. The question is what additional social costs result from such an outcome. The answer depends on what happens if the jury hangs and on the true state of nature.

Suppose there is no retrial. The jury's verdict is let stand as a nondecision. If the individual is truly guilty, this outcome has the same social costs as an acquittal except that society need not face the legal acquittal of a guilty individual but only his *de facto* acquittal. If, instead, the defendant is truly innocent, society does not forego any goods and services due to imprisonment as it does when a Type I error is committed. But society does incur costs similar to, but not the same as, all the other costs resulting from the conviction of an innocent individual. The two sets of costs differ because the stigma attached to an individual whose true innocence has not been affirmatively declared differs from that attached to an innocent person who has been declared guilty. Hence, the effects of the two situations are different for the individual and for the society that must recognize that it imposes this cost on individuals.

All of this assumes that the case is not retried. Suppose, to the contrary, that it is retried. If the defendant is guilty, then the additional social costs resulting from this particular hung jury are those associated with having a guilty individual free for the interval between the two trials. If, on the other hand, the defendant is in fact innocent, the added social costs are those associated with having a truly innocent individual not acquitted and therefore branded as a potential criminal during that interval.

The appropriate evaluation of the social noneconomic costs of a hung jury must be resolved, in the end, by empirical examination of the sequels to hung jury trials. For example, with what frequency are such cases retried? In examining a single case and asking about the optimal size and composition of the jury to decide that case, it is possible, though, to treat a hung jury outcome in either of the ways discussed. In what follows, we shall treat hung juries as final decisions, and we shall distinguish between those instances in which the jury hangs when the defendant is innocent and those cases in which the jury reaches no verdict when the defendant is guilty.

Once the given trial is specified, the social costs associated with making different errors are determined. The probabilities of making these errors may also be affected by the specific trial being considered. For example, the probability that a decisionmaker will err in deciding a murder case may differ from the probability that he will err in deciding a shoplifting case. But while knowledge of the defendant and of the crime with which he is charged suffices to determine the social costs associated with different kinds of errors, it is not sufficient for calculation of the error probabilities. On the contrary, the error probabilities and the economic costs of deciding the case depend on the size and composition of the jury selected to try it. A jury of a particular size and a particular composition will generate a particular set of error probabilities and engender a specific economic cost for society. The "social loss function" summarizes the various social "costs" resulting from the jury's fact-finding process, and the "optimal jury" for this case is the one with the lowest resulting social loss figure.

Without further assumptions about the nature of society's loss function—about how society weighs the different costs it incurs because it uses a jury to try the case—it is impossible to say very much about the nature of the optimal jury. To go further, I make assumptions which restrict the form the loss function can take and thereby confine the nature of the juror selection process. Nevertheless, these assumptions leave a fairly wide scope for the kinds of social trade-offs that interest us. Moreover, they yield a model which serves as a useful heuristic device for illuminating the process of optimal jury selection.

First, up to this point I have been intentionally vague about how one might measure the social noneconomic costs of the jury. I now want to assume that while these costs may not be monetizable, they are comparable with one another and can be measured on a scale which has properties similar to that of a thermometer scale. Second, we will assume that the social decisionmaker (society's agent) can compare different combinations of noneconomic social costs and economic social costs. Given two different combinations, he can indicate which one he prefers or whether he is indifferent between the two. Finally, I shall assume that in choosing among combinations of noneconomic and economic social costs this decisionmaker satisfies a set of conditions which at least many decision theorists regard as reasonable (even compelling) properties in situations of choice.

What choice situation does society or its agent—the social decisionmaker—face in selecting a jury? (The social decisionmaker is a fictitious jury selector who acts solely on the basis of society's preferences and who is not directly involved in the specific trial for which he is selecting the jury. In particular, I am not arguing that the common court procedure—employing the judge, the prosecutor, and the defense attorneys—fits this description.) We will assume that using a jury of a specific size and composition will engender the same social economic cost no matter what the true state of nature is—innocence or guilt of the defendant. In contrast, the social noneconomic cost of using that jury depends upon the true state of nature. Hence, the disutility associated with using a particular jury is conditional on the defendant's true state. In addition, since any jury's decision is uncertain to the social decisionmaker at the time he must select a jury, all he can compute is the expected social disutility of each potential jury conditional on the defendant's being innocent and similarly conditional on the defendant's being guilty. The social decisionmaker's task is to determine the characteristics of the jury which minimizes the social loss function.

Perhaps the broad outlines of the analogy with portfolio selection can now be seen. The acquisition of any portfolio of assets entails a specific expenditure of funds by the investor. As a result of his initial outlay and his choice of a portfolio, the investor will obtain a return, and this return will depend on which state of nature is the true one. At the time the investor selects the size and composition of his portfolio he does not know which state of nature will occur, which stocks or bonds will do well. If the investor satisfies certain plausible axioms—the same ones we assumed about our jury selector—he will use his subjective probability distribution over the possible states of nature and maximize his expected utility.

The problem society confronts in choosing a jury for a particular case fits quite well with this description of the investor's problem. While one might expect the typical investor to consider a fairly large number of states of nature—for example, many different levels of performance by the economy—there are only two alternative true states in the jury problem—guilt and innocence. The economic costs of using a particular jury are incurred no matter what the true state is, and they correspond to the investor's outlay on his portfolio. His initial outlay is also the same whether or not his assets perform well. The noneconomic costs of the jury depend on the true state of nature, just as the investor's returns do.

Perhaps the most important similarity is that, in both the jury problem and the investment problem, the outcome depends not only on the total resources expended—the economic costs in the one case and the size of the portfolio in the other—but also on the way those resources are expended. What securities are purchased by the portfolio investor? How many different kinds of securities are bought, and how much is invested in each type of asset? In the jury case, how many jurors are used to try the case and how is the jury composed? How many different "types" of jurors are employed and how many jurors of each type hear the case? To pursue this part of the metaphor, viewing jurors as assets to be optimally combined in the portfolio of the jury box, we need a model of the individual juror and of interactions among jurors.

Our model of the individual juror's decision-making process is quite simple. For any given trial, we assume that after the juror has viewed the in-court proceedings (which I shall loosely call the "evidence"), he first takes all that he has seen and heard in court, sifts through it, reflects on it, and arrives at a probability of guilt for the defendant. Second, he attempts to evaluate the degree of certainty he would require in making decisions in his own life where the risks to him were as substantial as those faced by the defendant in the case he has viewed. This yields his standard of reasonable doubt for the case. Finally, he compares his evaluation of the probability of guilt with his standard of reasonable doubt for the case. If the probability of guilt he calculates exceeds the probability required by his standard of reasonable doubt, he votes to convict the defendant. Otherwise, he votes to acquit the accused.

I am not asserting that any juror does, in fact, go through exactly this thought process; nor am I suggesting that any juror necessarily should. The model used here simply decomposes the juror's decision-making process into the three steps described for analytical purposes. It places a particular analytical grid on the "true" historical description of what the juror does. If you will, we are saying that no matter how *gestalt* the juror's decision process may actually be, we will view him as acting "as if" he proceeded according to the steps we have described.

The juror's decision-making process has random or stochastic elements in it; it is neither perfectly deterministic nor perfectly predictable. An outside observer who knew all there was to know about the juror prior to the trial and who was omniscient with respect to the trial itself, observing *every* element of the in-court proceedings, could not predict with certainty how the particular juror would vote after the trial and *before* any jury deliberation. Two sources of randomness seem important. First, there is the stochastic element in going from the in-court proceedings to the juror's evaluation of the probability that the defendant is guilty. There are random factors in the juror's observation and evaluation of the evidence. Even given the identical set of in-court proceedings (as perceived by our omniscient objective observer), on different occasions our juror could arrive at different values for the probability that the defendant is guilty. Second, randomness arises in the juror's standard of reasonable doubt. If we could confront the juror with the same trial on two distinct but hypothetically identical occasions, he might employ a different standard in the two cases.

I think the standard of reasonable doubt is sufficiently vague that we cannot expect a juror to be perfectly consistent in applying it.

Because there are random components in the juror's decision-making process—and hence uncertainty about his verdict—all that can be calculated before the juror reaches his decision in the case is the *probability* that he will vote to acquit and the *probability* that he will vote to convict. The juror's decision may be in error—he may vote to convict an innocent individual or he may vote to acquit a guilty defendant. The same configuration of evidence and in-court proceedings could probably be generated by a guilty defendant or by an innocent defendant, and jury trials are most likely to occur when there is substantial uncertainty about which of these is in fact the case. If the juror's standard of reasonable doubt depends only on the penalty the given defendant will face if convicted, then the juror must reach the same conclusion when the same in-court proceedings occur, whether the defendant is truly innocent or truly guilty. Hence, if the same "evidence" can be generated whether the defendant is, in fact, innocent or guilty, the juror necessarily has a positive probability of making at least a Type I error (convicting an innocent defendant) or a Type II error (acquitting a guilty defendant). In general, there will be a positive probability that the juror will make each type of error.

All of this can be formalized in a model of juror decision-making, and this model could be used to calculate the error probabilities for each potential juror. We would expect these error probabilities to differ among jurors since we expect people to differ in the way they process the same in-court proceedings and in their standards of reasonable doubt. They differ in their ability to understand arguments and in their ability to understand and interpret the testimony of expert witnesses. Alternative potential jurors might put the same set of in-court proceedings together in different ways. They might differ in their capacities to judge the credibility of witnesses and to sift what some might view as courtroom "drama" from the "hard facts." Of course, different people will have different biases, and they will also bring these biases to bear on their perceptions of the trial.

Clearly, one could go on to enumerate many other ways in which potential jurors might differ. The last one I shall point out here, and a very important one, is that they will differ in their life experiences and in the ways they have internalized these divergent experiences. To the extent that each juror draws upon his own experience to determine his standard of reasonable doubt for the case, this difference among potential triers of fact will lead them to use different standards in judging whether the probability of guilt each of them derives from the in-court proceedings is high enough to justify a conviction.

Differences among jurors are, of course, at the heart of the justification for the jury system. Use of the jury as a fact-finding unit is premised upon the view that different people see things differently, that "Twelve jurors have seen a larger slice of life than a single judge." Unfortunately, however, there has been little empirical research on how differences in jurors' backgrounds influence their verdicts. In terms of our formal model, jurors' verdicts might differ because the function which maps the in-court proceedings into a probability of guilt may differ from one juror to the next; because the standard of reasonable doubt may vary with the juror; and because the random factors affecting the jurors' decisions may not be the same. Hence, faced with a given set of in-court proceedings, two potential jurors deciding the case independently might have different probabilities of convicting the particular defendant of the specific crime with which he is charged.

The error probabilities calculated for different potential jurors do have some common determinants. They all depend on the social decisionmaker's judgments concerning the probability that a guilty (an innocent) defendant would generate a particular set of in-court proceedings and the probabilities with which different evidence configurations can be expected to arise. But each potential juror's error probabilities also depend on that individual's specific characteristics.

It is not only the error probabilities that differ among potential jurors. Using different potential jurors to try the case will also engender different social economic costs. If any particular potential juror tries the case, it costs society the incremental subsistence and incremental travel expenses of that juror *plus* the social opportunity cost of his time for the duration of the trial, that is, the value of the goods and services he would have produced had he not been serving on the jury. And, these quantities will differ among potential jurors.

Our description of the individual juror as a risky asset to be considered by the jury selector is now complete. Investing in a particular potential juror incurs the social economic costs just mentioned. If he were to decide the case alone, he would return one set of expected noneconomic social costs if the defendant were truly innocent and another set of expected noneconomic social costs if the defendant were, in fact, guilty. With this information, the social decisionmaker could now decide which potential juror to use *if* only one juror were to try the case. But if juries of a size larger than one are to be considered, this description of each risky asset will not suffice.

In considering the use of more than one juror, the social decisionmaker is essentially choosing a portfolio of risky assets. And, one of the main lessons of the portfolio theory developed in the last twenty years is that optimal portfolio selection requires consideration of more than the individual characteristics of a given security (for example, its mean and variance). It requires that careful attention be paid to the way in which the returns to one asset relate to the returns to another, that is, to the correlations in the returns to different assets. Analogously, in selecting the optimal portfolio of jurors, one must consider not only how "good" an asset each one is when considered by himself but also how he interacts with other jurors. The value of a portfolio of jurors cannot be determined from the characteristics of each juror acting alone.

Jury deliberations constitute a fascinating type of small-group decision process, and various kinds of information have been collected about them. Most of the available evidence comes from posttrial interviews with jurors in actual cases and from records of the actual deliberations of mock juries. But, while much data exist on jury deliberations, there is no single widely accepted theory of how juries reach their final decisions.

Our introduction of random elements into the individual juror's decision-making process and our incorporation of differences among jurors enables us to approach jury deliberations as follows. The individual juror verdicts and juror votes we have been discussing are viewed as final-ballot votes with the interpretation of the random variables which enter into the process of reaching that verdict broadened to include the results of jury deliberation. That is, the random variable in each juror's decision is interpreted as reflecting not only stochastic aspects of how the individual juror moves from the in-court proceedings to a probability of guilt and random aspects of his standard of reasonable doubt but also the effects of discussion in the jury room. It should be emphasized that modeling the deliberation process in this way does not imply that the discussion among jurors is haphazard. On the contrary, depending on the assumptions made concerning the random variables involved, that discussion can be portrayed as being quite structured indeed. Moreover, differences in the relationships among the random variables for different jurors are at the heart of our message about the instrumental case for representative juries.

To simplify our discussion of jury composition, assume that only three people serve on the jury and that the unanimity rule prevails. We could consider larger juries (as the conventional twelve-person or more recent six-person juries) but the discussion would become (more) cumbersome without additional analytical insights being gained. The issues involved in selecting the optimal jury and, specifically, the optimal degree of representativeness of the jury can be illustrated as well with three-person juries. In particular, since the individual juror verdicts discussed earlier are taken to be juror votes on the final ballot and since the unanimity rule is assumed to prevail, very little generality is lost by having an odd number of jurors. For example, all three types of outcome—conviction, acquittal, and hung jury—are still possible.

Since the social costs of different errors are assumed to be known once the defendant and the charge against him are given, all that must be determined for each potential jury is the probability that it will make each type of error and the economic cost incurred in using it. The latter, the jury's resource cost, is easily determined. Certain costs entailed in using a jury to try the case have been assumed to be fixed—including the judge's time, the lawyers' time, the time of other courthouse personnel, and the use of courthouse space. The variable economic cost of using a particular jury is the sum of the jurors' incremental travel and incremental subsistence expenses plus the sum of the social opportunity costs of their time. The economic cost of using a particular jury is the sum of these fixed and variable costs.

While the social economic cost of a particular jury can be expressed succinctly in terms of the social economic costs of using its individual members, it is much more difficult to express the jury's error probabilities in terms of the probability distributions characterizing its members' votes in the general case. Because of these difficulties, we shall consider a very simply structured situation which still serves well our investigation of the instrumental case for representative juries. Specifically, consider a fictional society in which individuals are divided into three groups (indexed 1, 2, 3) and the three groups are equal in size. Individuals are assumed to be grouped according to relevant socioeconomic and demographic characteristics, and we will think of the groups as income classes. In this society, factor markets are competitive, there is no difference between private and social marginal products, and members of a group have the same work-leisure preferences. Hence, the social opportunity cost of a juror's time will be the same for all members of a group. In addition, suppose that the incremental travel and subsistence expenses are the same for all jurors. As a result, in this fictional society, the economic cost of a juror depends only on the group to which he belongs.

The random variable describing the difference between a juror's estimate of the probability of guilt given the in-court proceedings and his standard of reasonable doubt will be assumed to be identical for all members of a group. Hence, the pretrial distribution of the verdict that would be reached is the same for all members of a particular group. In contrast, the distributions of the verdicts of jurors from different groups may differ. Furthermore, in this fictional society, the stochastic interaction among members of a group is the same no matter which particular members are involved, and the stochastic interaction between any member of one group and any member (or members) of another group is the same regardless of which members of the two groups are interacting. It follows from this characterization of individuals in this fictional society and the interactions among them that any jury in this community is fully described simply by indicating how many members of each group are on the jury.

Of course, defining the relevant groups in any real society will be difficult and somewhat arbitrary, as it will depend on the stratifier's perception of the society and its goals. In discussions of representativeness of juries and jury panels in the United States, one usually has in mind groups defined by socioeconomic and demographic characteristics—age, race, sex, income class, educational background, and so on. Exactly how many groups one would want to delineate is an open question, and, clearly, the verdict distributions of individuals in these real-world groups would not necessarily be identical. But I would argue that it is likely that jurors whose backgrounds and experiences are similar will view a given trial from similar perspectives and process the in-court proceedings in comparable ways. Moreover, to the extent that a juror's standard of reasonable doubt is based on his own experience, such jurors are likely to apply standards that are close to one another. The assumption that the random variable representing the difference between the probability of guilt and the standard of reasonable doubt is the same for all members of the same group expresses this looser, more tenuous, relationship in an extreme, though simpler form.

It is also easier to discuss representativeness of three-person juries in this fictional society than it is to discuss representativeness of juries or jury panels in any actual community. In this equally proportioned three-class society, a fully representative three-member panel would have one member from each group. A jury with two members from one group and one from another would be less representative, and all such juries—regardless of which group had two people on the panel and which had one—would be considered equally representative. Finally, the least representative type of panel would have members from only one group on it, and any such homogeneous jury would be as representative (or unrepresentative) as any other.

If the groups in a real community were well defined, the analogous approach would be to measure the representativeness of a jury by the degree to which the distribution of groups on it approximated the distribution of these groups in the population as a whole. One of a number of statistical procedures could be used. But there is no unambiguously superior method for gauging the similarity of these two distributions, and different approaches can yield different conclusions. Real communities would also present a number of specific difficulties that do not arise in the case of three-person juries in our fictional society. For instance, if the number of relevant groups were to exceed the number of jurors (or the number of people on the panel from which jurors are to be selected), some groups would necessarily be excluded from the jury (or the panel).

The problem the jury composer in our fictional society faces can be expressed as a particular type of mathematical programming problem which could be solved formally using standard mathematical techniques. Our current concern is with the way in which the solution to this problem changes as the structure of the community changes and, in particular, with whether one can make an *a priori* case for a representative jury—for a well-diversified portfolio of jurors. For this purpose, it is important to recognize the formal nature of the decision problem and its strong correspondence with portfolio selection problems. Nevertheless, the basic message can be conveyed by considering a set of examples in somewhat less formal terms, and this is what we shall now do. The critical elements determining whether or not to have a broadly representative jury are: the structure of the probabilities that individual members of different groups would err if they were to decide the case alone, the nature of the stochastic interactions within and across the three groups, the structure of the social opportunity costs in the society, and the relative disutility the society attaches to different kinds of errors. We shall see that a firm *a priori* case cannot be made for a representative jury when we focus on that institution's most instrumental function—fact-finding.

To simplify our examples, let us assume that the marginal disutility of noneconomic costs is independent of the level of economic costs and that the marginal disutility of economic costs is also independent of the level of noneconomic costs.

First, it should be clear that changes in the rate at which society is willing to trade off the expected disutility it suffers if the defendant is truly guilty against its expected disutility conditional on the defendant's being truly innocent might well result in changes in the optimal jury. For example, suppose that two differently composed juries drawn from our fictional society engender the same social economic cost, but the expected disutility of noneconomic costs conditional on the defendant's being guilty is much higher for jury 1 than for jury 2 and the opposite is true for the expected disutility of noneconomic costs conditional on the defendant's being truly innocent. Then, clearly, for very low values of the trade-off rate—that is, when low relative weight is attached to the expected disutility if the defendant is, in fact, guilty so that society manifests much more concern for erroneous convictions than for erroneous acquittals—the social decisionmaker would prefer jury 1 to jury 2. As the rate of trade-off increases, however, there would be a point at which the decisionmaker would be indifferent between using jury 1 and jury 2. Finally, for all higher values of the trade-off rate, the decisionmaker would choose jury 2 rather than jury 1.

Now, let us consider the special case in which society attaches no weight to the expected disutility it suffers if the defendant is, in fact, guilty. In this case, society's only concern is to minimize the expected disutility it faces conditional on the defendant's being innocent. Even with this extreme resolution of the question of the trade-off between the two conditional expected disutilities, the jury selector still faces important social trade-offs. He must still balance the cost of convicting an innocent individual, the cost of reaching no decision when the defendant is innocent, and the economic cost of the jury. Moreover, so long as there is some positive probability that each member of the society would convict an innocent defendant if he were to arrive at a verdict on his own, the "obvious" solution for this case—namely, choosing jurors who would always vote to acquit—is not feasible. And, because there are several costs to be balanced, the closest approximation to the "obvious" solution—selecting jurors with the highest probability of acquitting—is not necessarily optimal. Since the conclusion we reach is that diversification of the portfolio of jurors is sometimes but not always optimal, and since that result can be demonstrated using a social loss function which gives weight only to the expected social losses suffered conditional on the defendant's being innocent, using this simplification does not really impede our analysis.

Let us now consider what kind of jury the social decisionmaker in our fictional society would choose under alternative assumptions about the structure of the community. In particular, how representative is the optimal jury in each case?

In the first structure we will consider, *all* jurors act *independently* of one another. Knowing the way one juror would vote will not alter our probability distribution for any other juror's vote, regardless of whether the second juror is in the same group as the first juror or in a different class. If the probability of convicting a truly innocent defendant were the same for all potential jurors, then, regardless of the structure of economic opportunity costs for the several groups, there would be no reason for diversifying the portfolio of jurors. Either members of different groups would have the same economic costs or they would not. In the former case, it would make no difference in terms of economic or noneconomic costs which groups served on the panel. On the other hand, if the economic costs of members of different groups were unequal, then the jury selector would choose the entire jury from the group with the lowest economic opportunity cost.

Similarly, under the structure we are currently discussing where there are no stochastic interactions among any jurors, differences in the error probabilities of different groups do not suffice to ensure the optimality of a representative jury. For example, suppose that members of group 1 are least likely to convict the defendant if he is truly innocent, that group 2's probability of making such a mistake is higher, and that group 3 is most likely to commit this Type I error. Then if the economic opportunity costs of members of all groups were equal, the decisionmaker would choose all the jurors from group 1. The optimal jury would be the least representative kind, comprised of members of group 1 only.

If, however, the error probabilities *and* the economic opportunity costs differ across the groups, a nonhomogeneous jury may be optimal. Whether or not it will be depends, in part, on how large the differences in the error probabilities are and how large the differences in the opportunity costs are. The optimality of a heterogeneous jury in this case also depends on how the disutility of an erroneous conviction compares with the disutility of a nondecision when the individual is truly innocent, and on how these disutilities and the difference between them stand in relation to the disutility of social economic opportunity costs. If the group with the lowest probability of error has the highest economic opportunity cost, one can easily generate examples in which a mixed jury is optimal. In this case, the asset with the highest probability of paying off—the class of jurors with the lowest probability of erring—is sufficiently expensive that society cannot afford to hold a three-juror portfolio consisting only of it.

But the most representative type of jury—with one member from each group—may still not be optimal. The jury selector might choose to diversify, but only to the extent of holding two types of assets and not to including all three in the jury portfolio. Note also that if the most competent group of potential jurors—the group with the lowest error probability—has a sufficiently high opportunity cost, and if the disutility of economic costs is significant relative to noneconomic costs, the jury which minimizes the social loss function may not contain any members of this most accurate group.

In sum, when all potential jurors behave independently of one another, regardless of the group to which they belong, there are circumstances under which a fully representative jury is optimal. But there are also configurations of error probabilities, opportunity costs, and disutility levels for which a homogeneous jury minimizes the social loss function and situations in which a jury composed of members of only two groups is best. Essential to the case for broadening representation on the jury when all potential jurors act independently of one another are differences in the probabilities with which members of different groups will vote to convict when the defendant is innocent and variations in the opportunity costs of their time. When all potential jurors' verdicts are reached independently, the argument for a fully representative jury in our fictional community will be strongest when the ranking of error probabilities across groups is exactly the opposite of the ranking of economic opportunity costs.

The second structure we will consider for our fictional community is very different from the first one. In this case, the votes of individuals in the same group are *perfectly* correlated while the random variables representing the verdicts of jurors in different groups are *independent* of one another. Once we know the way one juror from a particular group would decide the case if he were deciding it alone, we know exactly how any other juror from that class would vote, but we know nothing more about what verdict an individual from either of the other two classes would reach.

The critical feature of a jury when society is structured in this way is that if one member of a particular group is on the jury, adding a second member of that group to the panel will not change the jury's probability of convicting a truly innocent defendant or its probability of acquitting him. In sharp contrast, increasing the number of groups represented on the jury decreases the probability of convicting an innocent defendant, and it also decreases the probability of acquitting the defendant if he is actually innocent. Since society would like the former probability to be as small as possible and the latter to be as large as possible, a trade-off must be confronted in deciding whether to diversify the portfolio of jurors, *even* in the absence of differences in the opportunity costs of members of different groups. As the jury becomes more representative, it becomes less likely that the panel will engender the disutility of convicting a truly innocent man. But, at the same time, it becomes more likely that the jury will not reach a unanimous verdict when the defendant is, in fact, innocent, and thus the probability increases that society will incur the associated hung jury costs. Even if the economic opportunity cost of an individual's time is the same for all individuals, regardless of group affiliation, variations in the optimal degree of representativeness will result from differences in the relationship between the perceived social costs of erroneous convictions and the perceived social costs of erroneous hung juries when the defendant is innocent, and differences in the structure of the error probabilities.

Suppose then that the economic opportunity cost of a juror's time is the same no matter what group the juror belongs to so that the disutility of economic costs is the same no matter how the jury is composed. Then, if the difference between the social disutility of an erroneous conviction and the social disutility of no decision when the defendant is truly innocent is much larger than the latter disutility itself, the social decisionmaker is essentially concerned only with minimizing the probability that a truly innocent individual is convicted. In this case, the optimal jury would be fully representative with one member from each group serving on the panel. Note that this would be the optimal solution regardless of the differences in the error probabilities—that is, no matter how much the probability of convicting an innocent defendant when reaching a verdict alone varies among members of the three classes.

This case provides an interesting illustration of the usefulness of the portfolio metaphor with its focus on interactions among jurors. One might casually think "If you want good fact-finders, you do not want representative juries." But here we have a case in which members of one group could significantly dominate members of the other two groups when performing the fact-finding function as individuals—say, the probability that a member of group 1 would convict an innocent defendant was much smaller than the corresponding probabilities for members of groups 2 and 3—and yet the optimal jury would contain only one member of that group. The social decisionmaker would choose a fully representative jury despite the apparently superior fact-finding skills of group 1 individuals. The explanation rests with the stochastic interactions among jurors—in particular, in this example, with the perfect correlation of the verdicts of jurors belonging to the same group in society. This example illustrates the point that the value of a particular juror as a fact-finder depends not only on how well he makes decisions in isolation, but also on the characteristics of the other jurors with whom he will serve.

Retaining the assumption that economic opportunity costs are the same for all members of the society, consider the other extreme—admittedly somewhat implausible—circumstance in which having the jury hang when the defendant is truly innocent is almost as costly (in noneconomic terms) as having it err by convicting him. In this instance, it turns out that the optimal jury will be homogeneous, comprised only of members of the group with the lowest probability of convicting a truly innocent individual.

Clearly, by considering values of the ratio of the noneconomic costs of a hung jury when the defendant is innocent to the noneconomic costs of a conviction when the defendant is guilty which lie between the two extremes we have examined (zero and unity) and by varying the structure of the error probabilities, we can generate other instances in which a fully representative jury would be optimal and yet others in which a homogeneous jury would be optimal. Examples could also be constructed in which the jury minimizing the social loss function would be composed of two members from one group and one from another. Differences in the economic cost of using members of different groups will affect the strength of the argument for a representative jury when our fictional society is structured as sharply along class lines as we are now considering it to be just as they did when all jurors' verdicts were independent of one another. The higher are the economic costs of those individuals with the lower error probabilities, the stronger is the case for diversifying the portfolio of jurors. On the other hand, to the extent that the ranking of the error probabilities matches that of the economic opportunity costs, the case for broad representation is weakened. But, as we have seen, in contrast to what we found for a community in which all individuals' verdicts were reached independently, representative juries may be desirable under the second social structure we considered even if all individuals' economic opportunity costs are the same.

We could go on to consider more complicated, less extreme structures for the stochastic interactions among individuals in the community. For example, the next logical step might be to retain the assumption of stochastic independence of the verdicts of jurors in different groups but to assume that the votes of individuals in the same group are (highly) positively correlated rather than perfectly correlated. Obviously, the strong argument for a fully representative jury which could be made in the second type of community we considered would weaken as the degree of correlation between jurors in the same group decreased. We could then go on to allow for positive or negative correlation between the verdicts of jurors in different classes, requiring only that the correlations between jurors in the same group be positive and higher than those between jurors in different groups.

In such societies, with richer structures of interrelationships, the conclusion would be the same as the one reached in the two very simply structured communities we have considered: Diversification of the portfolio of jurors is sometimes but not always optimal. For some sets of parameter values a fully representative jury is optimal, for others a homogeneous jury is best, and for yet other configurations of parameters, a somewhat (but not fully) diversified jury minimizes the social loss function. We have indicated the kinds of parameter structures that would tend to make more or less diversification optimal. But the *a priori* instrumental case for representative juries is inconclusive. Without empirical information—either actual data or empirical guesses—concerning the particular community, one cannot state how representative the best fact-finding jury would be.

Although representativeness of the jury does not necessarily serve the instrumental function of fact-finding, I would argue that it does serve a very important but much less instrumental function. It constitutes an important symbolic expression of our societal belief in and commitment to democracy. In this sense, representativeness of the jury is a value in its own right. One need not (perhaps, should not try to) derive its usefulness by positing some other goal and demonstrating the role representativeness plays in achieving that other goal.

The importance of jury representativeness as a political symbol can be suggested by considering the potential for such symbolic expression in each of the branches of government: the executive, the legislature, and the judiciary. While all citizens are meant to have an equal voice (one man-one vote) in choosing the executive, we do not expect the executive to be representatively responsive in each decision he makes. Similarly, while members of the legislature are elected democratically, they are not expected to take the proportional pulse of their constituents when voting on each and every legislative issue. Individuals who are sophisticated enough to recognize the interest-group nature of legislative politics certainly do not believe that each legislative decision is taken on a representative basis. And, even the individual who has not analyzed the workings of the legislature recognizes this lack of representative responsiveness on particular issues. Finally, we do not expect judges, be they elected or appointed, to decide cases on the basis of a proportional weighing of the opinions of individuals in the community. Judicial decisions may reflect the sense of the community or its "conventional morality," but individual judicial decisions are not to be rendered in a democratically representative way.

The jury, however, can be representative. It can provide symbolic reinforcement of the democratic myth (where "myth" is used in a positive not a pejorative sense) by being an institution which makes individual decisions on a representative basis. The communication of the symbolic value of representative juries is probably quite effective. While few people actually serve on juries, surveys have shown that many more people know someone who has served. And, at least some trials receive a substantial amount of publicity. People may not know about many jury trials, but they are at least aware of and informed about several major ones each year. To the extent that publicity is given to the courtroom juror selection process—the *voir dire*—in reporting these cases, the representativeness of the jury and the importance of having decisions made by representative bodies is brought into even sharper focus. Finally, the symbolic value of representativeness of the jury is heightened because that body is making a decision that everyone will recognize as being of major importance for one or more named individuals. The ordinary citizen can easily grasp the importance of the decision, as contrasted, for example, with some legislative issue whose ramifications he may find quite difficult to trace. Requiring that this jury decision be made by a representative group of individuals can provide a powerful restatement of our commitment to a particular political structure—democracy.

But we must still end with a question. If we accept the value of jury representativeness as a political symbol as one of its major justifications—perhaps the principal one—how representative does the jury have to be to give effective expression to the democratic principle? And, do the recent decisions upholding reductions in jury size and nonunanimous verdicts substantially reduce the politically symbolic power of the representative jury?

The Effects of Regulation of New Drugs

Sam Peltzman

I want to discuss government regulation of prescription drugs because government regulation in this industry is a prototype for a lot of government regulation that has come along subsequently, designed to protect the consumer. And I believe that the experience with the regulation of prescription drugs can tell us what to expect from much of the regulation that's emanating from the current consumerist movement.

Regulation of drugs has a long history, and I am going to focus on the more recent history, so I won't give you a very long history of the regulation of drugs. I just want to sketch very quickly, how it has evolved in order to place my discussion in some sort of context. The regulation goes back at least to 1907. The earliest regulation had to do mainly only with drug labeling. The original Food and Drug Act simply said that you had to say what was in the bottle. It is a little bit strange for us to read that regulation today, because it says that you must give the amount and the proportion of all the ingredients, including the amount of cannabis, opium, cocaine, and heroin. It was perfectly legal to market that stuff in those days as long as you told the consumer what was inside. In 1938, a drug purveyor sold an elixir of one of the early sulfa drugs, and he dissolved the drug in something very much like antifreeze, with as you might guess, rather unfortunate consequences. Congress responded to this particular scandal by requiring that there now be proof of safety before a drug could be marketed. You not only had to tell what was inside, but you had to prove to the government that the drug was safe. This turned out to be a fairly modest expansion of regulation. The Food and Drug Administration had to rule on the safety of a drug within a hundred and eighty days. If it did not do so the drug was presumed safe and could go on the market. The last major episode in this history of regulation, and the one that I am going to concentrate on, occurred over a decade ago in 1962.

Let me give you the background of the 1962 Amendments to the Food, Drug and Cosmetics Act. There were two major events that led Congress to change the law on drug regulation. The first was a series of congressional hearings held in the late 1950s under the chairmanship of Senator Estes Kefauver. Kefauver was concerned basically about drug prices and drug promotion. The second event, totally unrelated to this, was the introduction of a drug called Thalidomide, not into the American market, but into the European market, with some tragic consequences. The first push for a change in the law, at least chronologically, came from the Kefauver hearings which made the front pages with accounts of exorbitant prices for drugs and extravagant drug advertising expenditures.

To caricature Kefauver's argument, one starts with a presumption that the consumers were ignorant, and this includes the doctors who were prescribing the drugs for their patients. These doctors, after all, had long since taken their last course in pharmacology. The drug companies, according to this account, could exploit this ignorance. In those days, remember, as long as a new product was safe (which simply meant that it did not threaten to make you sicker), you could get a patent on it. And that meant that you would have no competition for seventeen years. As Kefauver saw it, the best way for a drug company to get ahead in the world was to try to get a new product on the market, promote the product very extravagantly, and claim that it cures everything, from acne to cancer. If this gambit worked—and because consumers were allegedly ignorant it worked often enough, according to this account—the drug company would be able to sell the proverbial sugar cube for the price of gold. And on top of that it would have protection from competition for seventeen years. Once the doctors caught on that they were paying the price of gold for what was after all a sugar cube, the drug companies would simply be ready to replace it with a new one heavily promoted, and pushed on the gullible public. A former research director of a large drug company, speaking at the Kefauver hearings, made this point very well!

Industry spokesmen stress that all research is on better medicinal product, and that there are many failures for every successful drug. The problem arises out of the fact that they market so many of the failures. Between these failures (which are presented as new drugs) and the useless modifications of old drugs, most of the research results in a treadmill which moves rapidly, but goes nowhere. Since so much depends on novelty, drugs change like women's hemlines. But rapid obsolescence is a sign of motion, not progress. The illusion may not last, but it frequently lasts long enough. By the time the doctor learns what the company knew at the beginning, it has two new products to take the place of the old one.

Now, if you would like, you can substitute cars, washing machines, and lawnmowers, almost any consumer product, and you can duplicate some of the current concerns, in this very early history of current drug regulation. That was one major concern that led to a change in the law. The other as I mentioned was the introduction of the drug Thalidomide. It was never marketed in the United States because of the way the pre-1962 law worked. That is, it never passed the safety screening. But it was distributed for experimental use, and on this there were no important restrictions. Before 1962, you could give a drug to almost anybody as long as you labeled it "for experimental use." You could not sell it in a drug store, but some doctors could give it directly. If you remember the history of this Thalidomide, it had a tragic effect. It caused birth malformations when it was taken by pregnant women. This did not occur very much here, but it did in Europe, where the drug was in fact put on the market. The response to this news added a new concern to the kinds of concerns that Kefauver was driving at. Not only were new drugs now frequently ineffective and expensive, but in the rush to get them on the market, the clinical testing process was being short-circuited. Humans were now being excessively exposed to dangerous drugs. The coming together of these two concerns led to a change in the law, the 1962 Kefauver-Harris Amendments to the Food, Drug and Cosmetic Act. These 1962 drug amendments have two important provisions, at least for the purpose of my discussion.

The first important provision was that the judgment of a regulatory agency, the FDA, was now going to be substituted for the judgment of the market place, with respect to which new drugs could be sold. The manufacturer now had to prove not only that a drug would be safe, but that the drug would be effective, before it could be sold. And this meant that it met its advertised claims. So, if you wanted to advertise that a drug would cure acne and cancer, you had to prove that that was what it would do, to the satisfaction of the FDA, and you were not permitted to advertise any more than you could demonstrate to the satisfaction of the FDA. The FDA could now, as part of this, require any amount of information on which to base a judgment about the efficacy of the drug. It could take as long as it wished to acquire this information. There was no longer a one hundred and eighty day limit to come to a conclusion on which claims you could advertise, if any, or whether you could sell it at all. A second important provision was that the testing of drugs was subject to very detailed regulation by the FDA, both to make sure that the FDA got adequate information on which to base its efficacy judgment, and also to prevent the premature testing of unsafe drugs on human beings. Essentially, the FDA can now tell manufacturers what procedures have to be followed in the testing process, and it can also order the modification or cessation of the testing process at any time. And again, it can force that testing process to take as long as it wishes in order to come to an evaluation of the drug's merits. The drug manufacturer is now in a position where, if you want to use the analogy, he is guilty until he uses his research and development to prove his innocence. Under the previous law, he was presumed innocent and the FDA had to prove him guilty.

The ideas motivating the 1962 drug amendments are still very much with us in the current consumer movement. The consumer is, in the first place, presumed to be ignorant, peculiarly susceptible to the lure of Madison Avenue. And sellers have promised more than they can perform. Product innovation is, in this view, largely a response to this ignorance, a search for the sucker who, Barnum told us, was born every minute. The incentive structure in the innovation process would, in this same view, frequently lead to short-cuts that produce not only overpromoted and ineffective products, but some that are dangerous as well. Since these notions drive the current consumer movement, whether it is talking about the regulation of cars or bicycles or what have you, I hope that the findings of my own research on the way that the 1962 Food-Drug amendments worked might have some implications for the increasing regulation of consumer products.

It is not too difficult to predict one outcome of the 1962 drug amendments; the testing of new drugs has obviously become a much more expensive proposition. To pin this down, my own research and the research of several other people who have looked at this indicates that the research and development expenditures that are put into a new drug that gets to the market have almost doubled over and above what they otherwise would be. It is also not very difficult to see the secondary consequence of all this. The number of new drugs has declined substantially by about 60 percent per year, compared either to what was happening in the American market before 1962, or what is happening now in other countries like Great Britain, which have less stringent regulation than we do. In part this result was intended by the law. After all, many of the new drugs that were being put on the market in the era before 1962 were supposedly bad. They did not work, or they were, like Thalidomide, sometimes unsafe, so a reduction in the number of drugs may be a desirable thing, at least in terms of what the law was looking for. The problem though, is that the desirable part of the outcome has a cost and a cost over and beyond the extra testing cost. The reduction in the number of new drugs that are being put on the market does not occur primarily because some drug is tested and somebody finds that in the testing process the drug does not work or is actually harmful and therefore the drug is not marketed. That is not really the important source of the decline in the number of new drugs. Usually, what happens is that the manufacturer, before he commits what are now enormous sums to the testing process, has got to decide whether the market for the drug is going to justify this sort of expenditure, or whether to take the risk that after he goes through a testing procedure and satisfies himself that he wants to put the drug on the market, he will be able to convince the FDA that he ought to be allowed to put it on the market. That risk has to be overcome. Even if he decided to go ahead, he also faces the prospect of waiting something like four extra years before he can get that drug on the market and begin to recoup his investment. That at least is the experience of most drug development since 1962, that something like at least two years or more, usually four extra years' time, is now required before you can come to market with a new product. Tying up capital in the research and development process for a period like that is another cost that deters new drug development.

What this means (although I am sure it was not intended by the founders of the 1962 drug law, and I am sure it is not intended by the people who are in charge of the FDA) is that at least some perfectly good drugs will never get to market, and those that do will necessarily get there later. The consumer is paying a price for the added safety that he is getting from the way the drug amendments work, and the presumably more effective drugs that come to market. And it is a twofold price. First of all there are the direct costs—those research and development costs that are now twice as large as they use to be. Those eventually have to be recovered in drug prices. Second, there is the lost opportunity to have access to some perfectly effective drugs that either are never developed at all, or come to the market two, four, or six years later. In that interval of time, some potential benefits are not realized.

I have tried to evaluate how consumers have fared in the balance. The answer, briefly, is: not very well. The reason for this really is implicit in some of the numbers that I have already given you. The decrease in the number of new drugs, as I have mentioned, has been on the order of 60 percent per year. There are 60 percent fewer new drugs being marketed each year than we could expect from past experiences, or experience elsewhere. For the benefits of the regulation to have outweighed the costs requires that a large fraction of the drugs that would be marketed today, were it not for the regulation (or that a large proportion of the drugs that were being marketed prior to 1962) would be ineffective and/or unsafe. This is simply unreasonable by any of the tests I was able to make. As nearly as I can tell, we could expect no more than 10 percent of the new drugs that would be marketed if there were no regulation, or 10 percent of those that were marketed if there was less regulation, to be ineffective. Let me try to tell you about some of the evidence that I looked at that leads me to the conclusion that consumers have not received nearly as many benefits from the regulation as the costs that they have been forced to pay.

Let me first focus on the efficacy issue, the issue that agitated Senator Kefauver so much. There are several ways to look at this. One way (although it is not the one that medical experts like very much, but it is one relevant piece of evidence) is to look at sales behavior of drugs in the market. After all, even if many doctors are stupid and lazy, some of them are going to catch on after a while that a drug is ineffective. Some will then tell their collegaues, and when the word gets around, sales of the drug will decline or at least stop growing. They do not have to disappear, but at least there will be some effect on sales, that one ought to observe simply with the passage of time, if a drug does not work. What I did was to look at the sales behavior of new drugs, those that were marketed in the bad old days, and those that have been put on the market with the blessing of the FDA in the post-1962 period.

I asked the obvious kind of question, do the new drugs that are being put on the market now, after this very extensive testing procedure, have more durable markets: do they grow faster, do they hold their market better than the drugs that were being marketed before? The answer, without boring you with a lot of numbers, is basically no. Both groups of drugs, the old new drugs and the new new drugs, behave about the same way in the market place. On average, what happens is, there are many duds and a few winners. The proportions are about the same today as they used to be; the winners hold up the same today as they used to, no better or no worse. I could show you a sales profile of new drugs before and after 1962, and basically, on average, you could not tell the difference.

On that basis, there has been no improvement and no deterioration, no effect at all—except, of course, on the total number of new drugs. I also looked at hospital purchasing patterns. This is relevant because many hospitals (the larger ones particularly) try to buy drugs in bulk, to take advantage of quantity discounts. To get these discounts, they try to restrict their purchases to a short list of drugs that they think are effective. If you have one of these minor modifications of some nostrum that is being promoted as a cure for everything, or some new drug that does not do very much more than a drug that is already on the market, they try to avoid those simply to avoid having to buy a lot of drugs in small lots. I wanted to see whether hospitals bought fewer new drugs before 1962 than the allegedly stupid consumer or whether they bought fewer new drugs in those days relative to their purchases after 1962. That is the sort of thing that they would have been doing if there were many ineffective new drugs being put on the market before 1962. They would have been culling out the ineffective drugs and focusing on a small fraction of the drugs that were marketed.

Again, what is surprising here is the absence of any discernible difference between the behavior of these supposedly more sophisticated purchasers between the pre-1962 and the post-1962 era. Hospitals devoted roughly the same percentage of their drug purchases to new drugs before 1962, as individual purchasers did, and the percentages (which of course are lower now because there are many fewer drugs on the market) are also about the same today. In addition, after a few years of experience with a new drug, these percentages tend to be maintained. Again, there is no difference between ordinary consumers and hospitals in this respect. What this seems to imply is that either there were very few ineffective drugs being put on the market before 1962, or that, in spite of the added testing, the proportion of drugs which are ineffective today has not changed very much.

To shed some more light on this issue, I looked at the medical literature. I am a layman in this field, but some of the medical literature is accessible to laymen. Let me just report the results of the rather crude examination of this literature that I made. The American Medical Association has a Council on Drugs, which evaluates substantially all of the drugs that are on the market. They published the results in a sort of consumers' guide for their membership. And, at least until recently, they would tell their membership whether a drug (at least in this particular expert panel's opinion) was effective, whether it worked, whether it met its claim, and so forth. I read through these evaluations and categorized these drugs by whether this group of experts was calling them effective or ineffective, and I found that for drugs that were introduced before the change in the law (before 1962) about 10 percent (at least in terms of sales) were judged ineffective. Interestingly, for the post-1962 drugs (the ones the FDA is calling effective by its definition) the AMA panel deemed 10 percent of them ineffective (10 percent, by sales, again).

Since the AMA got into the business, the National Academy of Science also has gotten into this business, this time under a provision of the 1962 law which requires them to evaluate new drugs put on the market before 1962 (and giving the FDA the right to remove those ineffective drugs that were put on the market before 1962). The National Academy of Science has gone through the whole list of the pre-1962 drugs and comes to very much the same sort of qualitative conclusion as the AMA. As a round number, 10 percent of the sales of pre-1962 drugs were for drugs that were deemed by these experts as ineffective. Compare this with what has been happening in the drug market and you will see why I was able to conclude, without very much difficulty, that the consumer has fared rather poorly. To get at the 10 percent of the drug sales that go for ineffective drugs (and not even to get at all of them but even to attempt to get at that 10 percent) the number and the sales of new drugs have been reduced by 60 percent.

These, as I surely do not have to tell you, are very heavy odds. Essentially, the consumer is losing the benefits from five effective new drugs in an attempt to avoid the costs of each ineffective drug. For those new drugs that he does get, the benefits are delayed, on an average of four years, and he pays a research and development bill that is double what he would otherwise have to pay. There is one more important fact that I should bring in here. It turns out that the consumer, the doctor, or whoever it is that makes the decision to buy a drug, is not as stupid as he is sometimes made out to be, and this lengthens the odds. As it happens, the 10 percent of the new drugs that were deemed ineffective by the AMA fared poorly in the market place. This is surprising in light of what you read in the Kefauver hearings about stupid consumers and uneducated doctors. However, drugs that in hindsight medical experts are now willing to call ineffective turned out to have a very much different sales curve than the majority of new drugs. Their sales had a short spurt at the beginning, and then there was a very quick decline in sales. This means that over the sales lifetime of these drugs, something less than 10 percent of total drug purchases each year was being wasted on ineffective drugs. Because doctors and patients responded to the fact that these drugs did not work, the consumers' loss from ineffective drugs in the past was mitigated. The fact is that these drugs were weeded out rather quickly.

I think this is a very often neglected but extremely important point to keep in mind, in evaluating not just drug regulation but the multitude of regulation that we are now getting, designed to protect the consumer. There are, in fact, very powerful forces at work to restrain a seller from marketing shoddy goods, whether they be shoddy drugs or shoddy anything else. Once the consumer discovers the truth, the market for the product will decline, and the chance that a producer will be able to recover his development costs will be smaller. The good products tend to last and to provide better returns to the development expenditure than the poor products. There is also the very important factor of seller reputation. The very advertising and promotion (the sales hype that was so much decried by Senator Kefauver) leads to a strong identification with the sellers of the drugs. The doctors are constantly made aware not only of the merits of a particular product, but of who is selling it. The name of the seller is imprinted on the doctor's mind, very ingeniously, with repetition, and with every kind of gimmick and stratagem available to the marketing department of the seller. Should the seller fail repeatedly to deliver the goods, the seller then knows that the receptivity of the purchaser to future goods is going to be affected. The customer will remember; that is the whole point of advertising, to make the customer remember who is doing the selling, and this memory is going to result in depreciation of the heavy advertising investment, if performance begins to fall short of promise consistently. That acts as a powerful check on the temptation to market poor quality goods.

I would like to say a little about the effects of regulation on drug safety. This is not the primary focus of the regulation I have been discussing, but the regulation does have effects on drug safety nonetheless. I would like to say something about what these effects are likely to be. The effects on drug safety are peculiarly difficult to evaluate, much more difficult than the efficacy issue that I have just dealt with. This is due to the fact that the rate at which clearly harmful drugs were marketed before the 1962 law was passed was very small. Maybe once every ten or twenty years would a drug like Thalidomide ever get to the market, or come to the verge of being marketed, as it did in the United States. There have been, at least to my knowledge, no similar drugs marketed since 1962. So, to the extent that the 1962 drug amendments have contributed to this result, there has been some gain. But, just as there may be a gain in terms of the prevention of unusual harm from the rare drug that is very harmful, there also are some unusual benefits that are sacrificed as a result of the regulation. Some drugs promise truly major reduction in death and sickness, and no drugs of this kind have been produced since 1962 either.

I am reluctant to blame all of this on the way that our drug regulatory process has worked, because it is really a worldwide phenomenon. Nowhere in the world has anything comparable to penicillin been marketed in the last fifteen years or so. But, by the same token, the absence of the Thalidomide-type drug is also a worldwide phenomenon, so it is difficult to credit our stringent regulatory process for that benefit either.

We are really left in the position of having to conjecture the net effects of the regulation, either in producing some benefit in the form of avoiding the usually harmful drug, or in generating a cost by sacrificing the benefits from the proverbial wonder drug. However, we have some history to guide us here, and I think the message of this history is very clear. That message warns us to expect more harm than gain from the way that our regulatory process has developed. Let me look at the problem in the following way: assume the very best result for the costs of regulation, the least possible damage. That is, assume that no major medical advance on the order of penicillin or the sulfa drugs will ever be blocked by the doubled research and development costs that are required by this regulation. Even if that happened, it is inevitable that the extra testing and screening will delay the introduction of the drug to the mass consumer market by something like two, four, or as it is rapidly becoming today, more like six years.

What is the likely consequence of just that delay? Remember, first, that in the past the major advance has come more frequently than the major mistake. Let me just look though at one major advance which I was able to study, one that is not nearly as important as penicillin or the sulfa drugs. This is the antibiotic treatment of tuberculosis. I can describe very briefly the conclusions of that study. I looked at the history of these drugs, which were put on the market after the end of World War II. One can see an immediate effect on the death rate from tuberculosis and trace out that effect over time. Since the effect is very dramatic, this is not very hard to do. One can then ask the following question: what would have happened if these drugs had been subject to the modern regulatory process, so that, as a result, they had come on the market a couple of years later than they did? Assume that they would have been developed, forget about the effect on the price of the drugs, just ask what would have happened had they come on the market two years later? The answer is that over fifty thousand more people would have died from the disease, and over a hundred thousand more victims of this disease would have had their suffering prolonged. That is the sort of magnitude involved in any major medical advance. If we ever have a major pharmaceutical advance in the treatment of something like cancer or heart disease, the numbers are going to be multiples of these. Hundreds of thousands of deaths would be involved for any major advance, in either of these two diseases, simply from the delay in getting the drug to the market for a couple of years.

Let me look at the other side of the coin, at potential benefits from drug regulation, again, in the best possible light. That is, let us assume that this added testing prevents the marketing of every single potential disaster like Thalidomide. That is, it weeds out every drug whose harm can show up in a few years of additional premarket testing. It is an unfortunate fact of life that no amount of this kind of testing will eliminate every possibility of harm, because some harm shows up only after a long period of time in mass marketing. So, I am talking about the kind of harm that can show up in the kind of premarket testing that is now required of the marketers of new drugs. Drugs of that type, as I have said, have been exceedingly rare. Thalidomide is one of a very small number. But let me use it to illustrate the potential gains of the regulation.

Even here we have to engage in conjecture because, as I have said, the plain fact is that it did not take contemporary regulation to keep Thalidomide off the American market, and it did not require very extensive testing for the information about Thalidomide to be produced. But since it is about the only good example that our history provides us, let me continue by simply supposing that it had been marketed widely here because the extra testing was not done. Judging by experience in West Germany, where the drug was most widely marketed, we could have had on the order of twenty thousand birth defects, or twenty thousand deformed children, if that hypothetical event had occurred. To put it differently, in terms of what we could expect for the future, that is the sort of thing that we can expect to be saved from as a result of the current regulatory system every ten or twenty years, which seems to be the rate at which Thalidomide type drugs appear. One has to weigh that against the kind of experience that we could expect with drugs like TB drugs, if they were merely kept off the market for a brief period. And I think the balance is heavily loaded here also against the consumer.

I recognize immediately the enormous moral issues that are involved in trading the potential suffering of some for the saving of others. But we are necessarily forced to make that kind of choice. The fact that the victim of the delayed introduction of some very beneficial drug is anonymous, that we will never know who the victim is, does not mitigate the suffering; it is there just the same. And even if we shrink from trying to make this choice, it is necessarily forced on us. You can save more people at the expense necessarily of harming others. If we shrink from trying to make this choice, I think we are going to logically end up banning all innovation, because any innovation might lead to unexpected harm to someone.

All I am saying is that we recognize clearly what the potential costs and benefits are. These are simply that by demanding less risk of harm we pay with a far greater risk of loss to others, on the order of five, ten, or even more times as much risk. Indeed, we may already be paying that sort of price. TB drugs and Thalidomide make the headlines; they are the truly major events in drug innovation. Much drug innovation, though, is much less spectacular than that, because it consists of the steady improvement on existing modes of therapy. In these cases the risk trade-offs will usually be more muted, and maybe the fact that it is not one dramatic drug against another dramatic drug makes it easier politically to suppress an innovation. But let me give you just one illustration of how the less spectacular kind of innovation is subject to the same harsh requirements of trading one form of risk against another.

Here I am drawing on the research of a pharmacologist, Professor William Wardell of the University of Rochester School of Medicine, who has done perhaps the best pharmacological research on the costs and benefits of our stringent regulation of new drugs. Wardell examined the pattern of the introduction of new sleeping pills in the United States and abroad. This is a rather mundane sort of product, and the major innovation in this product apparently has been the development of sleeping pills that are less harmful when they are taken in overdose. These newer sleeping pills are now on the market in the United States; they eventually got the blessing of the FDA, but they were delayed by five years compared to their introduction abroad. In that five-year interval, Wardell estimates that fifteen hundred extra deaths from overdose of sleeping pills occurred in the United States that would have been prevented had the new sleeping pills been available here, right from the start. There has never been an unsafe drug introduced prematurely that has had that magnitude of effect. There was one, the antibiotic chloramphenicol, that had on the order of half of this effect. Now, had a drug actually been prematurely placed on the market and killed fifteen hundred people, the outcry for still more stringent regulation would be deafening. Yet one hears only approval for a regulatory system that in fact seems to have produced that kind of unseen tragedy and promises a steady stream of them in the future.

I am personally dismayed by this continuing cost, but I have to tell you that I see little hope for avoiding it, not only in the drug market, but in many other areas that are now being subject to similar regulation. This is not because of maliciousness on the part of the regulatory agencies or anything of that sort. The reason is that consumers really do seem ignorant when you come right down to it, not when they have to buy something that they are spending their own money for, but in the ballot box. When costs are hidden and are borne by anonymous victims, we tend to delude ourselves that the costs do not exist. As long as that sort of delusion persists, the delusion that we can get something for nothing, I think we are actually likely to pay heavily and get very little.

Rail Transit: Hopes and Accomplishments

George W. Hilton

Unfortunately, the question of whether to build a rail transit system in a city tends to be treated as an issue of doctrinal purity: One chooses a group that one wants to be adjusted to, and decides whether the system should be built or, alternatively, a freeway should be built. I think this is a very poor way of going at things. The question of what the building of a rail transit system will do by way of generating external benefits is one which we ought to be able to discuss as dispassionately as any other. We do have a rather abundant body of information as to what the building of such a system does accomplish.

I think it is universally accepted that such systems are promoted not for their intrinsic output, but rather, in the hope of generating external benefits. In 1968, the rapid transit bond issue on the ballot in Los Angeles was promoted with radio commercials in which the announcer said, "Clean out our air, clean off our freeways. Vote for rapid transit." He did not say rapid transit will take some small percentage of the residents of Los Angeles downtown at speeds of between eighteen and thirty-five miles per hour, because he presumed no large number of people would be motivated by that. People were interested in the external benefits of reducing the use of freeways, which is to say, increasing the quality of the service for the people who would still be on the freeways, and also reducing atmospheric pollution. Rail systems are able to provide these external benefits, if at all, because of the superiority of the quality of their service to the bus service which they replace. Rail systems do not provide any new trip. They are so expensive to build, and so inflexible, that the only practical place to put them is along the route of the most heavily traveled bus lines already in existence. So, insofar as they can provide external benefits they do so through attracting some drivers by the superiority of their service to the preexisting bus lines, or of the preexisting rail lines if there was any rail service previously.

The federal Urban Mass Transportation Administration is devoting about two-thirds of its funds (about 64 percent) to the building and equipping of rail systems. It has to date provided funds for building two lines in Chicago, one in the median strip of the Dan Ryan Expressway, which runs straight south from the center of town (through the late Mayor Daley's neighborhood, past his favorite ballpark), and another running northwest from the central business district. It has built one line in Cleveland, an extension of an existing rapid transit system to the Cleveland airport, and it has built one line in Boston, a branch of the Red Line, the previous Harvard-Ashmont rapid transit line, into downtown Quincy. It has also financed a more recent line in Boston, a rerouting of the Orange Line, but I have not seen any literature on that. It has been operating just for a few months, so I cannot tell you anything about that one. What does the experience of these lines tell us?

Chicago has an old, established rail rapid transit system with its origins in an elevated built in the 1890s, mainly in anticipation of the World's Fair of 1893. It was originally steam operated. It was there that Frank J. Sprague invented multiple-unit control, which is the basic technological improvement which permitted rapid transit. He had previously invented the electric streetcar, and he developed the multiple-unit system so as to run essentially any number of cars from the first one with a single control. In fact, he invented it twice, selling the patent once to General Electric, and the second time to Westinghouse. In characteristic fashion, he really did the job. He did it so well it is almost impossible to improve on it. Admittedly, his cars were wooden ones with open platforms. The car bodies may be different, but the basic idea of transmission of the control impulses and the brake impulses through all the cars instantaneously, and electrically, is still Frank J. Sprague's idea of rapid transit.

That development on the South Side of Chicago in 1897 spread very rapidly, both by electrification of existing mileage and by allowing subways to be built. This technology spread, not only through Chicago, but to New York in particular, and to Philadelphia and Boston. Those were the only cities, essentially, that had dense enough populations and big enough central business districts to want this form of capital-intensive transportation. Chicago had the second largest rapid transit system. Admittedly, coming in second in that business is not much of an honor, because 81 percent of rapid transit passengers in the United States are on the New York subways. However, outside of New York, the principal rapid transit line in the country is the north-south line of the Chicago Transit Authority, which runs from Howard Street to 63rd Street, serving a string of high-rise buildings along the lake on the North Shore and a densely populated ghetto area on the South Side. This generates 20,000 passengers an hour or so in peak hours. It is one of the rapid transit lines which is most justified by its traffic density. However, it suffers from the fact that stations are close together, so it is not very fast. It does not go very far south. It goes as far as Jackson Park, site of the World's Fair of 1893, which is not a very relevant consideration by modern standards.

The Chicago Transit Authority was eager to build a line with fewer stations which would run out farther. It was built on the median strip of the Dan Ryan Expressway. The new line runs out from the Chicago Loop to 95th Street, with a parking lot for park-and-ride operations at the south terminus providing a much faster trip to a point about four miles farther south than the previous north-south line had done. It was opened on September 28, 1969. The trains were through routed over the Chicago Loop (the elevated structure that gives the central business district that rather mysterious name to nonresidents, the "Loop") and out the West Side over Lake Street. It parallels the existing north-south line, mainly within a half mile. It also parallels very closely the Rock Island Railroad suburban line. The South Suburban Safeway Lines, a bus operation, runs on the freeway or on major streets immediately parallel. Farther away, the Illinois Central Electric and one suburban train of the Norfolk and Western (formerly Wabash) parallel it. Thus, there were plenty of other forms of public transportation previously in existence.

Chicago, as you are doubtless aware, is the second largest city in the United States, and the second most densely populated. Actually, it is in a tie with Philadelphia, at about 15,000 people per square mile, which is slightly more than half the population density of New York, about triple the population density of Los Angeles, and about four or five times the population density of San Diego. As you are doubtless aware, it is a city of three-story walk-up buildings, the number of which I could not estimate in the thousands. It has a central business district, relatively well-defined, constricted by water barriers and railroads, which holds up fairly well, relative to most cities. Therefore, it is a relatively transit-oriented city. The Chicago Transit Authority (with its predecessors),

Table 9-1
Revenue Passengers of Chicago Transit Authority, 1967-1972

Year	Bus	Rail	Total
1967	389,770,830	120,737,566	510,508,396
1968	346,976,958	110,792,832	457,769,790
1969	317,024,210	103,071,290	420,095,500
1970	296,176,300	105,598,382	401,874,682
1971	282,659,196	103,499,016	386,158,185
1972	.277,152,147	100,468,879	377,621,026

Source: "Mass Transportation Riding Habits," March 12, 1973.

Table 9-2
Average Daily Vehicle Counts at Peak Points, Dan Ryan and Kennedy Expressways, Chicago, 1968-1972

Year	Dan Ryan	Kennedy
1968	122,300	103,000
1969	126,100	108,200
1970	121,500	104,300
1971	144,100	109,200
1972	159,000	117,000

Source: Chicago Area Transportation Study, letters of August 7, 1972 and February 13, 1973.

however, has lost more than half its passengers, going from 1,000,150,000 in 1946 to 420,000,000 in 1969.

The new line built in the median strip of the Dan Ryan Expressway served mainly to shift passengers between modes of public transportation. In mid-1970, the CTA surveyed passengers using the terminal station at 95th Street, which is the only station that has a parking lot. Therefore, the data which they collected on the number of passengers who had previously driven is presumably not representative of the number of passengers on the whole system. All the other stations are facilities simply for people who are walking to the station or are transferring from the east-west CTA bus lines. Thus, this would overstate the number of passengers who had previously used buses for the entire trip to the Loop. A reported 34.8 percent previously made a combination bus-rail trip, mainly by CTA buses, to the CTA's existing north-south line. About 8 percent had been diverted from suburban trains of the Rock Island, the Norfolk and Western, or the Illinois Central. Slightly over 80 percent of the existing passengers at the south terminus were attracted from preexisting public transportation. Eight percent only reported themselves as ex-drivers, and 6 percent had not made the trip at all previously, mainly people who had gotten jobs downtown after the line was built. The line at that time handled about 90,000 passengers per day.

The other line was an extension of the northwest line from Logan Square to a new terminal at Jefferson Park. This required slightly over a mile of subway to get into the median strip of the Kennedy Expressway to a station at Jefferson Park, at which an interface was made with CTA bus lines, Greyhound lines, and the Chicago & North Western suburban lines. The CTA rerouted buses extensively on the northwest side of the city to bring them together.

The CTA is, sensibly enough, trying to reallocate its long distance passengers from bus to rail on the ground that they move faster, and the marginal cost of moving them is not much different. This line has never had a survey of how its passengers formerly traveled. It would be unlikely that the percentage of ex-drivers is as large as on the Dan Ryan line because there is no parking lot at the end of it. Passengers mainly just transfer from the bus lines.

The impact of building these two lines can be seen in two fashions: one, on the vehicle counts on the freeways; and the other, on the passenger counts of the CTA bus and rail lines, and the total passenger counts on the CTA. The Kennedy line opened on February 1, 1970, so the year 1970 would show the impact of both lines on the vehicle counts on the freeways. It is not clear that all of the change in vehicle counts on the freeways is attributable to opening the rail lines. Building them required some closure of the inner lanes on the freeways while the construction was going on, which depressed vehicle counts in 1969. That is, the growth of vehicle counts in 1969 was less than it would have been if the lines had not been built. A mixture of that construction and other things caused the local highway department to resurface the road in 1970, and that resulted in vehicle counts in the summer months of that year being abnormally low. Nobody knows exactly how much this is to be attributed to either one. However, if all of the reduction in vehicle counts in 1970 is attributed to the building of the railway, you have a rather consistent pattern.

There is a heavier utilization of the Dan Ryan line than the Kennedy line. There is a parking lot on the Dan Ryan line, and there is none on the Kennedy line. So, you would expect the Dan Ryan line to have more impact on the use of the freeway. Also, it runs, almost its entire length, from Chinatown at 22nd Street to 95th Street, in the median strip, whereas the one on the Kennedy median strip is there for only the last two or three miles. Remember, the CTA, like the transit industry generally, has a declining rate of utilization. In general, like most mixed bus-rail systems, the rail lines lose more money because they are more expensive to operate, but they decline less rapidly because passengers spend less time riding them. In addition, as I have said, the CTA was pursuing a conscious policy of reallocating the passengers from its long-distance bus lines (mainly its north-south bus lines) to rail lines. Thus, they have a lower rate of decline on rail than bus.

First, the vehicle counts. The vehicle count rose on the Dan Ryan from 1968 to 1969 by about four thousand per day. In the first year the rail line was open, the vehicle count declined by about five thousand a day, or approximately the equivalent of a little more than one year's growth previously. But that growth was probably less than it would have been if they had not built the rail line. In 1971 there was an enormous increase in vehicle counts. The reason for this is easy to see. The freeway previously had fed into freeways running southeast, but it was then connected to I-57, the main north-south interstate in the center of the country, running south to Champaign-Urbana, the university town, and on to Memphis and New Orleans. Tying the Dan Ryan in enormously increased the vehicle counts by more than 20,000 vehicles per day. So, if the rail system had diverted some five thousand per day, the freeway was simply inundated by the additional 23,000 vehicles per day. But that was for only part of the year, so you got the full blast in 1972, carrying 159,000 vehicles per day.

The pattern on the Kennedy Expressway is not biased by any changes. Kennedy handles traffic out to O'Hare Airport, which is an enormous facility. As you are doubtless aware, it is the busiest in the world, with a margin of approximately 50 percent over any other airport. Kennedy also handles traffic to Milwaukee, the other major city in the area, and also out to Rockford in northwestern Illinois and Madison, Wisconsin. There is no change in the Kennedy Expressway. Nothing else was fed into it. You just get the increase in utilization which increase in population and increase in income tend to bring about: 103,000 in 1968 and 108,000 in 1969, and then down, by less than a year's growth in this case. You would have to expect it to have less impact than the Dan Ryan line, because there are less passengers on the trains, and there is no parking lot. So, it reduced the vehicle count by less than a year's growth. In

1971, that had been undone. The vehicle counts were back above the level of 1969, and in 1972 they increased very considerably, once again. What you got was a once and for all shot of somewhat less than one year's growth, in vehicle counts.

What about the rate of utilization of the CTA? All you can observe there is a reversal in an otherwise monotonic decline in the number of rail passengers. The number of bus passengers declined steadily, at a very rapid rate, from 347 million in 1968, to 277 million in 1972, which is a standard pattern of decline as they have been having since World War II. In the case of the rails, the decline reversed itself in 1970. The building of the two additional lines caused the number of rail passengers to go from 103 million to 105 million between 1969 and 1970. But it was down to 103.5 million in 1971, and down to 100,469,000 in 1972. So what it did was to reallocate enough bus passengers to rail to reverse the decline in the number of rail passengers by a year which was one of the city's intentions. But the total of the two continues downward monotonically 457,769,000 to 377,621,000, without any obvious consequence of building the lines. The first year the line was in operation, the CTA lost nineteen million people, and lost about fourteen million the year after that. If it is consistent with the behavior of declining industries generally, the rate of decline ought to slacken off. Declining industries decline first at an increasing rate, and then at a decreasing rate, and pass out of business (if allowed to do so) after a long period of relatively slow tapering off in the rates of decline.

There appears to be an entirely consistent pattern between the two lines, the freeways, and the CTA system. Is that consistent with experience otherwise? Yes it is. It is consistent with some earlier Chicago and Toronto experience. The building of a rail line in the median strip of the Eisenhower Expressway, which replaced previously existing elevated structure, running straight west, attracted about 10 to 12 percent of its passengers from the ex-driver category. The building of the Yonge Street subway in Toronto attracted 90 percent of its patrons from preexisting public transportation, and the Congress Street line in Chicago attracted about 88 percent of its patronage from preexisting public transportation.

This experience is consistent with an earlier line in Chicago, Skokie Swift, also built with Urban Mass Transportation Administration funds, but under a different category, the demonstration grant program. A nonstop service from the north end of the north-south line to the rapidly growing suburban community of Skokie, it had taken an estimated nine hundred vehicles a day off the Edens and Kennedy expressways. The Edens is the north branch of the Kennedy Expressway that runs up toward Milwaukee.

I mentioned that the UMTA has financed lines in Cleveland and Boston also. The Cleveland Transit System had built a rapid transit line from the east end of the city to a point about four miles from the Hopkins Airport, the principal airport in Cleveland, in the mid-1950s. It had a declining rate of utilization almost from the beginning. This extension was built at a cost of $18.6 million, mainly on the surface except for a short tunnel approach to the Cleveland Airport station. It also proved to have a declining rate of utilization. There were 1,444,000 passengers using the airport station in 1969, but this declined to 886,000 by 1971. It was carrying about 3,600 per day at the outset, and down to 2,400 in 1971.

The line was estimated early to have caused a maximum reduction of vehicular traffic to the airport of about 7,000 automobiles and taxi trips. This, it was estimated, removed from I-71, a parallel freeway, a maximum of about 500 vehicles per hour in the peak evening hour or 125 vehicles per hour per lane of a four-lane section, leaving the central business district. This was less than 10 percent of the prevailing level of 1,500 to 2,000 vehicles per lane per hour. Closer to the airport it diverted somewhat greater amounts, 170 per lane in counts of 1,213 per hour. This was estimated to reduce the running time between downtown Cleveland and the Hopkins Airport in the rush hour by about thirty seconds. I took these estimates, which are mainly from Martin Wohl of the engineering faculty at Carnegie-Mellon University, to the Cuyahoga County Highway Department to estimate how great this was relative to the growth of traffic on I-71. The county engineer estimated that this was approximately equal to six months' growth in traffic on I-71.

The other line is in Boston. As I said, it was a branch off the existing Red Line of the Harvard-Ashmont rapid transit line from Andrews Square to Quincy Center by North Quincy and Wollaston, built for $111 million. It is about six and a quarter miles of double track and opened in September of 1971. The Department of Public Works of Massachusetts did a before-and-after study in November and December of 1970, and in November and December of 1971. These were relatively peak periods because of Christmas shoppers. Joy riding to see the new line would presumably have been ended by December 1971. The line handled about nineteen thousand passengers per day and paralleled three highway routes in downtown Boston. There is a water barrier there (as you know, downtown Boston is on a peninsula), so all the traffic which is immediately rival to it would have to go across one of the three vehicle routes.

Over that period the vehicle counts increased from 16,578 to 17,800 in the two peak hours. The department concluded that vehicular through traffic on the major facilities of the corridor still exhibited the long-term characteristics of automobile orientation, after three months of new transit service partially serving the corridor. It estimated the rail line diverted between nine hundred and one thousand vehicles per day, about what the Skokie Swift was estimated to have taken off the Kennedy Expressway. The Southeast Expressway, the principal parallel facility, was designed for 70,000 vehicles a day but normally handles between 80,000 and 120,000 vehicles per day. There is nothing very unusual about this. The variance in vehicle counts on the freeways is enormous, depending on whether or not it is raining, whether the St. Patrick's Day parade is being held, whether the circus is in town, and whether the Celtics or Bruins are playing. If I include St. Patrick's Day, I should have said 135,000, because of the peak recorded of that magnitude on that day. The freeway's rate of increase is presumably about 4 percent per year, the rate on most freeways before the price of gasoline went up. Thus, the diversion is so small relative to the variance in the growth that you cannot perceive it.

This pattern appears to be a consistent one as between these three cities, and it appears consistent with respect to Toronto, Philadelphia, and San Francisco, as well. Subsequently, since the Bay Area Rapid Transit has been open, it is estimated to take about 2 percent of the vehicles off the San Francisco Bay Bridge, and about 4 percent off in the peak hours. You would expect the Bay Area Rapid Transit to be more successful than any already discussed, because it is a bigger system. It has more parking lots, and the stations are farther apart, so it can operate faster. It has a higher level of comfort than any of the systems discussed. More to the point, it parallels a water crossing, the San Francisco Bay Bridge, which has a toll on it which is a disincentive to driving. It appears to get about 70 percent of its passengers from preexisting buses, the Greyhound suburban buses to the Walnut Creek-Concord area, and Alameda-Contra Costa County Transit buses to the Berkeley, Oakland, Hayward, Richmond areas. It still mainly reshuffles passengers between modes of public transportation.

The Lindenwald line in New Jersey had an experience about parallel to that of BART. It's difficult to know what its impact was, because the bridge it crosses, the Benjamin Franklin Bridge, has a declining rate of utilization, owing to the decline of downtown Camden and Philadelphia. The bridge tolls were doubled, partly to pay for the rapid transit lines. So, as you would expect, it has been more successful than the other lines. However, Los Angeles and San Diego and most other cities that consider building rail systems, such as Atlanta, do not have water crossings with tolls on them, and thus their experience is more likely to be of the character of Chicago, Cleveland, and Boston, than of Philadelphia and San Francisco.

If this is a consistent pattern, then several things ought to be said about it. Did we know this previously? Yes and no. The Bureau of Public Roads made a rather well-publicized estimate in a publication of the House Public Works Committee, "Highway Needs Study of 1968" that rapid transit proposals in Atlanta, Seattle, Baltimore, and Washington, D.C., if implemented, would probably take off the roads approximately one year's to two years' growth of traffic on the roads, and that the system proposed for Los Angeles would be approximately half that successful, owing to the city's lower population density and greater diffusion of employment. It seems to be quite consistent with what I calculated casually in Los Angeles. If you took the growth rate for utilization of the freeway and took the projections of the proponents of the system on the ballot in 1968, you concluded that it would take off the equivalent of three months' growth of traffic on the freeways, or about peak load of traffic in fifteen months. After seeing the consistency of the Chicago, Cleveland, and Boston experience, I suspect that both the Bureau of Public Roads and I were overly optimistic. The systems, other than Los Angeles, projected in 1968 would probably have been about as effective as the Chicago, Boston, and Cleveland lines, and the one in Los Angeles about half as effective, or less effective than I thought at the time.

The question arises, is this experience consistent with what we know about the demand factors for public transportation and what we know about the geographical tendencies at work in major cities? What do we know about demand conditions for public transportation? In the first place, we know that the industry is confronted with relatively inelastic demands with respect to price. The elasticity of demand with respect to price for the transit industry is estimated by the American Public Transit Association (the trade association) at about −0.3 to −0.4, which translated from the trade jargon of economists is that a 1 percent increase in fares will reduce the ridership by about 0.3 percent to 0.4 percent. This, in turn, means that a transit enterprise can minimize its losses by raising its fares and contracting its rate of output. This is consistent with the industry declining endlessly.

The demand for automotive transportation is also relatively inelastic. The demand for gasoline was thought before the increase in prices in 1973 and 1974, to be of the magnitude of −0.1 to −0.2 with respect to the increase in price. It is now somewhat higher than that, but still relatively inelastic. More importantly, what do we know about the income elasticity of demand, how people behave with respect to automobiles and to transit in response to increases in their income? It is difficult to fit one income elasticity to the demand for transit, because it differs by income level. Conventional wisdom in this field, which is pretty well documented by studies in Atlanta and Boston and elsewhere, is that there is a positive income elasticity of demand for rapid transit only in relatively low income brackets, for example, under $4,000 per year, as of the late 1960s.

There is a very good reason for that. In low income brackets increases in family income are highly dependent upon more members of the family going out to get jobs. Somebody's wife goes out to get a job, and therefore the family's demand for public transportation doubles, because both the husband and wife go to work on transit. But that is true only up to about $4,000 per year in the dollars of nearly a decade ago. Beyond that level, there appears to be a negative income elasticity of demand for public transportation. As people's incomes go up, they desert transit for automobiles, which is quite consistent. The demands on time to ride it and the probability that one lives and/or works far from one line are so great that you would expect people to turn away from this form of transportation as their incomes increase. They appear to do so quite readily and quite consistently. This also is consistent with an apparently endless decline of this industry. There is a fairly extensive body of literature on people's evaluation of time in commutation which concludes that people tend to evaluate their time at about 40 percent of their base hourly earnings. Obviously, you would not expect them to value it as highly as the value of their time when working.

Thomas Lisco wrote a dissertation on this at Chicago in 1967, which is probably the best thing written on the subject. People who live in Skokie have a variety of ways of going downtown: driving, taking several rail systems, carpools, or buses. He concluded they behave consistently with the presumption that they know the alternatives facing them, that they evaluate their time at 4¢ a minute while riding and 12¢ a minute while walking, and that they are willing to pay $1.50 to $2.00 a day for the superior convenience of using an automobile for point-to-point service. That seems quite consistent with what we know about price elasticities and income elasticities. All this is consistent with a very low cross-elasticity of demand between transit and automobiles.

Essentially, advocacy of this form of investment is based on a bit of casual empiricism, which I mentioned at the outset, that people are so responsive to the increase in the quality of service when a bus line is replaced with a rail transit line that large numbers of people will get out of automobiles and take the transit line. But what we know about the elasticities of demand ought to indicate that is not true. Rail transit can usually provide the service between eighteen and thirty-five miles an hour, but a bus on the freeway can do about that well, and even an automobile on a very crowded freeway, say the Harbor Freeway in Los Angeles in rush hour, can usually go thirty-five miles per hour. So we should not expect changes either in the fares on transit or in the quality of the service of the transit to affect any large number of people. Again, to lapse into economic jargon, the advocacy of this form of investment is based on a presumption that the marginal rate of substitution between automobiles and transit is relatively high. But it is not. The marginal rate of substitution between freeways and ordinary streets is relatively high. Similarly, the marginal rate of substitution between buses and rail systems is relatively high. But the marginal rate of substitution between the automobile and rail systems is not high. The number of people who are on the margin between transit and automobiles is relatively small. It is not zero, but it is small enough to be consistent with shifts of the character we have observed.

An alternative way of saying this is that people are doing something with a positive income elasticity. They are driving a car. The income elasticity of driving a car is estimated to be about +1.2. People, in response to a 1 percent increase in income, increase their quantity demanded of automobile services by about 1.2 percent, which is proportionate to their increase in income. As we have previously seen, except in low income brackets, people respond to increases in income by reducing their demand for transit service. Under those circumstances, in the face of a strongly positive income elasticity, changing the mix of alternatives which have a negative income elasticity is not going to affect the behavior of any large number of people.

Furthermore, almost all the forces in cities are for diffusion, for decline of central business districts, as airports replace railroad stations, shopping centers replace downtown department stores, computers replace unskilled clerical labor forces, television replaces legitimate theaters, etc. To get out of economics to geography, practically everything about cities tends to make them less like New York and more like San Diego, or even more like Orange County, where you cannot even find the central business districts. If a reasonably large city like Garden Grove has a central business district, it has eluded me for years.

All this presents quite a consistent pattern that the external benefits of the sort sought are not achieved in any large volume, and they are achieved at very considerable costs. We should have known this on other grounds also. People in their demand for roads are responsive to the quality of the service of the roads. The principal purpose of the rail system is to improve the quality of the roads. If the quality of roads is improved, some people who did not demand the services of the freeways previously will begin doing so. So if the BART takes seven drivers off the Bay Bridge, it probably causes some smaller number, three or four to decide to start driving. About the best that institution of a rail system could do under the circumstances is shorten the duration of the peak of traffic. Even that is not an appropriate policy goal, for the service could be provided with less capital if the peaks were lengthened and made less severe.

In short, building rail systems is not simply a method generating the external benefits of the sort which they seek to produce. The systems are very expensive. BART cost $20 million a mile. The ones in Chicago were cheap. The one on the Dan Ryan Expressway was only $5 million a mile, because it essentially got a free right of way in the median strip which had been provided for it at the outset, but the one on the Kennedy was quite a bit more expensive because it had about a mile and an eighth of tunnel and two underground stations. While BART did cost $20 million a mile, it would now cost $30 million a mile. To build a Second Avenue Subway in New York, which was undertaken and abandoned because of the expense, might cost over $100 million a mile because it is so expensive to relocate underground facilities in Manhattan. The 64th Street subway paralleling the Queens main line in the New York system is costing $62 to $64 million a mile, and the New York subway has a very rapid rate of decline. All these systems, for the reasons I mentioned—because of the income elasticity, the price elasticity, in the nature of changes in the nature of the urban pattern—have a declining rate of utilization. But the pricing of a subway is as bad as the pricing of gasoline: it is just a flat fee, without regard to the hour of use. The Queens line cannot handle its peak twenty minutes of service in the morning rush, so public authorities pay an enormous amount of money to parallel it, which is just analogous to building parallel freeways or building rail systems elsewhere to deal with rush hour traffic.

This gets me to the punch line of all of this discussion. All of this is basically symptomatic of the way in which the roads are priced, and also the way in which transit is organized. The roads are priced in the fashion I mentioned, by an excise on gasoline. This is used for only one reason: because gasoline is the only input into automotive transportation which is regularly metered, it is cheaper to collect the charge in this fashion than any other. But this fee does not provide one of the functions of the price in society: to encourage economization of the existing supply of the resource. It also does not provide one of the other functions of a price: indicating society's demand for additional investment. This sort of charging creates queuing, as most nonprice rationing does. The queuing takes the form of congestion getting in and out of central business districts, which gives the totally erroneous impression that what society is demanding is additional radial facilities. The people who want to build the rail systems and the people who want to build redundant freeways paralleling existing ones, like the Junipero Serra freeway in San Francisco or the Pomona freeway in Los Angeles, and the people who want to build the rail systems consider themselves in opposite camps. But they are really both arguing for misallocation of investments, because of the fact that current road pricing neither encourages the economization of the existing supply of freeways, nor does it give accurate impressions of what society is really demanding. The increase in demand for trips is mainly for trips between suburbs, and for trips just going around cities for people who do not have any business there anyway. So, what society really wants more of, insofar as one can judge, is bypass facilities, like the San Diego freeway, which do not go anywhere near downtown, or the beltways around Baltimore and Washington, or routes 128 and 495 in concentric circles around Boston.

The problem essentially ought to be dealt with in two fashions. First, we ought to find some alternative method of pricing of the roads by some system of metering their use. This could be done with computers rather easily, by putting a meter on the automobile which would receive impulses from wires embedded in the road, a proposal of Professor William Vickrey of Columbia. Then, one could be charged five times as much for driving in peak hours as for driving in off hours. This would give people an incentive to fill up their automobiles. At present you pay for the service of the roads by the time you waste on them. It does not matter whether your car is full or empty. If it were a pecuniary price, you could split it with someone else in the car. It would give people incentives to stay out of business districts completely, and to live closer to central business districts if they work there, or for employment to follow people to the suburbs so people would not make such long home-to-work trips.

Building rail transportation systems tends to subsidize people for making long trips and trips in peak hours by increasing the comfort level of such trips. BART is fairly explicitly designed to do both of those things. So, in those respects it tends to worsen the problem it is intended to solve. Variable user charges would also give drivers incentives not to go through downtown interchanges, if they do not have any business there. The great majority of people, perhaps 80 percent of the people driving through the interchanges near the business district of Los Angeles, have no business there at all. Chicago, my beloved native city, is the absolute ultimate in ignorance in this. All of the radial freeways are free and the circumferential road has a toll on it. So, anyone driving from Minneapolis to Fort Wayne has an incentive to drive right through the interchanges to the west of the Chicago Loop which, to compound it all, are poorly designed, with a lot of left-side on-ramps and off-ramps, too many of them at intervals of every block.

The other thing which ought to be done is reorganization of transit to a competitive industry. Transit is a monopolized industry. The fact that it is publicly owned is not so important as that it is monopolized. Whether it is a public or private monopoly is only marginally significant. It is monopolized for reasons which are entirely historical, which sound irrelevant when you mention them. It had not been monopolized before 1888, but when the electric streetcar was developed, the cheapest way to distribute the power was to have a citywide distribution grid with one power station. Almost all cities gave out monopolies to the streetcar operators to have citywide systems, but required transfer privileges for a flat nickel fare. This resulted in the people who moved under two and a half miles cross-subsidizing the people who moved over two and a half miles.

This situation gave the economy the incentive to develop a device which could move people for short distances at higher speeds with higher levels of comfort, with a competitive economic organization, with greater facilities providing door to door service. This developed on July 1, 1914, on Broadway in Los Angeles in the form of the jitney movement, moving people in private automobiles—Ford open touring cars—as common carriers. This is usually looked upon as an historical aberration of no particular significance, but that is an incorrect interpretation. This was the origin of the bus industry. If the jitneys had been allowed to exist anywhere, preferably everywhere, they would have provided a competitive market in public transportation. You may think of the bus as something that runs on a fixed route operated by a local monopoly on a fixed schedule and at a fixed fare. If you read the trade journal which the jitneys had, you discover that the early bus operators said treating a bus like that robs it of its intrinsic advantages: you should not have a schedule or a fixed fare or a fixed route. Pick up the first passenger, go where he wants to go, then pick up anybody else who is going there. However buried in history that interpretation may be, that is the way in which a bus system ought to be organized. It ought to be run by owner-operators in a competitive environment.

People who would want to run jitneys would almost definitionally be people whose alternatives are relatively unattractive. Ghetto and barrio residents would probably provide the service for about 60 percent of present fares in smaller vehicles which could stop less frequently and be more willing to take people close to home. In long distance service between suburbs and cities, they would use probably forty to fifty passenger diesel buses like the present ones, but they would provide the urban collection and distribution facilities with vehicles of the character of Chevrolet vans or Volkswagen microbuses. They would provide a higher quality of service for a lower price, and would be much more demand responsive. The present transit monopolies provide the service with too-large vehicles to divide out the driver's wages over a large number of people simply because he belongs to a strong union. A transit system organized competitively would be impossible to unionize or cartelize effectively.

If we had a better road pricing system, taxation of noxious emission from vehicles to hold down pollution, and the competitive organization of transit systems, the problems would clear up. But by building rail systems, we are only aggravating the problem of an industry already too capital intensive because it is inappropriately organized.

However, I have always been rather optimistic that the efforts to build rail systems would blow over quickly. The lobby which has tried to generate a political demand for the systems could conceal what happened in Boston, Chicago, and Cleveland. After all, who bothers to find out unless he teaches a course in urban transportation? However, the people who promoted such systems had to point to BART as the prototype of what they wanted to build elsewhere. Once it was completed, I had great confidence that the movement for building such systems would collapse almost instantaneously. In fact, Professor Ross D. Eckert of USC and I wrote an article on the jitneys, deciding that there was no point in writing a book on urban transportation, because by the time we would get it out in 1977, at the earliest, the movement for building rail transit systems would be declining. You can rather clearly see that this is happening. The Secretary of Transportation and the head of the Urban Mass Transportation Administration in 1974 suggested Los Angeles consider a less capital intensive system more suitable to its low population density—which is double the population density here. That, I thought, was the milestone indicating the decline of the movement. At present, we are observing a brief movement of interest in building so-called light rail systems, streetcar systems on private rights-of-way. This I expect to be of a very short duration, a transitional phase in the complete loss of enthusiasm for building rail systems. Perhaps we will have to have one system of that character built, too. Dayton wanted to build one, but the UMTA disapproved its application, and UMTA now seems to be trying to get cities generally to think of alternatives. The building of rail systems is so expensive to create really negligible external benefits that the demise of the movement seems to me an inevitable development.

10 Law and the Invisible Hand

James M. Buchanan

I have often argued that there is only one "principle" in economics that is worth stressing, and that the economists' didactic function is one of conveying some understanding of this principle to the public at large. Apart from this principle, there would be no basis for general public support for economics as a legitimate academic discipline, no place for "economics" as an appropriate part of a "liberal" educational curriculum. I refer, of course, to the principle of the spontaneous order of the market, which was the great intellectual discovery of the eighteenth century.

The principle is perhaps best summarized in Adam Smith's most famous statement:

It is not from the benevolence of the butcher, the brewer, or the baker, that we expect our dinner, but from their regard to their own interest. We address ourselves, not to their humanity, but to their self-love, and never talk to them of our own necessities but of their advantages.[1]

Sir Dennis Robertson put the same point somewhat differently when he said that the economists' task was that of showing how to minimize the use of that scarcest of all resources, love. And he urged his fellow economists to emit warning barks whenever they observed proposals that required love for their effective implementation.[2]

The understanding of this principle is extremely important for the shaping of attitudes toward the economic process. To those who do not understand this principle, either from a lack of formal instruction in economics (or because of perverse formal instruction which is by no means uncommon), or from some failure to sense its fundamental elements from ordinary perceptions of social reality, the economy has no "order." The man of habit may seldom think, but if he is forced, for any reason, to look about him, failure to understand this principle requires some resort to "miracles" to explain such a simple fact as the observed presence of tomato juice on his grocer's shelves each time he goes to the supermarket. In this situation, the man of habit is highly vulnerable to persuasion by those who, from either ignorance or design, propose to subvert the workings of economic process. If the continuing availability of tomato juice is brought to the level of political consciousness, either by the chance occurrence of some exogenous event or by the deliberate effort of a demagogue, the economic illiterate would quite naturally tend to embrace governmental controls purportedly aimed at insuring stability in supply (of tomato juice or of anything else). The whole *raison d'être* of economics, as a discipline with some didactic purpose, lies in its potential for reducing to a minimum the numbers of persons who remain illiterate in this sense.

By implication if not directly, I have advanced here what is essentially a *political* justification for the understanding of this principle of spontaneous coordination. But there are two other, and different, justifications for understanding this principle that must be discussed. First, it has been alleged by Robert Nozick, in his much-acclaimed book, *Anarchy, State, and Utopia,*[3] that "invisible-hand explanations" of reality are intellectually-aesthetically more satisfying than alternative explanations. Nozick offers complex philosophical reasons for this that I cannot fully appreciate, but the common sense basis of this justification seems clear enough. We place positive value on those sorts of understandings-explanations that allow us to predict, even when there is no prospect of control. Contrast the Newtonion (and post-Newtonion) explanations of the movements of the planets with those which required explicit intrusion of "God's will." The economic sophistication that allows us to know why the tomato juice is on the grocer's shelves, and to predict what will happen if there is some increase in the demand, is something of intrinsic value in its own right.

A second, and more familiar, justification for understanding the principle of spontaneous coordination lies in the direct efficiency applications. We know that there will be tomato juice on the grocer's shelves, but we know also that we shall get *more* tomato juice, *more* potatoes, *more* shoes—more economic value generally if we allow market forces to operate than if we make attempts to interfere. If we can then accept aggregate economic value as an appropriate objective, an instrumental argument for understanding the coordinative principle is provided.

Or, we may introduce Michael Polanyi's application of the same principle to the organization of science. If we are interested in discovering the unknown, we had best allow individual scientists free reign in their searches. The jigsaw puzzle that is confronted can best be "solved" by allowing different persons to look for differing subpatterns, especially since the "big picture" has no defined borders and since no one knows what this would look like even with borders imposed.

It is useful to distinguish the three justifications for understanding the principle of spontaneous coordination which we may label the *political*, the *aesthetic*, and the *economic*. The failure to separate these may have been a source of some confusion in application. As a different example consider, not the supply of an ordinary commodity on the grocer's shelves, but the dumping of litter on the beaches near San Diego. (We assume, for now, that there is no law against dumping such litter.) We should be able to observe the results; beautiful beaches uglied by litter. We can explain and understand this result in the selfsame way that we understand the tomato juice on the grocer's shelves. Persons do not dump litter on the beach because they are evil or malevolent.

(Such persons may exist, but they are surely in a tiny minority, even in the world of the late 1970s.) Persons dump litter on the beach because to do so is in their own self-interest, which may be either narrowly or broadly defined. This does not imply that the persons who dump litter do not value a clean beach more highly than a littered beach; almost all will do so. But the private, personalized costs of cleaning up their own litter is probably greater for most persons than the differential value of the marginal change in the total appearance of the beach that their own activity can produce. In a large number setting, the change in the total amount of littering brought about by the change in the behavior of one person may be relatively insignificant. Hence, it may be to each person's interest to continue to litter, while deploring the overall appearance of the beach.

This is, of course, a familiar example to economists, an example of external diseconomies, of the generation of public bads, of a generalized prisoners' dilemma. Some economists would go on to suggest that the observed results arise because of the absence of property rights in the commonly-used resource, the beach. If this scarce resource were assigned to some person or group, it would then be in their interest to maintain standards of cleanliness, to internalize the externalities, and in so doing to insure economic efficiency. My purpose here, however, is not to discuss the particulars of this example, or to raise the more general issues concerning the uses to which various "market failure" constructions have been put. My purpose is the quite different one of illustrating that "invisible hand explanations" may be as applicable to "orders" that are clearly recognized to be undesirable as to those that are recognized to be desirable. We have "explained" the observed pattern of litter on the beach by looking at the behavior of persons, each of whom is maximizing his own utility. Out of this behavioral interaction, a result emerges, an order of sorts, which was not designed by anyone. It was not intended by any of the actors in the process.

We may now apply our three separate justifications of the basic principle of spontaneous coordination to this example. The "order" which emerges, the littered beach, has been produced by anarchy; there is no politically or governmentally orchestrated control or regulation which produces the result. We fully understand that the results emerge from the working of the "invisible hand." We can, as in the other examples, secure some satisfaction in our ability to explain these observed results in such a way as to make them seem "natural," as having been generated by rational utility-maximizing behavior on the part of the separate individuals involved in the interaction. The aesthetics of understanding the principle of order do not seem different from those present in the more familiar meat-bread-potatoes examples from Adam Smith.

An appreciation of the workings of the invisible hand also allows us to recognize that the littering of the beach will be kept within bounds, within the limits that are indeed explainable by individual utility-maximization. Anarchy need not generate chaos; the public beach need not be weighted down with tons of garbage in the absence of specific regulation and control by government-political authorities. For any given population, and for any given set of ethical norms for behavior, anarchy in the use of the acknowledged common resource will produce some equilibrium, one that can be predicted and described in general terms by resort to the economist's set of tools.

It is in the economic, rather than the aesthetic or the political, characteristics that our beach-littering example dramatically differs from Adam Smith's butcher, baker, and candlestick maker, or from the other standard and familiar examples drawn from classical and neoclassical economics, including my earlier tomato juice one. In the latter examples, an understanding of the principle of spontaneous coordination enables us to predict that we shall get more meat, more bread, more candlesticks, more tomato juice by allowing the forces of individual utility-maximization to work independently of direct political regulation (assuming, of course, a well-defined set of legally protected property rights). And if we make the widely-acknowledged value judgments that more is better than less and that individuals are better able to judge their own welfare than anyone else, we can label the results to be efficient. In somewhat more technical economist's jargon, we can say that the workings of the market generate Pareto-efficient results, which means that, under the standard conditions postulated, there will exist no possible rearrangements which could make one person better off without harming someone else.

But we cannot do this in our beach-littering example. In the equilibrium attained under anarchy here, under the uninhibited and unregulated utility-maximizing behavior of persons acting each independently or separately, no single person has an incentive to change his behavior, no incentive to reduce the amount of littering that he does. However, if *all* or even a relatively large number of persons should change their behavior in this way, by reducing the amount of littering, *everyone* might be made better off as a result. And "better offness" is here defined in precisely the same way as before, namely by the persons themselves. Each person who uses the beach may find himself with more utility after the general change in behavior than before. And no one would find himself with less utility than before the change. This is merely another way of saying that the results produced by the operation of the invisible hand, by the independent and separate utility-maximizing behavior of persons, are not necessarily efficient in the economic sense. The principle of spontaneous coordination, properly applied to our beach-littering example, allows us to understand and to explain the possible economic inefficiency that would characterize the anarchistic equilibrium just as it allowed us to understand and to explain the possible economic efficiency of the anarchistic equilibria (with well-defined property rights) in the market examples drawn from Adam Smith. The principle of spontaneous order, as such, is fully neutral in this respect. It need not be exclusively or even primarily limited to explanations of unplanned and unintended outcomes that are socially efficient.

So much for a very sketchy and capsule summary of the elementary principles of theoretical welfare economics. This is all by way of introduction to my basic purpose, which is that of examining the potential applicability of the principle of spontaneous coordination to human activities that are not normally classified as "economic," activities that are not normally discussed in terms of the production-exchange-trade of "goods" or "bads." More specifically, I want to look carefully at the emergence and evolution of "the law," which I define here broadly to include the whole set of legal institutions. I want to discuss the applicability of the principle of spontaneous coordination to legal institutions and to go beyond this to the implications for legal reform, notably for constitutional change. My discussion and analysis will be critical of the position that seems to be taken by Professor F.A. Hayek, a distinguished Nobel laureate in economics, and a social and legal philosopher whose ideas I respect and admire.[4] In his specific attribution of invisible-hand characteristics to the evolution of legal institutions, Hayek seems to have failed to separate properly the positive and the normative implications of the principle. Interpreted in a strictly positive sense, the principle of spontaneous coordination can do much to add to our understanding of legal institutions. But this understanding and explanation can be equally helpful in assessing the efficient and the inefficient elements of the order that we may observe, actually or conceptually. "The law" as it exists can probably be classified as some admixture of the bread-meat examples of Adam Smith and of the beach-littering example that I introduced earlier. In order to derive normative implications, we must carefully discriminate. The forces of social evolution alone contain within their workings no guarantee that socially efficient results will emerge over time. The historically-determined institutions of legal order need not be those which are "best." Such institutions can be "reformed," can be made more "efficient." The discussions of such potential reforms should, of course, be fully informed by an understanding of the principle of spontaneous order. But warnings against unnecessary and ill-timed interferences with legal institutions should not extend to the point of inhibiting us against efforts at improvement, which seems to me to be the position Hayek's argument forces upon us.

I shall elaborate this argument in several stages. A basic point that I stress in almost all discussion is the necessity of recognizing that "we start from here." Any evaluation or analysis of social institutions must commence with the status quo for the evident reason that this describes that which exists. For present purposes, there exists some body of law; there is in being a set of legal rules, legal institutions, and these may be described. A major part of law school training is indeed little other than the transmission of this description.

And it is surely appropriate for qualified scholars to devote intellectual energies to what may be called the "positive history" of these institutions. In such a history, some understanding of the principle of spontaneous order can be helpful. The legal historian who searches for some explicit or planned design in the existing structure, in whole or in every part, is surely destined for frustration. In a very important sense, as Hayek stresses, law "grows"; it is not "made." The legal historian must explain the sources of this "growth" as best he can, and by resorting to "invisible hand" explanations he can add clarity and understanding. But certain parts of the law are also "made," and have been explicitly designed for the accomplishment of particular purposes. The historian must classify the elements of law into these two sets. Explanation and classification—perhaps the work of the positive historian is complete when he has done these tasks.

For those who seek to evaluate the existing structure of law, however, the records of the positive historian offer little more than preliminary inputs. Return to the beach-littering example, and suppose that a careful history "explains" the absence of either a set of behavioral standards or more formally imposed constraints on private behavior. Population growth alone might explain why those behavioral standards that were deemed appropriate a half-century past may be inappropriate at the present time. But what is the conceptual basis upon which an evaluative judgment of "inadequacy" or "undesirability" may be established? How can the analyst attribute "inefficiency" to the results that he observes when the historian has explained how these results have emerged?

It is at this point that Hayek's argument seems misleading. He seems to suggest that those institutions that have evolved spontaneously, through the responses of persons independently to the choices that they faced, embody efficiency attributes. But, as the littering example is designed to demonstrate, an explanation of the results by the operation of "invisible hand" responses need not carry with it normative overtones.[5] But how can norms be introduced? It is here that my own position becomes what Hayek would call "constructivist," a term that he uses pejoratively. In order to distinguish my positive from constructivism of the idealist type, however, I should add the word "contractarian." My answer to the question posed is straightforward. We may evaluate any element of the existing legal structure in terms of its possible consistency with "that which might emerge" from a genuine "social contract" among all persons who are involved in the interaction.[6] This test applies equally to those elements of legal structure that may have evolved without conscious design or intent and to those elements which may have been quite explicitly "laid on" for the achievement of a particular purpose at some time in the past. The evaluative analyst must test all "law" on such "as if" contractarian criteria. But from such tests he can do nothing other than advance hypotheses of possible "failure." His understanding of the principle of order allows him to hypothesize that all of the beach-using persons would *agree* on some rule that would constrain their littering behavior, would agree on a change in the law that is in existence with respect to littering behavior. The ultimate test of his hypothesis is observed agreement on the change suggested.[7]

I am not clear as to how Hayek would classify this basically contractarian position that I have sketched. It seems clearly to fall within the "constructivist" category in the sense that it does "provide a guideline for deciding whether or not existing institutions (are) were to be approved."[8] But the position is not at all "rationalist" in the sense that rationality norms are applied to the group, as such. If properly qualified and interpreted, the contractarian position offers a plausibly acceptable alternative to both Hayek's implicit attribution of efficiency to whatever institutions that emerge from an evolutionary process and to the rationalist conception which posits the existence of a group mind. Hayek's criticisms of the latter position, which I fully share, seem to overlook the contractarian alternative, and his strictures may be taken, perhaps misleadingly, to apply equally to the contractarian construction.[9]

To imply, as Hayek seems to do, that there neither exists nor should exist a guideline for evaluating existing institutions seems to me to be a counsel of despair in the modern setting. There are, of course, many elements of the existing legal structure that would, without doubt, qualify as "efficient" in the technical Pareto sense. This would be true with respect to those elements that might have evolved in some evolutionary process, and in the absence of any design, and to those elements that might have been explicitly selected. There need be no relationship between the historical origins of a legal institution and its current efficiency properties. The latter relate exclusively to the institution's ability to command assent in comparisons with effective alternatives that might be suggested. In every case, the "as if" contractarian test must be applied, and existing institutions should be provisionally classified as "possibly efficient" only after meeting such a test. Note that efficiency in this restricted sense is not at all comparable to any concept of efficiency that may be defined with respect to the utility function of a particular individual or even of a group of individuals. That which is Pareto-efficient is that upon which all persons assent, at least to the extent that they fail to agree on any particular change.

Hayek properly stresses that many institutions that have emerged without conscious design are, nonetheless, efficient in the sense defined. But he fails to note that they must be subjected to the *same* test as those which are to be classified as inefficient.[10] There are surely many elements of legal structure that may be provisionally classified as inefficient in the Pareto sense. For these, explicit and deliberately designed proposals for reform can be, and should be, advanced by those whose competence offers them an understanding of the principle of spontaneous coordination. Framework proposals for change can be, and should be, "constructed" and then presented for possible approval or disapproval by the members of the relevant public, the participants in the interaction. The economist can, and should, suggest the enactment of a rule, a law, that would impose fines on persons who litter the beach, a rule that is deliberately constructed for the attaining of an end result, the cleanliness of the beach.

This example may, however, be somewhat misleading for two reasons. First of all, the example is deliberately designed to suggest that *all* persons can be made better off by a simultaneous and fully symmetrical change in behavior, and without the necessity of introducing more complex compromises, compensations, multidimensional exchanges, political log rolling, or side payments. Even for most strictly economic examples, things are not likely to be nearly so simple as in the beach littering case. Consider a situation in which the participants are not symmetrically engaged in the activity that creates potentially undesirable results. Consider mining activity in the desert, say, Death Valley. A few persons secure gains from undertaking this activity; to these persons the expected private benefits exceed the expected private costs. Many other persons, the set of nonminers, may be damaged slightly by the uglying of the desert that mining necessarily involves. Assume that there is in existence no law against mining and that the desert is not privately owned. Is the observed result inefficient or efficient? The economist who seeks to reach a provisional or hypothetical judgment here must reckon the costs that would be imposed on those who are now miners, whose behavior would necessarily be constrained by a new law, against the benefits or gains that would be promised to nonminers by the possible change in the level or type of mining activity. If the existing situation, with no law, is considered to be "inefficient," there must be some set of compensations possible which could "pay off" or "bribe" the persons who are engaged in mining, which would induce them voluntarily to modify their behavior.

This example is considerably more complex than the simple beach-littering case, but neither example presents difficulties in defining the end results to be evaluated. A second source of misconception may arise from these strictly economic examples, however, precisely because of the apparent ease with which the end result objectives are defined. For the more general elements of legal structure, the definition of an objective may itself be one of the most difficult steps in the process. Consider a familiar but highly useful example, the rules for ordinary games. Whether by some evolutionary and nonplanned process or by deliberate invention, an existing game is defined by its rules in being. Are these rules efficient in the orthodox Pareto sense? How can we apply the "as if" contractarian test? Would the players generally agree on any change?

This problem poses difficulties conceptually because it becomes almost impossible to specify the objective that might be sought through rules changes. There is nothing approximately akin to "cleanliness" or "natural beauty" here. Criteria of "fairness" may be adduced, but what can "fairness" mean independently of agreement.[11] The criteria for improvement in the rules that define the general game are necessarily more internalized by the participants than they are in the beach-littering example. In the latter, there is apparently an agreed-on standard of valuation (a clean beach is "better" than a dirty one), which the observing analyst can call upon in his development of suggested hypotheses for change. The tests of the hypotheses are identical; the agreement among participants. But the task of the analyst in advancing reform proposals is conceptually more difficult in the one case than in the other; the constitutional analyst must be considerably more sophisticated in his prognoses than the economic analyst who advances suggestions for economic policy changes.

My argument may be broadly accepted, but there remains the question: Why is a scholar with the sophistication of Hayek led to attribute efficiency to the results of the social evolutionary process, an attribution that makes such results analogous with those that emerge from the operation of markets, *within* a defined legal framework? Failure to understand the principle in the latter case has led, and will lead, to many ill-conceived and damaging interferences through the intrusion of political-governmental controls. But are not these intrusions themselves a part of general social evolution? How can Hayek adduce norms that will allow him to adjudge such interferences to be "out of bounds," while elevating the overall legal structure to a position that should not be called into question by potential constructivists? Surely Hayek must acknowledge that the rules that *emerge* (which need not be "constructed") to constrain market adjustments may themselves be inefficient. But what is his own test? While he seems to allow for reform, for "legislation" to correct for evolutionary aberrations, he offers no criteria for judgment. Hayek is, I think, led into what we must classify finally as a logically inconsistent position because of his implicit fear that politically orchestrated changes must, in most cases, produce social damage. He has been, I think, overzealous in transferring his wholly justified criticism of those who have failed to understand the workings of the invisible hand in the operation of markets, *constrained by law*, to the unjustified and partially contradictory criticism of those who seek to evaluate the emergence and operation of law itself in constructivist-rationalist terms.

In my discussion to this point, I have not distinguished between *nomos* and *thesis*, to introduce Hayek's terminology for the "law of liberty" and the "law of legislation" respectively. At base, my criticism of the invisible-hand or evolutionary criteria for evaluation applies equally to both. But it may be useful to outline Hayek's own distinction here. His emphasis is on *nomos*, that body of law that emerges from the separate decisions of judges in a process of spontaneous adjustment.[12] The evolution of the English common law in his historical model, and the implication is clear that the results that emerge from this process are somehow assumed to be "efficient" and that attempts to interfere with these results are likely to be harmful. As my argument has indicated, I see no reason to expect that the evolution of independent judge-made law insures efficiency or optimality.[13] Hayek elevates this set of legal institutions as prior to and conceptually different from legislation, which he defines as designed or constructed rules that direct the activities of governments. He has relatively little to say about criteria for evaluating legislation, which does not emerge from the invisible-hand process.[14] It is nonetheless clear that he assigns "legislation," which would include constitutional law, to a relatively insignificant role in the whole legal structure. *Nomos*, the law of liberty, "lawyer's law"—Hayek strongly suggests that this exists independently of and prior to "legislation."

Hayek's emphasis becomes almost the inverse of my own at this point. In a positive, empirical sense, many of our social-legal institutions have "grown" independently of design and intent. But man must look on *all* institutions as potentially improvable. Man must adopt the attitude that he can control his fate; he must accept the necessity of choosing. He must look on himself as man, not another animal, and upon "civilization" as if it is of his own making.[15] In some final analysis, Hayek's position may be taken to reflect a basic European attitude which is sharply different from the American. The European classical liberal, who is well represented by Hayek, can and perhaps should stress the evolutionary sources of many of the institutions that stand as bulwarks of individual freedom. The American cannot, and should not, neglect the fact that his own heritage of freedom, although owing much to its European antecedents, was deliberately "constructed" in large part by James Madison and his compatriots. Theirs were no invisible hands. They set out to construct a constitutional framework for the "good society," which they defined implicitly as "free relations among free men." For two centuries, their construction has stood the test. But who would dare, in 1976, to suggest that constitutional improvements are not possible, that the observed erosion of our traditional liberties cannot be reversed by deliberately designed reforms, motivated by something akin to the initial Madisonian vision. Americans, because they are Americans, must place their faith in man's ability to impose rules of law upon himself rather than in the rules of law that the historical process imposes upon him.

Notes

1. Adam Smith, *The Wealth of Nations* (Modern Library Edition), p. 14.

2. D.H. Robertson, *Economic Commentaries* (London: Staples, 1956), pp. 148-49, 154.

3. Robert Nozick, *Anarchy, State, and Utopia* (New York: Basic Books, 1974).

4. The Hayek position is expressed most fully in *Law, Legislation and Liberty, Volume I, Rules and Order* (Chicago: University of Chicago Press, 1973). My criticism is based on what I interpret to be the basic thrust of Hayek's argument, gained from a careful reading of his book. In particular places, Hayek seems to concede many if not all of the points that may be advanced in opposition. My purpose here is not one of exegesis, but is instead that of offering hopefully constructive criticism.

5. My position seems to be close to that taken by Ernest Gellner, in a lengthy critique of W.V. Quine. Ernest Gellner, "The Last Pragmatist: The Philosophy of W.V. Quine," *Times Literary Supplement*, July 25, 1975.

6. My position is developed in some detail in my book, *The Limits of Liberty: Between Anarchy and Leviathan* (Chicago: University of Chicago Press, 1975).

7. The basic methodological position outlined here is discussed more fully in my paper, "Positive Economics, Welfare Economics, and Political Economy," *Journal of Law and Economics* II (October 1959): 124-138.

8. Hayek, *Rules and Order*, p. 10.

9. I say "perhaps misleadingly" here, because in the Preface to *The Mirage of Social Justice, Volume II, Law, Legislation, and Liberty* (Chicago: University Press, 1976), Hayek states that he considers his own objectives to be closely related to those of John Rawls, as expressed in the latter's *A Theory of Justice* (Cambridge: Harvard University Press, 1971). The fact that Rawls is an avowed contractarian suggests that Hayek may not apply his constructivist-rationalist criticisms to the contractarian approach, properly interpreted.

10. In her summary paper on Hayek's work, Shirley Letwin suggests that Hayek does allow for "inefficient" outcomes under spontaneous adjustments. But she does not reconcile such recognition with the primary normative thrust of Hayek's argument. See Shirley Letwin, "The Achievements of Hayek," Mimeographed paper circulated for Mont Pelerin Society Meeting, Hillsdale, Michigan, August 1975.

11. Hayek (in *Rules and Order*, p. 76) notes that no one has probably succeeded in explicitly articulating the rules that define "fair play." This is in apparent contrast to the economist's articulation of the conditions that define efficiency, as normally understood. Even here, however, the contrast is not so great as it might seem, since the economist's criterion, like that of the observer of other social games, must ultimately reduce to agreement among participants.

12. Bruno Leoni has also analyzed judge-made law in a model of adjustment analogous to the working of a competitive market order. See, Bruno Leoni, *Freedom and the Law* (Princeton: Von Nostrand, 1961).

13. Richard Posner is more specific in his claim to the effect that the decisions made under common law rules are guided by considerations of economic efficiency. See, his *Economic Analysis of Law* (Boston: Little Brown and Company, 1972). For my own criticism of Posner's argument, see, "Good Economics—Bad Law," *Virginia Law Review* 60 (Spring 1974): 483-492.

Posner's claim is, however, less sweeping than Hayek's in one sense. Posner argues that the evolution of the common law has insured the satisfaction of criteria of economic efficiency, defined in the narrow sense. While he implies that this has also been socially desirable, he does not specifically make this the only criterion for the broader "social efficiency."

14. Presumably Hayek will deal with legislation more fully in the projected third volume of *Law, Legislation and Liberty*, which is not yet in final form.

15. I make this statement in order to contrast it explicitly with the following statement by Hayek:

Freedom means that in some measure we entrust our fate to forces which we do not control; and this seems intolerable to those constructivists who believe that man can master his fate—as if civilization and reason itself were of his making.

(F.A. Hayek, *The Mirage of Social Justice*, p. 30.) Of course, Hayek would acknowledge that some aspects of civilization are of man's making, just as I would necessarily acknowledge that some aspects emerge from the "growth-like" processes of social evolution. What is important, however, is the difference in emphasis or thrust here, a difference that has important implications for the development of attitudes toward the potentialities for social reform.

11 Economic Laws and Political Legislation

Armen A. Alchian

What is the fundamental premise of economic theory that I believe is informative? It is a conception of the animal called man. Law, political science, sociology, and psychology are social sciences. You would expect them to have the same conception, but they do not.

Many sociologists vision man as a pawn of convention and custom. He is what custom and society makes him. And society and custom are left unexplained. Psychologists flirt with a man who has a hierarchy of goals or drives. He satisfies one before embarking on another. That conception provokes such empty question as which drive or goal is more important. Political science and politicians espouse a man who is other-person oriented, who strives and sacrifices for the benefit of other people—to eloquently serve the public. All those conceptions are fatally defective. They are refuted by facts or are empty. Is the economists' man any more valid? The evidence says yes, in the extensive range of events now being made explainable—a range that began to be explored in the past few decades. Success has led to its adoption by lawyers and legal scholars with remarkable advances.

Briefly, the conceptions on which economic theory rests are: (1) Man seeks a multitude of goods and goals, not just one. He seeks bread, clothing, play, music, honesty, popularity, health, reputation, status, friends, athletic ability, knowledge, contentment, beauty, etc., etc. Obvious enough! (2) He strives for more than he has of these—a situation the economist calls scarcity. Also obvious. (3) He balances, substitutes, trades off, degrees of attainment of each relative to others, depending on feasible tradeoffs. In other words, he substitutes among the quantities of each according to the opportunities available—not satiating himself in one before striving for any of the next. *Not* so obvious to many so-called social analysts.

Indeed it is often denied. But it is true that he chooses a little *less* of this goal or good if he can have enough *more* of some other. He is not an all or nothing seeker. There is no minimum about of any good that is an absolute necessity. He does not have a hierarchy of amounts of goals or goods. All are attained to some degree; he compromises depending on (a) his tastes for more of this relative to more of that and on (b) the feasible tradeoffs. We foresake some personal integrity if we get more of other things, like good looks, athletic strength, high grades or good recommendations. It is the principled person, the one track, one goal seeker—no matter how much of other goods are sacrificed or foresaken—who drives us to despair.

The *total* amount we can claim from other people or produce ourselves is defined by our "wealth." In some societies that "wealth" is primarily in the form of exchangeable private property authority to goods and to services. But it also includes persuasive personalities, persuasive forensic oratorical powers, persuasive power in whatever form it may be; good looks, physical strength or skill in applying physical force on other people, political talents, i.e., ability to acquire access to governmental coercive power to control people and acquire resources.

I remind you that no place did I mention that man was concerned *only* with his own situation, or that he was a pleasure seeker. In his possessive interest we assumed he has *some* personal self interest, not *only* that. Sometimes for some simple problems we can usefully assume he is totally interested in his wealth only with no concern at all for others, but that is *not* the conception of man that underlies economic analysis.

Private property (production and use) was the constraint on one's attained degrees of goals and goods. By private property authority, entitlements, or rights of person A to a good X, I mean: (1) Person A has reliable private authority as against other persons to select uses of the good X. (2) He may exchange that authority with some other person for authority over some other good at mutually agreeable terms of trade.

I use the word authority, not power, to suggest a socially recognized or sanctioned control status, not one exercised by sheer force nor a natural inviolate right. Other people may alter the authority. But until they do, person A can do what he wants with his property, and that includes trading it for some ownership in other goods at mutually acceptable terms. Don't worry about my not including any clause such as "subject to not injure any other person or his property." In the first place, he has no authority to affect some other person's property, or its use, by the use of his own goods. In the second place, his use of his private property does not mean that other people are left uninjured or no worse off. If he produces a better lecture and outcompetes me, I therefore have a lower income. He is injuring the exchangeable value of my services by altering other people's demand for my services. That is permissible under the private property authority. Under private property entitlements one has no authority over what others must continue to offer in exchange for goods or services. No one "owns" rights to other peoples' offers nor their custom. We each bear the uncertainty of the exchange, market value of goods and services that are "ours"—that we choose to own.

Any perceivable present or future changes in valuations by other people for my goods is capitalized into the present price. Let a manager in a firm be foolish; let him be smart—whatever he does will have future consequences and if foreseeable, the consequences will be imposed on him now. The exchange value of the goods will be quickly altered to reflect anticipated future consequences. The owner suffers the loss now. If he is an employee, the employer suffers the loss now and is motivated to take corrective monitoring action over the responsible agent.

Capitalization of all foreseen future consequences into the present market price for some good, with the change in present value being borne by that private property owner is an essence of capitalism. Capitalization into the present price is the crux of the connotation of the word capitalist in the term "capitalist system." It is not some presence of capital goods or equipment. It is not that capitalists (who are simply people who have private property entitlements) control the economic system. They (we) do of course, by making bids and offers in the market. Since we all are capitalists (at least we own our own labor) we all affect the economic system and its outcome.

But capitalization of the foreseeable future consequences of one's present acts is *not* what happens—certainly not in the same degree and quickness—to resources that are not marketable or not held as private property. Let a New York City (or Socialist) mayor tolerate a couple of years of deficits. What wealth does he or someone else own whose capitalized value of the anticipated benefits and costs are so *fully* borne? The present capitalized value of future taxes or future implied consequences are not so clearly capitalized into the present price of some private entitlements. If the city of New York were a private stock corporation with common shares, the common share prices would drop immediately upon irresponsible financial activities. The behavior of Lindsay, Beam, and other mayors is not explicable by their personalities or odd tastes for irresponsibility, but rather by their constraints and rewards. The mayor of Los Angeles pleads for federal aid to New York. Does the mayor of Los Angeles see that trouble for New York enhances Los Angeles as a living area? Does he see rising stock prices of Los Angeles Incorporated? No, but local landowners do. Would stockholders of General Motors worry about the value of their common shares if their president pleaded for aid for American Motors on the foolish grounds that if American Motors fails, General Motors would fail?

I am not saying no cities are private. Most cities *are* private. What do I mean by private cities? I mean places where people sleep, eat, work, and recreate. If you live in an apartment—you are living in a private city. Its streets (hallways, elevators) are policed by the owner. Its residents are monitored and admitted or evicted by an owner. I am not being silly nor unrealistic. You work in factories or stores with other people. So you occupy two cities, one for sleep and one for work. And you may even recreate in a third private city where streets and living quarters are privately owned and policed with power of expulsion. For example, apartments, trailer courts, hotels, shopping centers are cities—private cities.

If a private city is successful as a working productive place of factories, the Socialist city—being a government—will tax the private city, but it will not return its share of sales taxes to the private city for operation of its streets and policing. Irvine found out. Rancho Sante Fe learned that too. The extending of political controls over private apartments in the form of rent controls, tenant unions, and tenant favors can be interpreted as constraints imposed—or found helpful—by politicians desirous of reducing private competition to Socialist cities operated by politically adept people. The consequent use of publicly owned-politically administered housing is not surprising. If the private city gets too big and threatens to become a place where people sleep, eat, and do everything in one private city—the Socialist city will eliminate it by force—before individual preferences and open competition eliminate the Socialist city—much as the Socialist postal system will not, indeed cannot, survive with private competition. Why? Because, for one reason, capitalization of effects of better or worse use of resources now and in the foreseen future are more quickly, fully and perceptively thrust on responsible agents.

I digress momentarily because I am displaying my prejudice against political power—not politicians—but political power. Yet, we cannot survive without political power and controls, or so I believe. And even if we could, we would not want to.

Frequently, my friends complain about the movement toward more socialism. Are Socialists more effective in persuading the public about socialism versus capitalism? If more people understood capitalism, would the move toward socialism be slowed or reversed?

I do not know. But my belief is that the move toward socialism and a wide span of government power is not the result of a rising ideology that socialism or government political power is better than capitalism. Rather, it is the result of competition by people adept in political competition. Those adept at the political processes advocate, for self-serving reasons, more government control or expropriation of or brokerage power over private wealth. Those adept at economic market activity advocate more use of the capitalist system, again for self-serving reasons.

The Tartars did not plunder because they believed plunder was a better system. Instead, they were better at it. People excelling in one form of behavior will, of course, extoll it and denigrate other forms. To excell is to extoll. I am good at golf and terrible at bowling. So golf is a good game; bowling is a poor sport. Those who are better at being productive and in outcompeting others in offers of exchange will denigrate the politically or militarily adept. Those who are superior at military or physical coercion (or intellectual pursuits) will use it more and extoll it and condemn producers. Neither necessarily understands what the other does. Indeed we have no theory of Socialist or government behavior. Our theory and analysis and understanding of capitalism is so far advanced over that of socialism that if that were what counted, socialism would be long forgotten.

Some ideologists contend expanding political power is a result of increasing economic complexity and interdependence. I believe that is naive. Primitive, noncomplex, independent societies are militarized and run by government: Socialist states. No inherent sweep of increasing political power over society occurs in history. It has been strong from time immemorial—but fluctuating like a drunk meandering in a wide corridor. We should expect a society initiated as ours was, at the extreme of little political power (little by *any* historical standards) to regress toward greater political activity simply because people adept at that form of activity find a wide territory ready for exploitation.

Do not misunderstand. I am not saying that is bad. I too would delight in having political power. It just happens that I have not been successful—the best I can do is ride the politician's coattails on the state payroll as a high paid professor—not unlike the high Mayan priests.

History reveals a contest among people of differing relative talents and modes of competition. The politically adept, who may say they prefer capitalism and indeed do, will nevertheless seek greater government authority. Some businessmen who *believe* in socialism, nevertheless work effectively in the capitalist sphere. Need I name some very successful businessmen who espouse socialism? Businessmen who think they would be good politicians advocate greater political authority—out of self-serving interest rather than ideology. We who are good at political power acquisition will exploit and extoll it—without necessarily being for socialism *per se* nor advocating political power because we happen to believe political power is a better way to order society. Instead, it permits us to better achieve enhanced status.

Education about socialism or capitalism will not, so far as I can see, change the future much. To change the move toward socialism we must change the ability of various forms of competition to be successful. I know of no way to reduce the prospective enhancement from greater political power-seeking; but I do know of ways to reduce the rewards to market-oriented capitalist competition. Political power is dominant in being able to set the rules of the game to reduce the rewards to capitalist-type successful competitors. It is rule maker, umpire, and player: by taxes, regulations, controls, national planning and directives, law suits, etc. But I have been unable to discern equivalently powerful ways for economic power to reduce the rewards to competitors for political power! Each capitalist may buy off a politician, but that only enhances the rewards to political power.

As I read history the influence of political power is typically greater than that which characterized U.S. early history. We may be simply regressing toward the mean of civilizations and that is not a prospect I enjoy. To look to the presumed good old days of our past century or two and when people were far apart, when we were less interdependent, is to forget the power of Elizabeths, Williams, Henry, Charles, Ivan, Murad, Lo, and countless smaller heroes.

Some, but not necessarily most, of my colleagues in academia are searching for ways to reduce political power of those who succeed in acquiring it or to make it less rewarding. I have no principles to bring to bear. Nor have I found anyone who does.

But what I do have is economic theory and economic analysis, permitting some implications about the effects of legislation in a capitalist society. What the effects are in a socialist economy is less sure, because economic theory is best developed in understanding feasible responses and adjustments in a capitalist system as people adapt or adjust to legislation.

Economics views the law as a price list or menu. That is why economic theory will not let me say punishment is not a deterrent even if not a totally prohibitive deterrent. The price of a Rolls Royce is a deterrent, if not a complete deterrence. Some people pay the price. Economics does not say any activities are bad and hence ought to be stopped. It says *if* you want to restrain them, you can raise the price—the cost of doing that action. Still, behavior in a capitalistic system is, by definition, more difficult to control by political authority because private property gives us more extensive authority over our lifestyles. That is why, whatever the legislated law, it does not follow that its intent will be achieved. Legislated law is overpowered by economic laws of capitalism which often nullify or pervert intended effects. So political forces are more and more designed to reduce the scope of private property rights, a bleak future. To see to what extent legislated law can be thwarted by economic law requires some notion of the intent of the legislation or order. Some legislation enhances property entitlements and their exchange ability in the market. Here intent and results may go hand in hand. Sometimes the legislated law reflects an an attempt by the politically adept and powerful to achieve more wealth and power.

I will take cases of each.

Laws against theft are an obvious attempt to enhance private property authority and the operation of the economic laws of behavior under a capitalist system. Laws providing for adequate payment for eminent domain appropriate are other examples. So are laws unitizing oil fields to enhance private property rights over the underground pools. Extending national boundaries to 200 miles is another.

Establishing property authority to some resources may be too expensive, as it is alleged to be for some wild animals, running water, air, and electromagnetic radiation. This argument gives politicians enhanced power and authority on sound economic grounds—or does for some cases. But is it valid for all water, all space, all radiation? Radio and TV spectrum could economically be controlled by private property rights to broadcast bands over designated areas. But in the 1920s Hoover, the advocate of private property, declared them government property—when he was a politician. Our subsequent, disquieting history of commercial radio and TV has been a result of that analytical error, and what, I think was undesirable policy. The consequent use of radio and TV for political purposes here and abroad is well known.

Surely control of our air quality is necessary. No ways yet exist to subject it to adequately defined and simulated private property authority. But are the effects of legislation and administrative edicts requiring cleaner air understood? The legislation and edicts are designed to improve the quality of life. But whose life? And at what cost? Let me give you a sample of some analysis of this particular issue. It shakes up my well-meaning friends who futilely implore me to donate to cleaner air efforts, to reduce disease and make the atmosphere more pleasant.

If the air in the polluted portions of the Los Angeles basin were somehow magically and costlessly removed, who would benefit? The landowners. The increased value of living with cleaner air will be evidenced by larger immigration and bidding up of land prices, possibly until the advantages of the better air are all bid in the offerings for the land. Landowners benefit in being richer. Occupants paying higher rent get cleaner, healthier air but by paying higher rents have less to spend on food, clothing, and other goodies. The net effect may be to make nonlandowning residents no better off or possibly worse off, because for the better air they must pay more and sacrifice other goodies. Would you be willing to *pay* to have the smog reduced? How much for each incremental reduction? Would you be willing to pay to change your life-style without improving your overall situation? There is more. Indeed, some of us landowners in the smog freer area will lose wealth as our land values decline as people move back into the smog freed areas.

Still there is a positive benefit if the smog could be removed or reduced costlessly. The benefit is not necessarily to the residents in the area now freed of smog, but more to those who live elsewhere or who subsequently move to the Los Angeles area. They are the ones who will benefit, and along with the landowners may get all the benefit while the tenant residents are literally made worse off. Whether you should regard this as a perverse effect or an intended effect, I leave it to you.

The answer is not to abandon the effort to heed costs and values of environmental use. The moral is to more clearly perceive and understand effects of alternative methods before deciding what to do. Indeed, in some instances more pollution of the air and water will get more than it loses.

A second class of legislative laws change our life-styles away from those permitted by a capitalistic system. These also enhance the politician's welfare by increasing demand for their services, assigning more power to them and increasing the wealth. Safety requirements on cars, drug sale admissibility under the pure food and drug laws, blue sky laws, energy use edicts, security sale regulations, warranty and guaranty obligations, occupational safety and hazard laws, minimum wage laws and compulsory social security are examples. I believe the consequences of these laws are not comprehended by the public, which is not to say that their effects were not foreseen and desired by some people.

Consider safety requirements on cars. Sam Peltzman, in an extensive study, concluded that the result has been no reduction in number of deaths but more property damages. Seat belts, collapsible steering columns, dual braking systems, resistant windshields, and improved bumper requirements have induced us to drive faster and less carefully with more pedestrian deaths and property damage.

These results are neither surprising nor undesirable. If safety is increased per mile driven, people will sensibly drive more miles. They will trade off some of the greater safety for a less attentive, easier, more extensive driving. Since we cannot control all goals and objectives attained by a person, if we impose more of one on them (safety) they will trade *some* of it away for *more* of other good things (travel) to restore a balance of values—which they can do by adjusting their manner and extent of driving. An increase in the number of people killed and amount of damage done does not mean the law has been ineffective or undesirable. On the contrary, it has been extremely effective—in unintended and possibly desirable ways.

Safer airplanes in the past half century have induced more people to fly more; as a result we have more deaths from air travel than if flying were less safe. The greater number of deaths was worth the extra miles of travel and time released for other activities. In less offensive words, greater extent of travel and of time for other uses was substituted for some of the greater safety per mile of travel. Man compromises, as I said earlier. Give him a lot more of this and he will trade off *some* marginal amount now worth less to him than some extra of other things whose amounts had not increased. Restraining him from doing so requires totalitarian control of life-styles.

Take strict liability laws, wherein a manufacturer must bear the losses or gains of uncertain performance. If risk bearing is undesirable manufacturers will have to be recompensed to carry that risk. Without those laws consumers could, if they wish, buy at a lower monetary price and bear some of that risk themselves, or pay more (have less of other goods) for higher quality goods. Under *strict* liability laws that option is closed off; all consumers pay more for less risk. So how do they respond? By being less careful with the product once purchased, thereby raising costs of "required" standards. People who are more careful or less risk-averse will suffer. As an exercise, try to predict effects of a *compulsory uniform* insurance system for breakdowns of automobiles. What would that do to the purchase price of a car?

Occupational safety and hazardous occupation regulations make jobs safer—and more expensive. Employees get safer jobs and lower money salaries. Consumers will not pay more for a product produced under safer conditions. Employees *are* more willing to work in the safer jobs, so the wage will become lower in those jobs. If you think riskier jobs do not command higher wages than less risky jobs, try hiring some people for some job and then make the job more hazardous; watch their response. Occupational safety laws reduce money income to those in the jobs made safer and raise them in jobs that were formerly the safer jobs. People forced to have so much safety are willing to foresake some money income or other rewards in the competition for that safer job. Also other working conditions will deteriorate if too much of one form of payment—greater safety—is provided—as people substitute by tradeoffs, as we stated earlier. This is one reason low pay jobs have poor working conditions as well. That is *preferred* by workers. Those of us on low income have less and poorer quality of *everything*, not just some things. We *prefer* that balanced package.

Political legislation prevents banks from paying high competitive explicit interest on deposits, because, presumably, they would compete excessively, offer too much interest, increasing the risk of bankruptcy. The error in this is that they compete in others ways to enhance income, letting the combined risks reach the same level as formerly. The possibilities are plentiful. People substitute unless their entire life-styles are controlled. Forcibly increasing one facet of their life-style or one good in their entire basket of goods does not prevent their compensating for that in the other goods, if they can buy and sell other goods.

Subsidies of education to students permit parents to divert funds from their children's education to other activities. Thus the low tuition subsidy at the University of California is in large part a gift to their parents paid for by the general taxpayers—undoubtedly the intent of low tuition.

Minimum wage laws ostensibly devised to raise wages of the lowest wage earners do not. The number of employees an employer can profitably hire is reduced. Some lose jobs and must work at lower paying jobs exempt from the law, or if none is exempt, work as self-employed for which there is no minimum wage law or simply leave the work force, or substitute poorer working conditions for the higher wages. Even those who retain jobs are not better off in the long run. Some who would be displaced will offer to work (at the higher wages) with less nonmonetary pay stricter discipline on the job, poorer circumstances such as less time off, fewer coffee breaks, vacations, fringe benefits. Employees will offer to foresake some of those things for the higher required wage rate to retain existing jobs, rather than take the inferior alternative of working in jobs not covered by the law, or becoming self-unemployed or departing from the labor force into "leisure." Economic law is not suppressed by legislated law.

Another class of political activity which directly enhances welfare of the adept political competitors is inflation. It is a tax without legislation. Expenditures are financed by explicit taxes and by printing new money—usually by first selling newly printed bonds indirectly to the Federal Reserve in exchange for new printed money. That, *and that alone*, is the source of persisting inflation, the politician's best friend. After printing more money to pay for promised benefits to their constituency—and thus maintain their hold on office—they then legislate vain attempts to restrain the consequent inflation by imposing wage and price controls (or an incomes policy—the same thing under a different name). But again economic law is not suppressed by legislated law. Inflation is not and simply cannot be restrained by wage and price controls. Inflation reduces the purchasing power of money. Price controls reduce purchasing power of money by creating shortages and forcing greater resort to nonmoney, nonmarket means of competing for goods and resources. Money loses some of its value when money will not buy the amount you want to buy at those prices. So you resort to other means of competition to establish claims to goods and services—like standing in line, supporting political candidates, spending time in protests and political action, and side favors of a variety too great to list, and of course, of reduced quality of goods and services—until the quality is reduced to just what the limited money price is worth to the producer. Is that what the legislation intended, and what economic law brought about?

Then to benefit themselves, politicians gleefully insist they must do something about the shortage—as if it had not been caused by the price controls and the initial inflation in the first place—as we should all have learned (but did not) during the gasoline and oil fiasco in 1974 and from the current natural gas shortages caused by price controls. But instead politicians and the politically adept have sought self-serving advantage in the situation created by their legislation. So they decreed we could not use power for outdoor lighting. They knew better than any of us that my value of *some* outdoor light exceeded the value to me of *some* more indoor light. They knew. They did not like my preferences. So, to make up for the loss of an outdoor light, I lighted *two* on the inside to be as well off. Did not think I was antisocial. Had I not used the power, what basis is there for believing it would have been used elsewhere to greater value? None. Indeed, there is *assurance* it would have been used elsewhere with less value—where the user had to pay only the low legal price that understates its true use value.

More recently the same "Only the kings shall wear purple and silk stockings" political authority appears in the California public utility commission's directive that outdoor swimming pools shall not be heated with natural gas because they are luxuries. The gas will instead be diverted to industry, making, I presume, *more* beer and aluminum cans rather than for *some* arthritic swimmers. My contrast of beer with arthritic swimmers is of course unfair. I have no basis to conclude that some *more* beer is in any sense less desirable than some *extra* swimming by arthritic people. But your friendly politician will pretend indeed, assert, he can, if he is carefully tuned to vote-getting or political staying-power of gas-use allocations.

The Federal Energy Agency's mandates for smaller cars with more miles per gallon will result in less comfortable, less durable, less resalable cars, but then they know what we prefer. What sparked that drive for mandated kind of cars? The initial inflation with price controls jointly with environmental legislation. But economic law took over and the present results are evident. Did you realize that you, who must drive more-expensive-to-operate cars in California, in order to reduce pollution, are doing so for the benefit of special landowners and people who now live in areas not plagued with smog? Know it or not, it is true. Do you know that using less gasoline for cars permits more petroleum for plastics, perfumes, heating of vacant rooms? Getting back those rights from politicians will be done only by paying them to do so. That is how political activists confiscate wealth.

Collective Bargaining in the Public Sector

Harry H. Wellington

Government has been a growth industry, and in our states and municipalities its growth has been particularly marked. The decade ending in 1974 saw civilian federal employment increase 15 percent; those same years witnessed state and municipal employment increase four times as fast. Nearly twelve million men and women now look to our states and cities for their livelihood. And some 9.2 million are full-time employees.

This growing municipal work force has produced an expanded municipal bureaucracy. And bureaucracy has brought with it increasing isolation and alienation for the individual worker. Long chains of command depersonalize the employment relationship. They contribute mightily to the frustration and powerlessness felt by many who inhabit bureaucracy's lower echelons. If the individual worker is to share in the governance of his employment relation, it must be through the device of representation. It should come as no surpirse, then, that the rapid growth in public employment has been attended by an even more striking growth in public employee unionism. Between 1972 and 1975, the number of full-time state and local government employees in labor organizations rose from 41 to 51 percent. And this at a time when the percentage of union members in the total work force has remained level, or declined.

There are those who decry the advent of the public employee union as an evil in itself, the beginning of the end, the first step along the slippery slope. Their position is, I would submit, extreme. Collective bargaining is the preferred method of ordering private labor relations in our country. Imperfect though it is, collective bargaining remains the best available means of facilitating industrial peace and enhancing industrial democracy. There is reason to believe that, in the long run, collective bargaining will contribute to the realization of these goals in the public sector. What should give us pause is not free collective bargaining, but excessive union power.

The problem confronted by those who seek to transplant collective bargaining from the private to the public sector is the problem of accommodating bargaining to a dramatically different environment. The danger is not that collective bargaining will fail to thrive: it has thrived. The danger is that it will badly distort the political process and contribute to the fiscal difficulties of the cities. Some of this has already happened. It is bound to get worse before it gets better. It will never get better unless we understand the nature of the problem.

The new sophistication in labor relations holds that the wage claims and other demands of organized public employees can be handled exactly as they are handled in private industry. Pressure has been mounted, furthermore, to persuade the public that, in the absence of a genuine emergency, there is no justification for a legal ban on strikes by municipal workers. Arguing from these propositions, union spokesmen call for a simple translation of collective bargaining practices into the public sector. The validity of their position depends upon the validity of their underlying premise, namely that a city, as employer, is no different from a private corporation, as employer. Government, it is insisted, is "just another industry."

On its face, this seems a dubious premise, indeed. The functions performed by city government are not chosen randomly, or by lot. These functions are generally undertaken precisely because they have unique characteristics which distinguish them from those typically performed privately. Among those characteristics is the real, and often remarked, fact that the disruption of public services is more apt to endanger the health, and safety, of a municipality's citizenry than the disruption of operations privately performed.

The distinctions between government and industry, however, involve more than the comparative essentiality of the services they render. Fundamental economic and political differences distinguish public from private business, and these differences enable municipal unions to wield excessive power.

The economic distinctions between the public and private sectors may be illustrated by comparing two models, neither of which is thoroughgoing nor detailed. I fear there will be too little rigor here. The models, however, will serve, at least, to highlight the more salient features of each sector's physiognomy.

Although the private sector is, of course, extraordinarily diverse, the paradigm is an industry that produces a product which is not particularly essential to those who buy it, and for which dissimilar products can readily be substituted. Within the market, or markets, for this product, most (but not all) of the producers bargain with a union representing their employees, and this union is generally the same throughout the industry. In most institutions, when the union demands an increase in wages greater than would be justified by an increase in productivity, one must expect an increase in the price of the product if the union's demand is met. A price rise of this product relative to others will generally lead to a decrease in the number of units of the product sold. In some oligopolistic situations, of course, the firm may be able to raise prices after a wage increase without suffering a significant drop in sales. But one does not want to exaggerate the number of situations in which this occurs.

In the paradigmatic case, the decrease in sales will mandate a cutback in employment. In general, then, the union is faced with some sort of rough trade-off between, on the one hand, larger benefits for some employees and unemployment for others, and on the other hand, smaller benefits and more employment. Because unions are political organizations, with a legal duty to represent all employees fairly, and with a treasury bolstered by per capita dues, there is pressure on the union to avoid the road which leads to fewer jobs.

The extent of the restraints which the market thus imposes on collective bargaining settlements will vary as union organization of the industry becomes more or less complete. To the extent that nonunion firms remain within the product market, restraints upon union demands will be quite severe, since consumers will be able to purchase identical products from nonunion and, presumably, less expensive sources. On the other hand, as union organization of competitors within the product market nears completion, the restraints will relax. The principal barrier to union bargaining goals will then be the capacity of consumers to react to a price change by turning to dissimilar, but nevertheless substitutable, products.

The impact of market restraints upon union demands is conditioned by two additional factors. First, where the demand for an industry's product is relatively inelastic, and where all the firms in a product market are organized, the union need fear less the employment/benefit trade-off, for the employer is less concerned about raising prices in response to increased costs. By hypothesis, a price rise affects unit sales of such an employer only minimally. Second, in an expanding industry, wage settlements that exceed increases in productivity may not reduce union employment. They will, instead, retard expansion, so that the employment effect will be experienced, not by workers who belong to the union, but by those who do not. This means that, in the short run, the politics of the employment/benefit trade-off will not constrict the union in its bargaining demands.

In both of these cases, however, at least two restraints continue to operate. One is the employer's increased incentive to substitute machines (capital) for labor, a factor present in the paradigm and all other cases as well. The other restraint stems from the fact that large sections of the nation are unorganized and highly resistant to union organization. Accordingly, capital will seek nonunion labor, and the market will again discipline the organized sector.

What all this means is that, in private industry, the demands which the union can afford to make of an employer are delimited by powerful market forces. These forces are visible to both labor and management; they are visible, in fact, to anyone who can see the forest for the trees.

The paradigm in the public sector is a municipality with an elected mayor and an elected city council. Decisions that cost the city money will generally be paid for from taxes, and tax revenue may be available from several layers of government: federal, state, and local. Formal allocation of money for particular uses is made through the city's budget, which may have within it considerable room for adjustment. A union, consequently, will bargain hard for as large a share of the budget as it thinks it possibly can obtain, and even try to force a tax increase if it deems that feasible.

While market-imposed unemployment is an important restraint on unions in the private sector, the trade-off between benefits and employment is much less certain in the public sector. Government does not generally sell a product, the demand for which is closely related to price. There rarely exist close substitutes for the products and services provided by government, and the demand for these products and services is relatively inelastic. Such market conditions are highly favorable to unions in the private sector. They permit the acquisition of benefits without the penalty of unemployment, subject to the restraint of nonunion competitors, actual or potential. But no such restraint limits the demands of public employee unions. Because much—but not all—government activity is, and must be, a monopoly, product competition, nonunion or otherwise, does not exert nearly so insistent a downward pressure on prices and wages. Nor will the existence of a pool of labor, ready to work for a wage below the union scale, attract new capital and create a new, competitively less expensive, governmental enterprise—a new Jerusalem, or even a new San Diego.

The fear of unemployment, however, might be thought to restrain public employee demands in one of two ways. If the cost of labor increases, a city, arguably, will reduce the quality of the services it furnishes, by reducing employment; alternatively, it will seek, like a private employer, to replace labor with machines. While the feasibility of either response is not open to question, it is the case that the ability of city government to reduce its services is limited both by union pressure and by the pressure of other affected interest groups in the community. Until a city confronts the prospect of bankruptcy, political considerations tend to deter any serious reduction in union employment. If there are to be reductions, they are apt to occur in areas where union members do not work. The poor, who need government most, are the ones who suffer first.

The strategy of replacing labor with machines encounters problems as well. The absence of a profit motive is one, a political concern for unemployment is another. Absent a New York-type crisis, the public employer that decides it must limit employment will find that the politically easiest decision is to restrict new hirings rather than to lay off current workers.

A comparison of these two models, then, suggests that unions in the public sector operate under decidedly more favorable circumstances than their counterparts in private industry. The primary reason is that the close relationship between increased economic benefits and unemployment (which often acts as a strong deterrent to unions in the private sector) often is only a weak deterrent in the public.

But what about the argument that the taxpayer is, in some sense, the public sector's functional equivalent of the consumer. If taxes become too high, in other words, the taxpayer can move to another community. Surely there is a point at which a tax increase will cause so many taxpayers to move that it will decrease total revenue. And at that point, the market can be said to discipline or restrain the union and public employer in the same way, and for the same reasons, that the market disciplines unions in the private sector. Moreover, does not the analogy to the private sector suggest that it is legitimate, in an economic sense, for unions to push government to a point just short of the exit point?

153

Two questions are involved here. The first is whether the analogy holds at all, and the answer, I would suggest, is that it holds only to a limited extent. The reason is the rather obvious one, that it is much easier for a consumer to substitute products, than for a taxpayer to substitute communities. The second question is whether the union's conduct in pushing the government almost to the exit point is legitimate. This question, I believe, must be judged not by economic, but by political criteria.

In the first place, there is no theoretical reason to suppose that it is desirable for government to liquidate its taxing power. In the private area, profit maximization is a complex concept, but its approximation is generally both a legal requirement and a socially useful means of allocating resources. The liquidation of taxing power seems neither imperative nor useful.

Second, the tax structure is exceedingly complex, and different kinds of taxes—property, sales, income—fall differently upon a given population. In many cases, the taxing authority of a particular governmental entity may be limited: many municipalities, for example, lack the power to impose an income tax. What is necessarily involved, then, is principally the redistribution of income by government, as opposed to the allocation of resources. Questions of income redistribution are essentially political questions—very important political questions. And I for one hate to see them resolved at the bargaining table. The poor, who need government most, have no seat at that table.

While these economic factors often tend to make the bargaining position of municipal unions strong, union strength derives mainly from political considerations. Municipal strikes are political events because the employer is the government. When a private corporation faces the prospect of a strike, its directors can plan their campaign with cold economic realities as their principal guide. Management can estimate the cost of a strike, and the cost of the union demands. The costs will be compared; the lesser evil chosen. Since private corporations are motivated largely by profit, their reaction will be conditioned, largely, by economics.

The mayor of a city cannot be so single-minded in his response. His office is a political office, and his response is apt to be that of a political man. By settling with the municipal union, the mayor will earn the plaudits of labor at large, and labor, as every elected official knows, is a potent ally. The costs of a wage settlement to a private corporation will show up, at once, in its balance sheets; its directors will be held accountable for those costs at once by its shareholders. The costs of a wage settlement to a municipal government, however, often do not become a burden until the next mayor has taken office. Consider as an example of these "deferred burdens" the pension plans which New York City's municipal workers have won in the past. The pension payments, of course, did not fall due until some years after the agreements were concluded. Today their weight seems insupportable.

Moreover, when pay increases cannot be deferred, they can frequently be concealed: municipal budgets are labyrinths, and the real costs, to say the least, can be difficult to trace.

Most of all, of course, the people want labor peace. Stockholders will be content that their corporation endured a strike if they believe that a strike makes economic sense. The citizens of our cities are not likely to be so sanguine. Precisely because the services rendered by city unions are so vital, citizens will clamor the louder for their reinstatement. And their cries will have force. Discomforted by interruptions of vital city services, citizens may resent unions, but they will blame their mayor. These citizens have the power to punish at the polls any mayor who is too stubborn in his defense of fiscal responsibility. No one is more conscious of this power than the man in City Hall.

If this intense political pressure induces the mayor to settle on unfavorable terms, what of the cost? To some extent, it may be concealed, as we have seen, or passed on, for the present. Until a city reaches the point of bankruptcy—as in the position of New York today—the received political understanding is that citizens are more incensed by garbage piled on their front stoop than by the prospect of a future tax increase or yet another addition to the municipal debt.

These economic and political facts mean that, all too often, the municipal union's wish is its command. And such concentration of power not only injures our cities, it is bad as well for our democratic process.

Viewed from City Hall, the unions should be one group among many competing in the political arena for the attention, and favors, of municipal government. Not infrequently this competition is over issues upon which the unions, and other groups of citizens, disagree. The policemen's position regarding a civilian review board, for example, may pit them against citizens concerned about the accountability of police officers. The teachers' position regarding classroom size, discipline, or curriculum may pit them against parent groups whose priorities are different. If the competition were confined to the usual political arena, the protagonists would have access to like weapons: propaganda, persuasion, and the vote.

Increasingly, however, the battle is being transferred to the bargaining table. There, the balance of power is not so well preserved. There, the union's weapons are indeed coercive; for their arsenal is augmented by the strike, and the threat of a strike. Questions of school curricula, or review boards, are preeminently questions of public policy; questions which traditionally have been resolved by the people's elected representatives. When such questions are transferred to the bargaining table, there is the likelihood that many interested groups will find no chairs provided for them. And even if they are dealt in, the union's predominant position at the table may enable it to dictate public policy. For at the appropriate time, the union may play its trump card—the strike. This imbalance of power can leave no one happy who is concerned about the vigor of our democratic form of government. And remember—it is the poor, who need government most, who are most apt to be hurt the most.

The problem then is this: because government is not "just another industry," collective bargaining should not be transplanted from the private sector to the public without alteration. I now propose to trace the various phases of private collective bargaining, and to suggest how it should be altered.

A first step in the collective bargaining process is to define the parties who shall bargain. To define the employer in the private sector is a task of little difficulty. The pyramidic structure of the private corporation ensures that the corporation will present a single, unified, and coherent position against the union. In the public sector, the task of definition is not so simple. Who is the public employer? The mayor's office, which is responsible for hiring and firing? The legislature, with its power of the purse? An independent board with budgetary powers? The civil service commission, which oversees hiring procedures? The consequences of fragmented authority were dramatically illustrated some years ago in Hartford, Connecticut, when the organized firefighters played off the city council against the city manager to win a 34 percent wage increase. The consequences of fragmented authority were again illustrated, last year, in San Francisco. The solution lies in local ordinances which carefully define the governmental employer, and restrict or eliminate the role of each governmental body, save one. The locus of responsibility must be clear.

Once it has been determined who shall bargain, it must be determined what shall be bargained about. Increasingly, public employers are encountering union demands to extend the scope of bargaining beyond the traditional subjects of wages, hours, and fringe benefits. Increasingly, unions are seeking to bargain about political questions, and disputes over these questions often hold the seeds of racial and ethnic strife. Accordingly, the unions' attempt to extend the scope of bargaining should be confined by law.

Of course, the crucial moment for municipal governments comes when the collective process breaks down, and the threat of a strike becomes real. Three questions might be asked: First, whether strikes are to be permitted at all; second, what alternatives can be developed to replace strikes; and finally, what steps can be taken to reduce the impact of strikes when they do occur.

Public employees argue that a total and effective ban on strikes would make their union a paper tiger: the public employer would become intransigent, and collective bargaining would become a euphemism for "collective begging." Whatever may be said of this argument—and it is not invulnerable to attack—the attitudes and convictions of public employees cannot be put aside. While most states ban strikes by government workers, no ban can be effective—and few have been—if the employees themselves believe they are being treated unfairly.

For this reason, I would suggest that only where a strike will create an immediate danger to public health and safety should the strike weapon be outlawed. Although the line separating true emergencies from severe inconveniences is not always easy to discern, common sense provides the best guide. Police and fire services cannot be wholly disrupted for any length of time without endangering public safety. On the other hand, the disruption of utility services may not create an emergency for some time, and even hospitals can maintain partial services.

Where the strike weapon is outlawed, alternative post-impasse procedures must be developed. Public employee laws in many states provide for fact-finding with recommendations, offered by a tribunal whose task it is to work out an agreement acceptable to union, executive, and legislature. Studies indicate that these recommendations have frequently succeeded in forming the basis for a negotiated settlement—a settlement that the parties had been unable, on their own, to reach.

In contrast to this purely advisory method is compulsory and binding arbitration. It aims to impose a final settlement under threat of sanctions. The advantage of compulsory arbitration lies in its comparative certainty: in most instances, it can prevent an illegal strike by persuading public employees to accept an award they find less than ideal. The primary disadvantage of compulsory arbitration is that the union may get more than it should. And this, I take it, is the reason why so many government officials oppose arbitration. Arbitration, moreover, may convert the collective bargaining which precedes it into a masquerade. Collective bargaining is the preferred mode of reaching labor-management agreements; arbitration is called in only when bargaining has stalled. However, if either the public employer or the union believes that it will get a better deal from an arbitrator than it will get from a negotiated settlement, that party will take unreasonable positions during bargaining, thus guaranteeing an impasse and arbitration.

This danger can be reduced substantially by a procedure known as "last offer" arbitration. In this procedure, the arbitrator's choice is limited to the final position of either the employer or the union. With this refinement, neither party can afford to persist in unreasonable demands: if its stubbornness produces impasse, it can be sure its opponent's offer will be accepted.

Fact-finding and compulsory arbitration represent alternatives to strikes, where strikes, because of the emergencies they would create, have been banned. Strikes may unfortunately occur despite the ban, and when they do, the role of sanctions becomes paramount. The penalties must be more than hortatory, but within the community's sense of fairness. Within these bounds, each locality must experiment and find its own way.

In cases where no emergency is involved, however, the strike, should it occur, must be tolerated, and mechanisms developed to diminish the severity of its impact. A city with a potential for municipal labor trouble can reduce its vulnerability by planning carefully for contingencies. Prepared emergency traffic patterns and parking facilities can offset some of the consequences of a transit strike; contingency plans for the use of neighboring hospitals may avoid disaster in a hospital strike. Another approach meriting serious consideration is the partial operation of struck facilities: policemen can keep order without giving out parking tickets; welfare checks can be processed while other welfare services cease; garbage can be collected, but less often. The goals of any partial operation scheme are to ensure the performance of essential functions, and to avoid severe inconvenience, while maintaining pressure on both sides to settle. This gives the union the advantage of some continuing income for its members, and of a strike which, though partial, is legal.

These changes in municipal strategy may render strikes less damaging to cities; other changes in municipal organization may render them less attractive to unions. Where nonemergency strikes are permitted, strategies can be invented to deter their use. One approach is a referendum in which registered voters must approve settlements which have been reached *after* a strike has been called. Such a referendum would ask voters to approve any tax increases or new bond issues which the settlement has necessitated. This heightens the visibility of the cost, and makes explicit how that cost must be borne. Union leaders, furthermore, are encouraged to reach an accord with the city, since by calling a strike they risk the unknowns of a referendum. Most valuable, perhaps, in the referendum strategy is that it would reduce the political pressure of a strike on a mayor. As things stand now, the mayor faces the dilemma of choosing between voters enraged by strikes, and voters enraged by taxes. The referendum would enable him to pass this, essentially political, question on to the voters themselves. Once an impasse has been reached and a strike called, the issue would be in the electorate's hands: the mayor, having surrendered the power to make a final settlement, could assume a less pressured, and more neutral, stance.

The changes in the collective bargaining structure which I have suggested so far are statutory, or administrative, in nature. These changes may succeed in reducing the inconvenience caused to city dwellers by public employees' strikes. The ultimate judge of inconvenience, however, must be the people themselves, and for this reason I suggest that the essential change has yet to be mentioned, and that is a change in public opinion.

I have stressed earlier that the most valuable asset of the municipal union is public exasperation. This exasperation exerts powerful political pressures upon mayors to settle strikes swiftly, without sufficient attention to future costs. What is needed is to bring the message to the people: labor peace is sometimes a luxury that a city cannot afford. Our citizens must learn that a city official who gives in easily is both a poor official and a poor politician. In the long run, the best hope for successful municipal labor relations is an informed and enlightened public opinion. What we require is a determined and principled public spirit, which will shout to a wavering city official, "Get tough, or get out." The people must tell their mayor that he can bargain hard and determinedly with organized labor. The people must tell their city official that he will reap political rewards if he takes a fair, firm line. The people must tell their officials that it will be political suicide for them to give away their future.

New York indicates just how close the future is. I have seen it. It does not work.

Regulating the Use of Land

Bernard H. Siegan

In the preceding chapters, a number of the authors have attempted to compare regulated and nonregulated markets. It is not a simple undertaking. One reason is that most of the market they were concerned with was regulated, and there was little left for purposes of comparison. Professor George Stigler complained about this situation in an article he wrote in 1966 about the antitrust laws for the *Journal of Law and Economics.*[1] He said that a Congress which had good will toward scholars would have exempted from the Sherman Act a random sample of industries. He also thought a world more favorable to scholars would have had many United States, some of which did not have antitrust laws.

Fortunately there is one area where a great deal of evidence exists with which to compare the regulated and nonregulated market. I refer to the use of land in this nation, most but not all of which is locally regulated. The regulation is known as zoning. Over 95 percent of municipalities with populations of five thousand or more have adopted zoning ordinances. There are, however, significant areas that are not zoned. Many counties in Florida, Texas, Missouri, Illinois, Iowa, and Indiana have never adopted zoning ordinances. Augusta, the capital of Maine, is not zoned. Six cities in Texas of substantial size have not passed zoning ordinances and those are cities that I shall be concerned with in this chapter. They include: Baytown, population 45,000; Victoria, population 40,000; Laredo, population 70,000; Wichita Falls and Pasadena, each having a population of 100,000; and of course Houston. Houston is now the nation's fifth largest city with a population of 1.4 million and is one of the most rapidly growing. On two occasions, in 1948 and 1962, voters of that city rejected proposed zoning ordinances, and as a result, one has never been adopted. In a municipality that has adopted zoning, the local legislature, that is, the city council, board of supervisors or equivalent, regulates the use of land within its boundaries. The legislators are advised by lay planners (planning commissions) and professional planners (planning departments) but the final authority usually rests with them. No such process exists in the nonzoned cities.

Although Houston does not have a zoning ordinance, it has land use controls, but they are primarily economic. Specifically, the use and development of land and property in that city are controlled in three different ways: First, by the normal economic forces of the marketplace. Second, through private legal agreements primarily restrictive covenants. Third, through a relatively limited number of land use regulations adopted by the city. Houston also controls indirectly and to a limited extent building and development through subdivision, building, pollution, traffic, and minimum housing regulations that do not appear to differ appreciably from those of other cities in that region of the country. But the contrast with zoning is clear: Unless the property is subject to an enforceable restrictive covenant, the city exercises minimal authority over the use of that property, as I shall subsequently describe.

Consider the first control that I have referred to, the ordinary controls of the marketplace. You will find that in Houston most commercial uses locate on major thoroughfares and not residential streets. An example is provided by the gas station.

Oil companies in Houston have this opportunity. They can buy for, say, $75,000 or $100,000, a lot on a major thoroughfare for the construction of a gas station. The companies have the alternative of purchasing the same sized lot on a residential street a short distance away and paying only $5,000 or $10,000 for it. They frequently can save more than $50,000 to $75,000 by building on an interior lot instead of on a major thoroughfare. Do they? Never. The economic imperatives of that industry require gas stations to locate only on major thoroughfares. That is where the traffic is and where accessibility is the best. Stations on inside streets will not remain very long in business. A major thoroughfare is the only street or road on which it is profitable to build them. When I read zoning literature that says, if not for us zoners, the gas stations would be on residential streets next to mansions, I think one has to take that with more than a grain of salt, because it is simply not accurate. The same location controls hold for most commercial uses such as McDonalds, Jack-in-the-Box, major shopping centers, minor shopping centers. They also want to go where traffic is. There are small commercial uses that will locate on inside streets and I shall discuss these subsequently. For the moment, let me suggest that these other uses are likely to be compatible with the area in which they locate.

There is likewise a great tendency for industrial uses to group and concentrate separately from residential. A comparison of maps showing the location of industrial uses in the metropolitan area of Houston with comparable maps of Los Angeles or Dallas, cities with which Houston is often compared, suggests that the proliferation of industry in the Houston area probably is no greater than in these other metropolitan areas, although the large territories involved and differing definitions of industry make measurement very difficult.

It is generally too costly in terms of land prices and potential residential hostility for heavy industry to locate near new residential subdivisions. The plants and factories in the Houston area which are contiguous to and were erected subsequent to homes are usually "light" rather than "heavy" in character. In most instances their existence appears to pose no more, and possibly less peril to residential values and tastes than would be the case if the same property has been developed for an alternative use such as apartments.

Close examination of the land use maps of Baytown, Pasadena, Laredo, and Wichita Falls show that market processes have not been completely effective in avoiding the proliferation of industrial uses. When compared, however, to land use maps of Texas cities long zoned, it is difficult to detect a difference. The zoned cities I refer to are: Amarillo, population 130,000, zoned since 1931; Lubbock, population 150,000, zoned in 1941; and Abilene, population 90,000, zoned in 1946. Because land use maps are difficult to obtain, I do not know if these zoned cities are representative. At the very least, however, these land use maps do create doubt as to whether zoning is more protective than nonzoning against the proliferation of industry.

The major land use control employed in Houston is popularly known as "deed restrictions" or "restrictive covenants." They are most often used to exclude buildings other than homes from single family areas. They are also used by developers of industrial parks and townhouse projects. When a developer subdivides acreage into, say, three hundred or four hundred lots for houses, he imposes a legal restriction on each one limiting its use solely for a single family residence. The developer imposes these restrictions because of market demands for assurance as to the use of neighboring property. It is done because of the self-interest of the person imposing that restriction and works to the advantage of the entire community. The restrictions will contain provisions in accordance with market conditions—what consumers want who might be attracted to buy homes in that area. Restrictive covenants are as a general matter enforcible unless they violate public policy such as controlling occupancy on the basis of race.

The bulk of the covenants imposed in Houston subsequent to World War II offer a reasonably practical solution to the conflicting desires of allowing for change and yet maintaining stability. They contain an automatic extension provision which provides that after an initial duration period of, say, twenty-five to thirty years, there will be an unlimited number of ten or more year automatic extension periods. Agreement on the part of 51 percent of the owners (usually one vote per lot or on the basis of frontage) may cancel or amend the covenants before the end of the initial period or before the end of any subsequent ten year period. Under this provision, a majority of homeowners can control the destiny of their subdivision.

In the wealthiest areas, restrictive covenants usually control aesthetics, maintenance, and architecture to provide an exclusivity that the most restrictive zoning code could not legally achieve; for they have virtually forbidden any construction that might injure values. Restrictive covenants have also served well the interests of the less well-to-do. The covenants affecting less wealthy subdivisions are usually not as restrictive or often not as strictly enforced as those for the higher incomes, and this is a market response to the life-style of these income groups. There is consequently greater variety among subdivisions than would be found under the aegis of a monolithic zoning ordinance.

The restraints operative under the covenants generally imposed in Houston differ in at least four respects from those of zoning. First, the terms and provisions of the covenants, including the size of lots (provided the city's minimum has been met) are established by the developer, possibly in conjunction with a lender or with the FHA or VA if either of these agencies is involved. The basic objective is to cater to consumer demand and enhance sales. In subdivisions where covenants have expired, homeowners will decide the contents if new ones are to be imposed. Second, the rights of homeowners are generally limited by the boundary lines of their subdivision. Unlike zoning, homeowners have little influence over the use of land beyond the perimeters of their subdivision. Third, covenants cover primarily land improved with buildings, and only a small fraction of vacant land is subject to them, largely the unsold portions of platted subdivisions. Landowners are ordinarily reluctant to restrict their land unless it is programmed for development since different market demands may arise in the future which might bring a better return. Possibly no more than 10 to 15 percent of vacant land in Houston is subject to restrictive covenants whereas 100 percent would be controlled by zoning. This permits much greater flexibility in land use outside of the restricted areas. Finally, because the city enforces them and draftsmanship has improved over the years, it is likely that covenants will control usage for every lot covered throughout at least the initial period. This probably allows for greater reliance by homeowners and lenders as to the future since "rezoning" will not occur almost regardless of changes in conditions and public pressures.

There are regulations in Houston that do control land use and development, but compared to even the most minimal zoning ordinance, they are relatively few. These regulations include a minimum size requirement of 5,000 square feet for a lot adjoining utilities, and 7,000 square feet for one without utilities. The city has an off-street parking ordinance for residential construction, some controls over townhouses for individual ownership and over trailers and trailer parks. Houston enforces the deed restrictions and forbids development contrary to them. Otherwise there are no significant controls over the use of property. So if you go to Houston and look at a vacant lot not subject to a covenant, be aware that you can build on it a glue factory, a mansion, a gas station, and most anything else you can think of. But I doubt if you will build anything unless economic forces favor that decision.

Let me discuss some of the reasons why I think Houston has greatly benefited from the absence of zoning. For one, rents are lower in Houston than they would be if zoning were in existence. The best evidence we have to support this conclusion comes from comparing Houston with Dallas. The latter is within 250 miles and adopted zoning in the early 1930s. The economic statistics of the two cities are quite parallel. It costs about the same to live in one as it does in the other and about the same to build. Median and mean incomes are similar. There is one major exception, however, in the economic statistics between the two cities: the cost of rent. U.S. Bureau of Labor Statistics figures show that rents were an average of over 15 percent lower in the Houston SMSA than in the

Dallas SMSA for the period 1966 through 1974, the years for which such statistics were available.[2]

There are four explanations for this substantial difference in rents. First, is the matter of supply and demand. A larger amount of land is "zoned" in Houston for apartments because virtually all of the land except that restricted by covenant is available for this purpose. This means that the land cost for apartments is cheaper in Houston than it is in Dallas and this should be reflected in rents. Second, as a result of lesser land costs, more land will be purchased in Houston than Dallas for apartment production. Third, no controls on multi-family density exist in Houston, thereby permitting a greater number of units in a single project. There should be cost reductions in buying greater quantities. Labor costs may also be reduced. Fourth is the operation of the zoning process. Most large multifamily developments in recent years have required rezoning or other special dispensations. The authorities usually are reluctant to permit construction of projects with which they are not comfortable and this leads to requirements for more expensive exteriors, landscaping, street improvements, and possibly even interiors. The developer who proposes a minimal development will have little difficulty in erecting his project in Houston, whereas it may not be possible to obtain permission to construct a similar one in Dallas without costly additions.

This raises the question of government making business and professional decisions that are ordinarily left to the marketplace. When you think about going to see a doctor or lawyer or hiring a carpenter, the least you want to do is hire someone who has competence, experience, and knowledge in the field. This should be the objective in the use and development of land. But under zoning it is not. The powers are being given to people who either are not experienced or knowledgeable or have only textbook information. I refer, of course, to planners and politicians. That seems to me very wrong; we should not let people of limited knowledge make judgments that can be made better by those trained and highly motivated to perform the tasks.

Measured in overall effect, the power local legislators have over land use is probably the most important one they possess. Their decisions on the real estate market have affected substantial portions of the population. Biographical sketches of local legislators are not likely to inspire confidence that they as a group have the competence or motivation for such responsibility. While there probably are notable exceptions, the office of council-person, supervisor, or trustee, or member of a zoning board is not likely to attract many individuals with any special abilities or technical competence in the field of land use regulation. Probably the reverse is more often the case, with the result that these powers are vested in many who could not possibly be hired for this task by private industry. Yet they are exercising powers far greater than those exercised by any builder or developer. Even when they have some expertise, it may have to be subordinate to the commitments they must make to obtain and hold public office.

This is a day when we are very mindful of conservation. We all want to save land; we want to save resources. One of the other benefits of the Houston system is its conservation of the land. Why is that? Because when builders create lots they are guided by market forces. They will size their lots in accordance with demands of the market, and consumers will get about what they want whether that be five acres or a fifth of an acre.

How does that compare with the zoning process? Politicians tend to be concerned with consumer demands only when these translate into political pressures. In many instances, potential purchasers do not live in the community where the houses are being built. The existing residents usually want less people in the community and achieve this by seeking bigger lots. They have joined with environmentalists who regularly demand more open space. Together these groups have brought much pressure for less density and bigger lots. Once you could build in certain places, one unit to the half acre, now it is one unit to the acre; soon perhaps it will be one unit to two acres. That means the use of more land for urban purposes and that, in turn, reduces the amount of land available for farming, grazing, mining, and other purposes.

Land is a precious resource and it should be used with great consideration. Because of the pressures I have referred to, the tendency is to waste greater quantities of land for urban development; more and more land is being used for less and less housing. Major exceptions are the areas that do not have zoning. In Houston, land will not be used to require people to purchase land they do not want just because somebody in City Hall thought that was a better idea or was converted to that belief by the innumerable pressures to which politicians are subjected.

Zoning causes urban sprawl in another respect. Urban sprawl usually denotes a spreading or scattering of development. It is characterized by bypassed tracts of land, so-called "leap-frogging," and low density development. A certain amount of urban sprawl is an inevitable consequence of urbanization and will occur under any system of private or even public ownership since vacant land next to existing development may not be appropriate or desirable for a certain use at a particular time.

The adjoining land may no longer be in demand for housing or other purposes. It may be too expensive or too big or small; sewer and water facilities may be inadequate. It may not be for sale, be subject to title and legal problems and possibly have unusual topographical or soil conditions. (And, of course, the zoning may be entirely wrong for a proposed use.)

Normal market conditions, however, will tend to minimize the amount of sprawl. First, it is ordinarily more economically advantageous to builders and developers to build consecutively rather than to leap-frog. This is borne out by the fact that land located next to existing development tends to be more expensive than land farther away. This occurs chiefly because the demand for land abutting development is greater, causing its price to be higher.

Second, as I have indicated, developers will conserve on the size of vacant lots to accommodate consumers. Likewise, in the instance of multiple family dwellings, there are equally strong economic pressures to build for substantial density. Again, this practice uses up less land and makes possible a lower land cost per unit. And, as I have indicated, greater densities will tend to reduce the cost of producing an individual unit. Competition will, however, deter many builders from achieving maximum densities, since there can never be a saving if no one is willing to buy.

Nor should sprawl always be regarded as undesirable. Because close-in land can be very expensive, it may not be possible to develop lower cost housing projects except by leap-frogging. Developers of such projects must evaluate the trade-offs involved in distance, land cost, and demand. When localities attempt to prevent this kind of bypassing, they deny the opportunity for housing which requires less costly land. Distance, however, is a strong restraint upon developers. Transportation to work and shopping from more remote areas is costly and time consuming and would necessarily be a factor in the decision to buy or rent. Schools, shopping centers, churches, and cultural institutions are not likely to be as convenient or accessible.

Economics, consequently, is a strong deterrent to sprawl and will operate to balance its positive and negative effects. No such limitation exists in the political sphere. Sprawl is being caused for highly irrational and counterproductive reasons. Restrictive zoning closer in causes development further out. Localities with highly exclusionary practices force development to occur in more remote areas where the pressures against development are not yet as great. The affluent suburbs and a number of cities have surrounded themselves with invisible walls, causing the excluded housing to be developed in places that should be used for other purposes.

Some people insist that money directed to the right places will remove such obstacles. Such practices of course are a very serious blot on the system. The one thing you cannot do in Houston, or in any nonzoned area, is pay off a politician to get a windfall zoning change. There is nobody who says this land can be used for this and not for that. It is controlled by the very impersonal market and it is very hard to bribe a market.

In this day and age, we ought to consider and appraise carefully any institution that easily gives rise to graft. Bribery is always a temptation; and it is not difficult in zoning for a politician to accept it without fear of exposure. One reason is because the result can be camouflaged by the planning rhetoric. This is not because the planners are sharing the graft; but because there is so much subjectivity in the process that you can always get a planner to say, "I believe this is the best use of land." I am not in this sense criticizing planners. Planning is highly subjective; many competent professionals have different opinions. It happens that the world of urban planning is virtually one of unlimited options.

Houston, up until recently, was the sixth largest city in the country.

However, during this period it always was third or fourth in the amount of new construction. Houston is a city where there never seems to be an absence of substantial residential construction. That means greater business and employment and the continual addition of more units to the market. People have a greater opportunity to have new apartments and homes. But there is something else significant about housing construction that is often overlooked. When people occupy new housing units, they vacate their former residences for occupancy by others. These others, in turn, vacate their accommodations, and so on down the line. A filtering process occurs and it can operate quite effectively to improve housing conditions. When new units are built, not only do people benefit who will actually occupy them, but people further down in the housing chain also gain. The leading source of information about this process comes by way of a study conducted at the Survey Research Center of the University of Michigan in 1966.

The results were published in a monograph called *New Homes and Poor People*.[3] The researchers attempted to find out whether and to what extent the poor benefit from the construction of new homes and apartments—or was it only the rich? The survey showed that for every one thousand new units, about thirty-five hundred moves resulted, twenty-five hundred of which were to existing houses and apartments. More than one-third of all those who moved were likely to be in the lower and moderate income categories, and that while more new construction occurs in the outer portions of the metropolitan area, these moves extend to the older areas near the center of the cities.

The low and moderate income groups have been and are the subjects of enormous governmental expenditures for subsidized and public housing; something like $40 to $80 billion has been spent for subsidized housing in the 1970s to improve the economic housing conditions of these groups. The Michigan Survey reveals that these groups can also be benefited through the normal operation of the construction industry; more residential development will provide better housing conditions for them. It also indicates that the prohibition of new housing starts can seriously harm those most in need of a better environment.

Let me return to a point I made earlier about the existence of some commercial uses in residential areas. Zoning attempts to eradicate diverse uses within residential areas in the belief they are incompatible. Houston suggests something to the contrary; the so-called incompatible uses may well increase rather than decrease the viability of a lower income section. The elimination of small commercial enterprises within these areas, such as groceries and even auto repair shops, can inconvenience the family and seriously reduce its desirability for many residents. Although auto repair shops may seem highly undesirable neighbors to those imbued with the delicacies and ideals of middle class housing, they do offer much convenience and service for a lower income family, owning one usually older car in an automobile city. They are within walking distance, frequently stock used parts, and may provide liberal credit terms. Such commercial uses, therefore, are neither incompatible nor undesirable in the circumstances, and their elimination would be more harmful than helpful. It is hard to believe that these diverse uses could possibly remain against any determined opposition (which could well take the form of vandalism).

An illustration is provided by a section of Houston known as Denver Harbor, where the population is in the lower and lower middle income categories. In 1969, land uses on interior streets in a selected rectangular-shaped portion of this section consisting of over eighty-five square blocks were surveyed.[4] The area studied was first subdivided in 1911 and the balance in 1913; there were never any restrictive covenants imposed controlling land use or building. I doubt that government planning could have accomplished the same degree of viability as exists in this area. Although it is bordered on one side and at one corner by heavy industry and about 13 percent of the land was vacant, only approximately 1 percent of existing structures were occupied by industry. About 7 percent of the structures contained commercial uses (about one-third of which were auto repair shops and groceries), about 5 percent were duplexes and apartments, and about 2 percent were trailers. New homes probably had been built in every decade since the 1920s, including some in the late 1960s. Real estate values have been generally stable in the area.

Evidently the character of the area is satisfactory to its residents. In the 1962 zoning straw vote in Houston, those precincts of Denver Harbor encompassing the area surveyed voted against zoning by a margin of 995 to 205.

Inasmuch as a large majority of the restrictive covenants still in force in Houston contain an automatic extension or comparable provision, it is not likely that a substantial number of subdivisions will become unrestricted in the near or distant future. Moreover, due to Houston's policy of enforcing them, few, if any, restrictive covenants will become ineffective prior to their initial termination date. There are some covenants that will expire at a date specified by their terms and, of course, a majority may agree to cancel or amend their covenants as provided under automatic extension provisions. The pace at which property becomes unrestricted will thus be gradual, and will benefit the balance of the community by allowing for a greater adjustment to economic pressures that have arisen subsequent to the imposition of the covenants.

When restrictions expire in single-family subdivisions, changes to other uses occur in accordance with economic pressures. This means that in time, commercial uses, apartments, and possibly a few (probably light) industrial uses will develop on properties adjoining the more heavily traveled streets. For land on local or interior streets, economic pressures for commercial uses are generally much less. As a result, despite the absence of covenants for long periods, relatively few such uses will develop, probably involving no more than 5 percent to 7 percent of the structures on the interior streets of a subdivision. As I have suggested, the commercial uses that do develop tend to have some compatibility with the area. Thus, in interior areas where the population is more affluent (and therefore more mobile) there are less commercial uses than in Denver Harbor and the "heavier" ones such as auto repair shops have not developed.

Substantial changes in interior areas come about only where there is a strong demand for multiple family use. Since many areas tend to be immune to the demand for apartments and commercial establishments, there are substantial portions of Houston where despite the expiration many years ago or absence of covenants, the existence of any use other than single family is a rare occurrence.

The major thoroughfares in Houston are largely similar in appearance to those in most zoned cities. Areas adjoining heavy traffic streets contain homes, apartments, townhouses, and businesses similar to what occurs under zoning. There are likely more businesses and apartments along the thoroughfares than there would be under zoning because such uses bring a better land price there than does single family. The result is also a greater number of houses on interior streets, all of which makes for a separation of uses not inconsistent with conventional planning objectives of compatibility and desirability. One can hardly fault economics that cause homes to be built on the local rather than on heavily traveled streets and of course, vice versa, with respect to commercial uses.

Moreover, the absence of zoning restrictions allows for maximum development of strip areas. In zoned areas with their many classifications and subclassifications, it is often a matter of chance whether a particular parcel is zoned for the use intended. There is no such problem under nonzoning. The results in Houston appear even more favorable when compared with what develops when the planners, politicians and possibly even the courts juggle the land to determine where the various uses along the thoroughfare will go. What land will get the least valuable R-1, the more valuable C-1, and the most valuable C-6? Where should the B-1 district begin and where should it end? Which uses should be permitted in the B-2, B-3, B-4, and B-7 districts? Who will be allowed to live where? I submit that the process is considerably more chaotic, disorderly, and inequitable than what takes place in the nonzoned cities.

These zoning controls, by impeding development, serve to increase consumer prices and reduce local tax receipts. An excellent source for local revenues is commercial and industrial development, which often pay, per square foot of land, more in taxes than homes, and send no children to school. There are minimal legal impediments in Houston to interfere with such construction.

One among many examples of this difference stands out. It is the story of Greenway Plaza, which will soon be one of Houston's major commercial complexes. As of 1968, it consisted of a 55 acre high-rise commercial development. In that and the following year, Greenway's developer purchased almost all of the 237 homes and one apartment building in two adjacent subdivisions. To induce everyone to sell, Greenway made a generous offer. Homeowners would be paid a price above market and given five years of rent-free occupancy. Since there were few governmental barriers that had to be overcome, the major problem confronted by the developer was buying piecemeal the two subdivisions from the many homeowners. He obtained from each owner willing to sell an option for the period of time needed to determine if everyone else would also sell.

If the property had been zoned, it would have been classified as single family and the time required to determine the city's pleasure would have lengthened the necessary option period substantially. Not many owners would have allowed their property to be legally bound for the many additional months or perhaps years needed by the city council to arrive at such an important zoning decision. This would have dissuaded a developer from undertaking such a project.

The total cost of new construction in the two subdivisions is now estimated at about $1 billion. This amount of building will generate an enormous amount of business and employment activity, and an annual real estate tax obligation in excess of $9 million. Taxes on the land will add to this amount. Total yearly taxes on the homes and one apartment building in both subdivisions were under $125,000. The difference is enough to purchase many school rooms, parks and open space—or, alternatively, simply reduce taxes. The site of the complex is close to two expressway intersections and is a short ride from downtown Houston, obviously ideal for the development contemplated. It would in all likelihood have been financially unfeasible to substitute a site with similar potential. Many of the benefits that will accrue to the community would have been lost under zoning.

As this last illustration shows, Houston is responding well to the demands and desires of people who live in major cities. It is a most viable place and at the very least, life for its inhabitants is as comfortable as elsewhere, without the pernicious political pressures, petty tyrannies, coercions, and inequities that have characterized zoning throughout its existence. Let me respond briefly to some criticisms that have appeared in print on the Houston system. The dearth of such comments about a place whose system is anathema to proponents of controls attests to its success.

It is said that nonzoning has resulted in a large number of billboards. Many billboards are seen in Houston (only on the major thoroughfares), but the absence of zoning does not account for them. There is nothing that prevents the city from adopting an ordinance curtailing billboards. Many communities have passed sign ordinances separate from their zoning regulations. Strict controls over billboards have been advocated by some in Houston over the years and the failure to pass them reflects the sentiment of the city council.

Critics have discovered that there has been subsidence and destruction of homes in certain areas because groundwater has been pumped from under these houses.[5] Those all-knowing zoners who have done such a remarkably poor job elsewhere would somehow have come to the rescue and there would have been no such problem if only Houston had zoning. I beg to differ. As I have indicated, Houston has passed a limited number of land use regulations, covering even such a mundane matter as off-street parking for residential construction. There was no reason why a regulation could not have been adopted concerning the groundwater problem if the city had considered this course of action advisable. Legislation was some years ago passed to control these difficulties, and is presently in force.

Some might contend that if Houston had zoning, and the larger planning department that goes with it, the subsidence problem might have been recognized and treated earlier. Again, I disagree. Countless ills of cities remain despite zoning, and many are the direct result of zoning. Zoning is so bogged down in petty matters that the important problems of the city frequently get lost. Those tightly zoned suburbs west and northwest of Chicago with which I am familiar provide a good example. I spent many late hours at public meetings and hearings listening to arguments between neighbors and developers and learned discussions about whether the setbacks should be 25, 30, or 40 feet from the lot line. The hour was late and frequently most everyone still present was quite exhausted by the time the meetings adjourned. I rarely heard about the potential of floods and I think had the subject been brought up it might have been tabled to allow some local citizens to expound on city planning or the evils of apartments and townhouses. Well, these areas had enormous floods in the early seventies and were unprepared for them. The absence of zoning might have permitted the officials to concentrate on matters that truly involved life and property.

I began this discussion by suggesting that nonzoning would tell us something about the operation of the regulated and nonregulated markets. Let me close with an example that is at the crux of any such comparison.

In the absence of controls on production, there has been over the years a significant vacancy rate in the Houston rental market. Construction is more likely to continue there than elsewhere because builders do not have political as well as economic barriers to overcome. Still one could not help wondering why apartment buildings continued to be produced in spite of the high vacancy rates.

The basic reason is the developer of each new project believes that he can provide something better than what is currently available and will be able, therefore, to attract people to rent his housing in preference to that of his competitors. He has detected some void in the market and believes he can satisfy it and still obtain a profitable return. This may involve providing extra amenities, larger rooms, more green space or recreational facilities, or perhaps lower rent. It requires skill, ingenuity, innovation, and much time and effort on the part of the developer. This is the means by which enormously valuable services are rendered the consuming public, without cost, by highly productive and skilled people. There is no government agency that can possibly provide or demand such benefits.

Contemplate what is occurring. Very productive people using their ingenuity and imagination, skill, and creativity to serve the consumer. They are engaged in private and free enterprise and the invisible hand (Chapter 10) is operating at a high level. It exists in zoned cities but to a much lesser degree because of the very visible and heavy hand of government. The primary beneficiary in Houston is the general public, which is also the most seriously harmed when these productive processes are curtailed. And there lies the difference between a regulated and a free market.

Notes

1. G.J. Stigler, "The Economic Effects of the Antitrust Laws," *J. Law & Econ.* (1966): 225.

2. B.H. Siegan, *Land Use Without Zoning* (Lexington, Ma.: D.C. Heath and Co., 1972), pp. 95-122, sets forth figures from U.S. Bureau of Labor Statistics for 1966 through 1969. The Bureau's statistics for subsequent years through 1974 show a similar pattern of rents for the two cities. Most of the Houston SMSA is not zoned, whereas most of the Dallas SMSA is.

3. J.B. Lansing, C.W. Clifton, and J.N. Morgan, *New Homes and Poor People: A Study of the Chain of Moves* (Ann Arbor, Mich.: Univ. of Michigan, 1969).

4. Siegan, *Land Use*, pp. 37-39.

5. J.B. Costonis, " 'Fair' Compensation and the Accommodation Power: Antidotes for the Taking Impasse in Land Use Controversies," *Columbia L. Rev.* (1975): 1021, 1030.

List of Contributors

Armen Alchian
Professor of Economics
University of California at Los Angeles

James Buchanan
Professor of Economics and
   General Director of the Center for
   Study of Public Choice
Virginia Polytechnic Institute

George W. Hilton
Professor of Economics
University of California at Los Angeles

Alvin Klevorick
Professor of Law and Economics
Yale University

Michael E. Levine
Luce Professor of Law and Social Change,
California Institute of Technology, and
   Professor of Law
University of Southern California

Wesley J. Liebeler
Professor of Law
University of California at Los Angeles

Henry Manne
Director of the Center for Studies in Law and
   Economics and Distinguished Professor of Law
University of Miami School of Law

Sam Peltzman
Professor of Economics,
Graduate School of Business
University of Chicago

Warren F. Schwartz
Professor of Law
University of Virginia School of Law

Herbert Stein
Robertson Professor of Economics
University of Virginia

W. Allen Wallis
Chancellor and Professor of Economics and Statistics
University of Rochester

Harry Wellington
Dean of the Law School
Yale University

About the Editor

Bernard H. Siegan is a distinguished professor of law at the University of San Diego School of Law. He writes a weekly syndicated newspaper column and is the author of *Land Use Without Zoning, Other People's Property*, and the editor of *Planning Without Prices* (all published by Lexington Books). He is also a contributor to professional journals and other publications, with articles pertaining to land use, zoning, and urban planning. Professor Siegan received the J.D. degree from the University of Chicago and was in private practice for many years.